BANGLADESHI FAMILY LIFE IN BETHNAL GREEN

ROSEANNA POLLEN MSC
DEPARTMENT OF SOCIAL ANTHROPOLOGY
LONDON SCHOOL OF ECONOMICS AND POLITICAL SCIENCE
THESIS SUBMITTED IN PARTIAL FULFILLMENT OF THE DEGREE OF
DOCTOR OF PHILOSOPHY AT THE UNIVERSITY OF LONDON
2002

ABSTRACT

This thesis is about Bengali[1] family life in Bethnal Green. This part of the East End of London is a place of paradoxical darkness and light where Victorian gloom, economic polarisation, Cockney traditions, racism and heart-warming kinship all coincide.

Bengali families form the largest non-white ethnic group in the borough. They evince marked heterogeneity of biography, language, religious practice, occupation and household composition, yet certain themes such as chain networks of masculine support, the institution of arranged marriage and patrilineal joint households endure. Despite demographic density, the overall social atmosphere (*batash*) in Bethnal Green is experienced as attenuated and thin for many Bengali people, and for some, distorted and disfigured. Social knowledge is thick and pervasive through village connections with Bangladesh, but practical knowledge can be obstructed by living in a mixed-ethnicity area. The destabilising effects of this social atmosphere are shown to be compounded for those who also feel that they are vulnerable to gossip and spiritual modes of harm. Racism, in violent, institutionalised, banal and culturalised manifestations is a pervasive social practice in Bethnal Green which affects the lives of all its residents.

I use the notion of the distribution of social predicaments as a heuristic device to present the ways in which cultural effects work in synergy with, or independently of other social facts. Whilst economic resources, gender and racism predictably have the most leverage in determining outcomes, the likely social trajectory for any individual cannot be extrapolated from these three factors alone. The interactions of cultural effects and social facts are exemplified maximally in the predicaments of young British women who marry husbands from Bangladesh. They take on burdensome engagement with enduring traditions of patriliny, novel reconfigurations of kin relationships, feminist discourse, relations of difference and changing expressions of Islam.

---

[1] For simplicity, I use Bengali in the text of this thesis to denote British citizens of Bangladeshi-Sylheti origin. I am aware that Bengali only describes the regional and not the political origins of this transnational population.

PREFACE

This thesis is presented as a published book for the benefit of social science students who from time to time email me asking for a copy. Over the years Bangladeshi people on meeting me for the first time have on occasion asked me how I knew so much about their family because they found marked similarities between the ethnography and their own life histories. Of course I knew nothing of their individual families but it is a mark of my research that I only wrote down things that were said or experienced by more than one person or family. As a doctor I have preserved confidentiality of my patients by elision of conversations and descriptions of several people to present the named 'persons' in this book. Academic readers have raised the question then as to the veracity of an ethnography that uses such amalgamations. In response I can only say that I would not have been able to do research from my position as a doctor without doing so. If anthropological research is confined to those who work as full-time academics I think it is a shame and many voices from interesting field-work positions would thus be silenced. To my patients and friends I state simply that if you feel that you recognise yourself or friends and family within these pages it is very likely that you are reading about someone else.

Note to researchers: this published format has changed the pagination of the original printed thesis.

TABLE OF CONTENTS

CHAPTER 1: INTRODUCTION

1.1 Introduction   1
1.2 Motivations   1
1.3 Methods   9
1.4 Outline of the chapters   7

CHAPTER 2: THE FIELD

2.1 Introduction   10
2.2 History   11
2.3 Current social geography   14
2.4 Migration history of the Bengali population in East London   17
2.5 A walk in the street   21
2.6 Urban anthropology and methodology   23

CHAPTER 3 SOCIAL PREDICAMENTS

3.1 Plight and Predicament   29
3.2 Dynastic success   35
3.3 Irregular marriage   37
3.4 Marital difficulty   40
3.5 Troubled young men   42
3.6 Boundaries

     3.6.1 FAZLUL AHMED   44
     3.6.2 RAHMAT KHAN   46
     3.6.3 MAMUN   47
3.7 Sequestered women   49
3.8 Discussion   50

CHAPTER 4 HOUSEHOLDS

4.1 Introduction   52
4.2 Preliminary ethnographic description

     4.2.1 CONTRASTING FAMILY BIOGRAPHIES   55
     4.2.2 WEDDING PARTIES   62
4.3 The Developmental Cycle of the Bengali Domestic Group

     4.3.1 INTRODUCTION   69
     4.3.2 DATA   70
     4.3.3 DEMOGRAPHY   72
     4.3.4 HOUSING RESOURCES   74
     4.3.5 TRANSNATIONAL AND INTRA-NATIONAL EXTENDED HOUSEHOLDS   76
     4.3.6 COROLLARIES OF THE DEVELOPMENT CYCLE OF THE BENGALI
         DOMESTIC GROUP   78
4.4 Household economics and changing roles for women   81
4.5 Roles within households

     4.5.1 INTRODUCTION   86
     4.5.2 OLDER MIGRANTS' GENERATION
         4.5.2.1 A woman's view   86
         4.5.2.2 The husband's view   90
         4.5.2.3 Discussion   92
     4.5.3 MARRIAGEABLE CHILDREN   93
     4.5.4 THE INSTITUTION OF THE JOINT HOUSEHOLD   97
     4.5.5 THE PARTICULAR PROBLEMS OF LONDON WIVES
         AND BANGLADESHI HUSBANDS   100

4.6 Conclusions   103
    4.6.1 CONTINUITY   103
    4.6.2 CHANGE   105

CHAPTER 5: NETWORKS OF SOCIAL RELATIONSHIPS
AND KINSHIP

5.1 Introduction   107
5.2 Learning about kinship   109
5.3 Thick and Thin   112
5.4 Making friends and knowing who people are - the village network   116
5.5 Migration distorts kinship   121
5.6 Batash   129
5.7 Summary   131

CHAPTER 6: NEGATIVITY

6.1 Introduction   133
6.2 Fieldwork discovery   133
6.3 Gossip
    6.3.1 INTRODUCTION   135
    6.3.2 GOSSIPS   137
    6.3.3 BODNAMI   138
    6.3.4 DISCUSSION   144
6.4 Nozzor
    6.4.1 DESCRIPTION   145
    6.4.2 DISCUSSION   148
6.5 Jinn
    6.5.1 DESCRIPTION   151
    6.5.2 REDRESS   155
6.6 Discussion   161

CHAPTER 7: RELATIONS OF DIFFERENCE

7.1 Introduction   165
7.2 Multicultural Bethnal Green and Dual Discursive Competence   168
7.3 Three Practices of Relations of Difference
    7.3.1 UNSETTLED STRATEGISING (AND THE DISCOURSE OF CULTURE)   171
        7.3.1.1 Episodes   173
        7.3.1.2 Young men   174
        7.3.1.3 Young women   175
        7.3.1.4 Young mothers   176
        7.3.1.5 Culture   178
    7.3.2 COMMON-SENSE MULTICULTURALISM (AND THE DISCOURSE
        OF ETHNICITY)
        7.3.2.1 Ethnicity   180
        7.3.2.2 Class effects   181
        7.3.2.3 Different Languages 184
    7.3.3 CULTURAL AGONISM (AND THE DISCOURSE OF RACE)
        7.3.3.1 Racist violence   189
        7.3.3.2 Banal Racism   192
        7.3.3.3 Traditionalism   193
        7.3.3.4 'Asian gangs'   195
7.4 Summary   197

CHAPTER 8: CONCLUSIONS

8.1 Introduction   198
8.2 Static and dynamic I: position and trajectory   198
8.3 Static and dynamic II: predicament and strategy
    8.3.1 INTRODUCTION   199
    8.3.2 VIOLENCE AND RACISM   200

8.3.3 FAMILIES WITH OLDER CHILDREN   201
8.3.4 YOUNG MARRIED COUPLES   202
8.4 Discussion   203

BIBLIOGRAPHY   208

LIST OF TABLES

TABLE 1 *Household types*   71

TABLE 2 *Bengali adults of working age*   82

TABLE 3 *Long term sickness among Bengali adults of working age*   82

TABLE 4 *Economic activity, working age, not sick*   82

TABLE 5 *Occupations*   82

TABLE 6 *Sources of household incomes*   83

TABLE 7 *Future trajectories of Bengali households in Bethnal Green* 85

ACKNOWLEDGEMENTS

Mature, part-time students are less in need of encouragement and support than the chance to have time alone. I gratefully acknowledge the benign neglect afforded by my family, friends and work colleagues in this respect. My contemporaries at the LSE thesis-writing seminar were similarly indulgent of my irregular attendance over the years. During three months unpaid leave during 2001, Richard Chenhall, Manuela Ciotti, David Crawford, Stephan Eggs, Luke Freeman, Peggy Froerer, Sigrun Hardardottir, Annu Jalais, Kriti Kapila, Eva Keller, Isabella Lepri, Lucia Michelutti, Massimiliano Mollona, Benedetta Rossi, Ed Simpson, Patti Taber, Barbara Verardo and David Yang were generously inclusive. I thank Chris Fuller and Johnny Parry for their sustained and positive critical attention throughout.

CHAPTER 1: INTRODUCTION

1.1 Introduction

When a local doctor presents an anthropological thesis which appears to be 'about' Bengali people in Bethnal Green, a number of important questions are raised as to motivations and methods. This is particularly necessary since the presentation resembles a 'village monograph' where domains of Bengali kinship, households and spiritual beliefs form the bulk of the ethnographic chapters. Moreover the descriptions are provided by someone who is outside that 'community', although I am placed in Bethnal Green by virtue of my work. The thesis is not about *their* culture, nor is it simply an account of urban-village life. The project in its most condensed form can be stated thus: I have set out to use a form of participant-observation to discover the contours of, and the reasons for, the distribution of salient social predicaments that are particular to the Bengali population in Bethnal Green.

1.2 Motivations

Research was undertaken while I continued to work full-time as a family doctor (GP) in a four-handed practice in Bethnal Green. I have been a doctor in the practice since 1984. In 1994/5 I took a sabbatical year and studied for the MSc in Social Anthropology at the London School of Economics (LSE). My interest in anthropology at that time had two aspects: first, the obvious and immediately applicable project of enhancing the quality of my medical practice through an anthropological understanding of multicultural societies; secondly I was interested in using the methodology of social anthropology for research from the position of a working doctor. It was not possible for family reasons to change two careers and two school placements as well as four persons' social lives in order to pursue research anywhere else apart from the East End of London. In addition, I felt that such a radical change of place would uncomfortably over-determine the importance of my research. The insights that I might achieve were unlikely to be so momentous as to justify loading the research position with such a burden of responsibility. Nevertheless, the unorthodox position of staying put and studying as well as writing from my place of work made its own demands (as does any field area) to be thoughtful about the precise setting, methods and goals of my research.

Missing from social science research, to date, is anything that looks like a full-length, general monograph for the East End Bengali population. Eade has published extensively on the subject of Bengali involvement with local and national politics, community groups and Islam (Eade 1990a, 1990b, 1994, 1996, 1998). Gavron's thesis (1998) is a study of the attitudes of young Bengali women in Tower Hamlets towards traditions of marriage. In addition there are numerous smaller studies such as Adams's (1987) account of early Bengali settlers in Britain,

1

Carey and Shukur's (1985) brief overview of the population (see also Alam 1988), studies of community organisations (Asghar 1996, King 1994) and accounts of discrimination and racism (BG & STC 1978, Cohen 1997, Cooper & Qureshi 1993, CRE 1979, Husbands 1982, Keith 1995, Phillips 1988, Runnymede Trust 1993). Census analysts have evaluated demographic data (Eade, Vamplew & Peach 1996, Peach & Rossiter 1996, Ratcliffe 1996). Others have researched particular aspects of British Bengali populations (Alexander 2000, Barton 1986, Centre for Bangladeshi Studies 1994, Chalmers 1996 & 1998, Summerfield 1993, Wrench & Qureshi 1996, see also the CBS database of relevant literature: Eade & Momen 1995). Complementary to this British-based work is the transnational work of Gardner who has studied social change in Bangladesh in relation to migration (Gardner 1992a, 1992b, 1993a, 1993b, 1995), as well as aspects of the East End Bengali population (Gardner 1998, Gardner & Shukur 1994).

The East End of London is a location where studies of migration and ethnicity are of obvious relevance. Working-class social history, criminology, urban change and popular culture are also subjects for which the area offers rich material. The fact that the borough's Bengali population represents the largest single non-white ethnic group of any borough in the United Kingdom, and that the local history of racism is almost metonymic for British racism (Cohen 1997: 76, Keith 1995: 551) makes the inclusion of relations of difference essential to any study of the Bengali population in Bethnal Green.

1.3 Methods

As I am not Bengali, the question arises as to whether it would be more appropriate to conduct a research project concerned with racism among those most similar to the researcher, or among the perpetrators of racist behaviour, or among those most vulnerable to racism. The attitudes of those who are socially similar to myself, as well as those who are racist in their behaviour are included in this thesis, but I was unwilling to place them in centre-stage with the most disadvantaged group at the periphery. I can only state that having given the matter considerable thought during the last six years I have not been made aware from any quarter that the differences between myself and informants are an insuperable obstacle to serious research (cf. Kuper 1994: 545).

I neither valorise nor deplore the fact of difference in the anthropologist-informant relationship. My written accounts of analytical medical case-work, prior to this thesis, included people similar as well as different to myself; the question of difference was considered an important matter in this respect. Similarity and difference each pose their own obstacles as well as suggestive possibilities. I have recognised that the existence of sharp differences in the doctor-patient relationship calls for a greater degree of concentration and attention to what precisely is going on in such encounters compared with those where there is a lesser degree of apparent difference (Pollen 2001: 9). If I used this experience from the outset to reflect on how best to collect data, write field-notes and present ethnography, I also recognised the need to modify my technique from one suited to individual case-work, where generalisations are guarded, cautious or avoided, to one appropriate to an aggregated analysis.

Gupta and Ferguson (1997b) summarise anthropological critiques of the position of the anthropologist in relation to informants. They and others are critical of hierarchical and fastidious classifications of fieldwork into categories such as insider, indigenous, native, inter-cultural or non-Western (Yan 1997). Such classifications look suspiciously like essentialist labelling of fieldworkers which most anthropologists would hesitate to apply to informants. Gupta and Ferguson are less interested in generalised opinions and hand-wringing on this matter than in the specifics of any particular fieldworker's position. My position as a white middle-class doctor among Bengali migrant families is radically asymmetrical, so I was unable to participate on the basis of fictive kinship or 'passing' in the way sought by some fieldworkers (Mascarenhas-Keyes 1987: 182, Okely 1996: 23). On the other hand, the facts of difference in my position are clearly defined and I am habituated to being thoughtful about the variety of ways in which patients of similar and different backgrounds interpret our relationship and choose to present some subjects but not others for discussion with their doctor.

A typical working day at the surgery comprises two surgeries, morning and evening, each with eighteen booked appointments plus any emergency consultations. Telephone advice, home visits, antenatal and well-baby clinics as well as considerable amounts of paperwork take up the middle of the day. Out of hours emergency care is shared by all local GPs through a local co-operative. The organisation of the practice is managed by the four doctors together with a team of employed staff in conjunction with other primary care workers such as midwives, district nurses and health visitors. Each doctor in the practice has a personal list of about 1700 patients who only see another doctor if their own is absent and the case is urgent. Patients in poor districts such as Bethnal Green attend their doctors frequently so it is not difficult, over time and without any unusual curiosity, for GPs to become knowledgeable about the family circumstances of local households, excepting those who are transient, short-term residents. The informants in this study therefore includes people from about sixty households whom I know well and about eighty households in all where I have sufficient demographic, economic and health data on which I can draw with reasonable confidence.

Throughout fieldwork with patients (which was subject to scrutiny by the local medical ethics committee) I worked entirely with the material that they chose to bring to consultations even when an important insight could possibly have been gained by moving from medical consultation to anthropological interview techniques. Nevertheless, towards the end of fieldwork, some patients became aware that I was unusually knowledgeable about Bengali 'culture' and this, in a way, marked the end of the possibilities of continuing fieldwork in this opportunistic manner.

In addition to being attentive to what patients said and did, I added a form of 'triangulation' to my methodology by seeking out a small number of key informants who were not patients (cf. Kuper 1994: 548). At first these relationships were framed by my need to learn the Sylheti dialect of standard Bengali spoken by the majority of informants (*pace* Chalmers, 1996: 5-8, who suggests against the majority opinion in Bethnal Green that Sylheti is a separate language). With some women I added on the wish to learn about Bengali cookery so as to make the language lessons practical, given that my teachers had no experience of teaching Sylheti, and some spoke no English at all. From these initial relationships others developed, some transient acquaintances, others friendships which have grown to be independent of the needs of this thesis. Whilst data from patients are unprompted, fresh, sometimes intimate but unstructured, non-patient informants are a resource for more systematic information. Data from outside informants and from patients are used recursively to check context and relevance. Whereas with non-patients it is relatively straightforward to introduce material by saying something like, 'Some people tell me that such a such a custom means this', with patients I only introduce externally gained knowledge tentatively or indirectly, and only if it is relevant to their present medical problems.

This method of privileging material presented spontaneously and avoiding interrogative formal or semi-formal interviews originated in post-graduate medical training. Apart from undergraduate medical school, house jobs (internship) and post-graduate GP training, I spent four years (while working as a GP) in seminars run by the Institute of Psychosexual Medicine (IPM). After a year at LSE I felt that each discipline, the IPM and Anthropology had complementary defects. The IPM offers only a slim, if growing, body of published work that is low-profile in terms of academic recognition, but has intellectual and practical confidence in a specific understanding of its methodology, that is, the analysis of the doctor-patient relationship. Anthropology, on the other hand, has *gravitas* in the sense of an established corpus of prestigious scholarship, but the discipline seems to me to be less confident about the theoretical underpinning of its fieldwork methodology beyond the general descriptive term 'participant-observation'. Whereas the interpretation of subjectivity and empathetic understanding are written about extensively, at times tellingly, or obscurely (Crapanzano 1992, Fabian 1983, Knauft 1996: 47, Reyna 1994, Rosaldo 1989, Sangren 1988) there is little consensus as to how the analysis of the professional anthropologist-informant relationship can, may, or should be taught to students or translated into ethnographic text (Geertz 1973, Gupta & Ferguson 1997b: 2, Levy 1994: 188, Russell Bernard 1994, Sperber 1985: 9-34, Stocking 1983).

Heightened critical awareness of the position of anthropologists in relation to informants, particularly in unorthodox settings, could itself be analysed as betraying a deep-seated anxiousness about such relationships (Kanaaneh 1997, Kuper 1994, Passaro 1997, Ryang 1997, Strathern 1987, Weston 1997). I see this as entirely understandable given that any serious engagement with other people in the hopes of making an accurate analysis about precisely what is going on is arduous, troubling and often exhausting, particularly when undertaken with only remote supervision in the field.

The IPM technique for analysing doctor-patient relationships can also be described as participant-observation. Participation is undertaken not by the doctor seeking to identify with the patient but through bilateral empathetic sensitivity. This means trying to get as close as possible to the emotional inter-subjectivity of the consultation in all its phases: history taking, physical examination and discussion. Analysis is possible when the doctor mentally and emotionally steps back from empathetic moments to consider the doctor-patient relationship thus revealed, *in conjunction* with the observable facts of the encounter. With patients, these observations might include their age, gender, appearance and method of access (routine or emergency appointment), where they sat in the room, posture and gesture as well as their social and cultural backgrounds. The observable context of the doctor is also taken into account since an encounter with a patient on a day when they are running late and have just dealt with a terminally ill patient, or someone who was aggressive, is likely to be very different from one with a patient on a day when appointments are less pressured and the problem is one in which the doctor has a specialist interest.

These two types of data, participant-subjective and observation-objective, put together and carefully thought about, may allow the doctor to formulate an interpretation that can be put with greater or lesser success directly to the patient in order to bring fresh insight to their presenting problem. The important point that deserves emphasis is that the power of empathetically gained *subjective* knowledge neutralises the tendency to bias or prejudice that is often prompted by the so-called *objective* observations (Pollen 2001: 5). For all doctors, rapid problem-solving techniques that are much needed in busy clinics make it all too easy to become someone who makes snap judgements about patients as they walk in the door, sometimes thoughtlessly and detrimentally. The IPM technique mitigates this slide towards stereotypy by emphasising the value of information gained empathetically so as to contextualise the observational data. For example, a woman in orthodox Islamic coverings, chaperoned by male relatives, might, from her appearance, seem to be in a submissive, even subservient role within her family. This assumption must be modified if consultations frequently result in the doctor feeling indecisive or pressured into giving more prescriptions or orders for tests than is her usual practice. The patient may be the controlling personality in this relationship and the apparent restrictions of her cultural customs belie her authoritarian approach to others.

A cultural difference between doctor and patient may mean that there are practical obstacles to managing consultations effectively. These may be to do with language problems, and sometimes different experiences of health care and the roles of doctors and patients in other places. Secondly, cultural matters have a qualitatively different effect on the doctor-patient relationship compared with other features such as age, gender, occupation and so on, even where there are no significant language barriers. In my experience, clinicians are far more likely to have difficulty with and make an issue of what they perceive to be cultural differences than do our patients (see also Smaje 1995: 110). This is commonly a defensive strategy protecting a sense of inadequacy in the face of difficult encounters. After all, if patients have a specific cultural question that needs answering they could ask an expert from the same background as themselves. The fact that cultural issues are brought by a patient to a consultation with a doctor in a direct way may suggest that a comparative view is being sought rather than a straightforward 'correct' answer. Throughout my research I found that my attention was always alerted if I felt that cultural issues became an explicit part of cross-cultural encounters of any significance.

The key difference between my work as a doctor and fieldwork within the practice, is that I do not enunciate interpretations to patients about my analysis of our relationship if it is not relevant to their medical needs. In fact, analytical insights which were potentially useful as ethnographic material nearly always took place outside consultations when I was writing up field notes at the end of the working day.

The Bengali patients on my medical list form a reasonable cross-section of the local Bengali population since we do not select our patients and the scarcity of local doctors means that they in turn have little choice as to registration with a particular practice. Most are families derived from original male migrants from the Sylhet district of Bangladesh and have had working-class occupations since settling in Britain. The concerns of patient-informants that come to my attention, apart from their medical needs, are, on the whole, family matters. This means that my research has not been involved to any great extent with community groups, religious institutions or party politics. Since these have been the subjects of other local studies referred to earlier, I did not see this as a deficiency in need of redress. Interestingly, very few patients whom I know appear to have much knowledge of the services of local Bengali politicians. The very fact that their social problems were revealed to me suggests that in part this is because they are people who have little access to Bengali community leaders or who place more trust in the opinions and resources of non-politicians.

This extended description of my methodology answers Gupta and Ferguson's call for specificity as well as the recurrent enquiry from others who have been interested in my research to explain what I do. It should be emphasised that the IPM technique is designed for ordinary and short encounters. I have not pursued 'exotic cases' with curiosity, nor extended for research purposes, the seven-and-a-half minutes allotted to the forty or so consultations that take place on any normal day at the surgery. The time-demands of this technique are in thoughtful reflection afterwards and writing field notes. The IPM seminar training has been invaluable in this respect since it fosters disciplined skills of recall and detailed reflection without recourse to audio or video recording.

1.4 Outline of the chapters

Chapter 2 contains background information on the history, geography and sociology of Bethnal Green, as well as an account of the development of local Bengali society from a group of single male migrants to a large population of established households. It becomes apparent, even in a straightforward précis of local historical data, that the representation of Bethnal Green and the lives of its residents is problematic. This difficulty is discussed in the context of a review of the literature of urban anthropology.

Chapter 3 consists of a set of case histories from my practice. In the first instance this illustrates the kinds of people and lives that make up the Bengali population of Bethnal Green, and the precise way in which I collected data from patient-informants. Some case histories are only episodes while others describe long-standing relationships with patients. I have chosen case-work that highlights the ways in which cultural effects and cultural interfaces may emerge in unanticipated ways within a setting that should be confined generally to straightforward medical matters. In some instances cultural issues are found to be an obstacle to medical care, in others they appear to be absent or unobtrusive but, on reflection, a particular bias or strategy of cultural boundary management can be discerned. This bias may arise entirely or partly from the doctor or from the patient, or grow in dialectical fashion within the doctor-patient relationship. At this stage, a more precise analysis as to why people with similar social positions may have very different kinds of predicaments is left to one side although the large scale parameters of gender and socio-economic position can already be seen to be important primary determinants of differential experiences. These large-scale effects are modulated by the three descriptive chapters that follow and the argument then returns to the central concern with relations of difference in the last two chapters.

A description and analysis of Bengali households is used as a middle-range location of ethnography in Chapter 4. This settles data within a more general perspective than Chapter 3, and a more particular perspective than Chapter 2. Diversity is illustrated as well as continuity of traditions. The notions of patrilineage, arranged marriage and masculine chains of hierarchical utilitarian relationships are strong themes, as well as divergent practices of Islam. The tensions between these themes and any individual strategies for household life operate with particular force in the lives of young Bengali women who marry men from Bangladesh. The household description and analysis are central resources in this thesis for factual sociological data about the Bengali population of Bethnal Green. This allows the ethnography to move into more specific areas of kinship, social networks, negativity and relations of difference.

Subsequent chapters look at contrasting kinds of relationships. Chapters 5 and 6 describe and analyse the ways in which relationships are shaped by the ideals and norms of Bengali kinship, friendship, social knowledge and social harm. Positive relationships form an apparently limitless network of connections within and beyond Bethnal Green, Britain and Bangladesh. The network is nevertheless shaped by Bengali understandings of hierarchy, patriliny, gender relations and marriage. More significantly, transposition from Bangladesh to Bethnal Green, as well as juxtaposition with non-Bengali society are found to attenuate customary social comfort and to alter important kinship practices. These changes affect some people more than others but most particularly those parents with teenage children. Negative sociability, in the form of gossip, evil eye and spirit affliction, compound these problems and retain much of their force in transposition to Bethnal Green since they are not so vulnerable to attenuation and distortion as are positive social networks.

The third of this set of chapters about social relationships is concerned with relations of difference. In approaching this issue, Chapter 7 is an explicit engagement with the contradictory goals of ethnographic research as discussed by Kuper (1999) Sahlins (1999) and Knauft (1996). In summary, Kuper finds that conceptualising culture as a solid social formation endangers an accurate and nuanced presentation of all the processes which have significant effect on the lives of the people under study. In effect, a hard definition of culture risks the stereotyping of any individual by playing down the contingent nature of cultural effects. Sahlins disagrees with Kuper's preference for replacing nouns such as culture and society with adjectives (cultural and social). He points out the dangers, argumentative and political, which result from disaggregating what he sees as solid social facts. Noting the long history of this debate, Sahlins argues that deconstruction in analysis is liable to impoverish both the explanatory possibilities of any research as well as the scope for finding an acceptable moral perspective on research conclusions. Disavowing vulgar cultural determinism, he vigorously defends the continual and prolific production of 'cultures' against 'afterological' notions of cultural contingency in a globalised world. Knauft (1996) recognises the contradictions of these two positions but dismisses neither. He argues that social science research which takes a critical humanist stance must take account of its dual and contradictory goals. One goal is 'to document and valorise the richness and diversity of human ways of life' (ibid: 48 emphasis removed). This presentation of diversity, exceptional cases, contingency and contestation of norms will deliver a more subtle and sensitive account of the population under study. The second goal is 'to expose, analyse and critique human inequality and domination' (ibid: 50 emphasis removed). To this end, it is often necessary to present cultures and societies as essential social facts in order to show how socio-economic inequalities and injustices are aligned with identifiable cultures and societies.

My thesis is written in the light of Knauft's dualism rather than adopting the mutually exclusive positions of either Sahlins or Kuper. I found a diversity of alignments with Bengali culture, however defined, within the study population. Nevertheless the study group has a shared experience of injustice and racism through being identified by others as being of Bangladeshi origin. I found scant evidence of a visibly bounded community but many examples of commonalities of experience as well as emic discussion of Bengali culture. At times I present Bengali culture as a solid social formation and at others as a contingent aspect of social relationships. Bengali culture is experienced as a rich resource for some people, but an oppressive system of social control for others; for many it is an automatic or routine part of daily life. I argue that it is when personal difficulties arise, especially in relation to living in a mixed society, that the contingencies of culture, relative values and the appropriateness or not of bringing culture and cultural differences to the fore become evident.

In the concluding chapter the salient and significant social predicaments of the Bengali population as a whole are described in the light of the ethnographic chapters. The case histories of Chapter 3 are revisited in order to illustrate the summary generalisations. The distribution of predicaments is shown to be polarised: while a significant minority of Bengali people are seen to be shaping successful future trajectories, persistent inequalities inhibit the scope of possibilities for the lives of others. The light and dark of Bethnal Green described in Chapter 2 remains a constant for the foreseeable future.

CHAPTER 2: THE FIELD

2.1 Introduction

Bethnal Green is an area in the East End of London's borough of Tower Hamlets, so-called because of its proximity to the Tower of London. The Tower is no longer visible from Bethnal Green, its view blocked out by tall buildings in the financial district that intervenes, nor does it retain its former symbolism of political power. Instead the towers of commerce in Canary Wharf can be seen from all parts of the borough, and their height and geographical location signal two dominant social themes of the area: the polarisation between high and low (Riseboro 1996), and the point of arrival for immigrants. Canary Wharf is the high point of new enterprise in the Docklands area of Tower Hamlets. Although a little distant from Bethnal Green, the old Docks were, until final closure in 1981, an important source of employment throughout the borough, and in earlier times the disembarkation point for refugees and migrants. These themes colour the history and social geography of Bethnal Green which, together with the migration history of its Bengali population, forms the first half of this chapter. This is followed by an appraisal of the methodological problems that such a field area poses for research.

'The East End' is sufficiently descriptive for most British people to understand the topographical reference, given its fame in history, journalism and fiction. It is a place that is dominated in its historiography and all other representations by a chiaroscuro effect formed by a contrast between the downward darkness of poverty, degradation, violence, disorder and despair with the upward lightness of cheerful resilience, strong social roots, fierce loyalties, independent individualism and rags to riches social mobility. The compelling and persistent nature of this chiaroscuro, leaving aside for the moment the question as to whether or not it has any basis in reality, lends itself readily to melodramatic and sentimental genres alike and thus impedes dispassionate representation of East End society. Although markedly contrastive lives are indeed juxtaposed in the East End, it is also the case that many people continue a humdrum and unremarkable existence in the neutral mid-zone between dark and light. What is certain, however, is that any analysis, description or statement that seeks to generalise beyond the narrowness of a particular case, as well as any significant social action on the part of individuals or local groups in the East End is likely to be amplified, exaggerated and distorted in its interpretation as well as in its consequences by being read against this dominant trope.

The chiaroscuro can be demonstrated by reviewing references to the East End in Porter's (1994) social history of London. In conjunction with other sources, this review serves the purpose of orientation for readers unfamiliar with the area. After this historical section, a summary of present day social geography and demography is given as a similarly conventional background section in advance of my ethnography. Throughout this chapter, however, the issue of polarisation as a social fact and chiaroscuro as a questionable and even fictional trope continues. Thus, while the format and content of this chapter is conventional in one sense, I have already lost the opportunity to present 'background information' about Bethnal Green in a cut and dried manner. This is therefore a piece of urban ethnography that is both 'of the city' and 'in the city' (Hannerz 1980: 3).

2.2 History

Bethnal Green emerged as a pleasant semi-rural parish in 1743. By 1851 it had become the poorest parish in the expanding urbanisation of London, and its population had grown from 15,000 to 85,000 (Porter 1994: 143). Even in the eighteenth century it was notorious for its maverick political regime when Joseph Merceron a 'local political boss' ran a distinctly undemocratic popular political regime that encouraged gaming and all-night taverns (ibid: 182). By the middle of the nineteenth century the expanding population made it 'infamous for slums' (ibid: 267). East London was, because of its location near the river and the availability of unskilled labour, 'a magnet for the destitute and the displaced from all over Britain and the world' (ibid: 268). By the 1890s, Bethnal Green became symbolically the heart of the East End and 'the land of the outcast' (ibid: 268). If not quite the poorest London district overall, Bethnal Green had the highest proportion of the two poorest classes (Baker 1995: 127), a polarised distribution of wealth which will be seen to continue to the present day. Mid-century, detailed reports about the poverty of the East End were published by journalists and social reformers (Booth 1891-1897, Chadwick 1842, Mayhew 1861-62). Titles such as, *'Bitter Outcry of Outcast London'* (Mearns 1883), *'The Great Army of the London Poor'* (Wright 1875) suggest lurid contents. Porter's summary of these accounts is in keeping with the genre, 'Life was tough, and the street people's work exotic. But most were self-sufficient, law-abiding, and fiercely independent' (Porter 1994: 349).

Cohen notes that these accounts have been deconstructed by others as voyeuristic hallucinations or fantasies which perhaps reflect, in their recurrent interest in sewers, a suppressed Victorian anal eroticism (Cohen 1996: 174). He is critical, however of those who suggest that a frank disregard for the fantastic will allow a 'purely proletarian authenticity' to emerge. Removing the fantastical overlay raises the contrary problem that the more unpleasant social traits of the area must then arise from within East End society itself (ibid: 175). This is incompatible with other local narratives of identity, particularly that of the warm-hearted Cockney, but also those of joking mimicry and creative subversion (ibid: 178). There is little doubt, however, that the shocking conclusions drawn from Victorian accounts, particularly the more sober survey of Charles Booth (1891-7), prompted the late Victorian movement of concerned gentility to improve the hard lot of the poor through charitable institutions. Porter is sensitive to the trope of chiaroscuro here, 'Movements like Toynbee Hall show the paradoxes of late-Victorian London, a world of two cities in which the poor were described as degenerate while being sentimentalised as cockneys.' (Porter 1994: 370). In Bethnal Green itself, the mission institutions of Oxford House and St Hilda's remain community centres that have not entirely shaken off their Victorian roots.

The clichéd image of the working-class, sharp and streetwise Cockney emerged in Edwardian times. The Cockney became the classic irreverent East Ender, associated with street-markets, rhyming slang and the music hall (Porter 1994: 368-9, Stedman-Jones 1989: 278). Cohen questions whether the classic, respectable Cockney in the later era of conservative working-class patriotism was, as some suggest, the product of 'naturally' racy and radical East Enders internalising the missionary ideals of patriotic conservatism. If East End racism is not product of overly enthusiastic missionary zeal, the alternative notion of an enduring, almost 'in-bred' cultural trait is equally unpalatable. Nevertheless, simplified versions of these extrinsic and intrinsic explanations of East End social characteristics continue to be presented in the media (Cohen 1996: 175-180). It is clear that the burdensome quantity of competing representations, which abound in the East End, does not allow for simple resolution into neat typologies (Stedman-Jones 1989: 300).

Racism in the East End has been evident from the earliest days of Huguenot immigration and grew apace as Jewish refugees, fleeing pogroms in Eastern Europe, followed in Huguenot footsteps to Spitalfields which adjoins Bethnal Green. Anti-Semitism flared during World War I when Bethnal Green showed its patriotism in achieving the highest record for voluntary enlistment in London. The local Jewish population was largely exempt from conscription because of their essential tailoring work which was co-opted for making uniforms. Those who returned from the trenches readily interpreted Jewish trade as theft of jobs from local people and there were violent uprisings in the area in 1917 (Baker 1995: 132). British Fascism of the 1930s is remembered most significantly in the march of Mosley's blackshirts through the East End culminating in the battle of Cable Street in 1936.

The proximity of the Docks meant that the East End suffered particularly in the Blitz, both directly as people and homes were hit by bombs, and indirectly through the upheaval of child evacuation and the worst civilian disaster of the war (173 people died in an air raid shelter crush in 1943). The image of heroic cockneys was exploited by journalists for patriotic effect (Stedman-Jones 1989: 314). Post-war regeneration of the area continued the earlier projects of slum clearance. Between 1945 and 1962 the London County Council built over 2000 flats in Bethnal Green (Baker: 135-47). Such efforts of municipal social democracy brought decent housing, education and health services within the reach of nearly all (Rustin 1996: 4).

By the mid 1950s the Jewish population had declined through out-migration to other parts of London. Those who remained assimilated, or appeared to do so (Baker 1995: 145). Other European migrants (Irish, Maltese, Italians, Cypriots) followed a similar trajectory after initial periods of racial conflict. During this time, immigration from the New Commonwealth had not yet become noticeable. For a brief period, nonetheless significant in social memory, a sort of utopia existed of decent doorstep-scrubbing working-class society (Young & Wilmott 1957). Change continued apace thereafter: increasing traffic pushed some traditional street-trading away from the main thoroughfares to uncongenial purpose-built market-places in a repetition of the failed attempt by Baroness Coutts and Charles Dickens to create a model market place in Columbia Road (Porter 1994: 330). The number of dwellings declined and there was a continuing fall in the local population and a contraction in industry. Between 1931 and 1955 more than 40,000 people from Bethnal Green were rehoused in new estates, mainly in Essex (Young & Wilmott 1957: 123-4). This displacement forms the counterpoint to these authors' account of close-knit kinship in the traditional streets of Bethnal Green. The break-up of the old social order and the contraction of privately rented housing, coupled with the abolition of council housing waiting-lists in the mid 1950s increased the number of homeless.

The 1960s were characterised by increasing social and racial tensions and a climate of criminality typified by the notoriety of the Kray twins who had their headquarters in Vallance Road. The influx of Bangladeshi migrants accelerated throughout the 1970s and 1980s. It is to Bethnal Green's shame, but typical of the notorious strand of its social history, that the phrase 'Paki-bashing' was coined in its estates at the end of the 1960s (Runnymede Trust 1993: 21).

Porter, writing at the end of the Thatcher era takes a dismal view of contemporary inner London.

'Many indices of decline suggest a new urban order is emerging. In place of the employed, self-sufficient and respectable working classes.........A new outcast London is coming into being, poorly integrated into the disciplines of work, family and neighbourhood. Homelessness, family breakdown, classroom violence.......racial attacks - all aggravate spirals of deprivation, alienation, despair, and antisocial activities among a proliferating lumpenproletariat. Poverty and deprivation deepen, and an underclass is emerging that is perceived as a threat by the respectable, law-abiding and integrated.' (Porter 1994: 453-4).

If, as this quotation shows, it continues to be difficult to write about places like the East End without the contagion of a Victorian obsession with dirt, then we might hope that the disciplines of sociology, and geography should yield objective data with which we can contextualise such narratives.

2.3 Current social geography

Avoidance of the excesses of a lurid genre can lead to the opposite extreme, that is, the portrayal of the East End as place of uniform drabness. (This dreary version of the East End is portrayed in Jack London's abjectly titled, *'The people of the abyss'*). The two-dimensional nature of statistical profiles are always a problem when the aim is to produce an objective account which is not entirely lifeless. One method is to use illustrative life-histories to vivify the tables of numbers: the Runnymede Trust, a charity based in Spitalfields provides information and advice on matters relating to racial equality and justice and warns against inflammatory and cursory judgements about Tower Hamlets. Prompted by the election of a fascist to Millwall ward in the borough, the Trust's report (*'Neither Unique nor Typical: the context of race relations in the London Borough of Tower Hamlets'*) echoes, in its title, the chiaroscuro trope discussed earlier but the authors demand that readers should approach the problems of the area with 'humility, respect and slowness of judgement........particularly if they come to it from outside' (Runnymede Trust 1993: 3). The Runnymede Trust has need to lighten the gloom of its factual data with colourful extracts from life-history sources (Runnymede Trust 1993: 5). Mere juxtaposition of life-histories with statistics has, I argue, a tendency to sentimentalise the former while not adequately explaining the latter.

Alternatively, a perspective of evolution and progress may soften the impact of statistical facts. Rustin introduces a multi-disciplinary volume concerned with the regeneration of East London by suggesting that there is light at the end of the tunnel. He arranges the chiaroscuro along a historical time line. Thus the darkness of poverty and social disorganisation belonging to the Victorian past is left behind as industrialisation and political progress lead to the light of the respectable working-class of Young & Wilmott's Bethnal Green. He predicts that the darkness of economic hardship from the 1970s onwards will be left behind as he speculates on a globalised future. If the East End should now be categorised as a post-industrial global city, he suggests that an underclass may be an inevitable corollary and the darkness threatens to return (Rustin 1996: 2-8). Rustin is generally more optimistic than Porter in his hopes that ethnic diversity will contribute to the development of a more balanced society (ibid: 10), a hope which is not shared by Rix in the same volume.

Rix's (1996) survey of East London as a whole, including the outer as well as the inner boroughs, lends statistical weight to the view that the East End has a highly polarised society. Her account of the demographic changes and social geography of the area reveals continuing problems of scarce social resources and both relative and absolute social deprivation. Her data show evidence of a simultaneous upward and downward drift in opportunities and life-chances in the inner East London boroughs that are in contrast with the rest of the country. Rix's perspective thus suggests a dynamic model of East End life. Rather than trying to categorise East End people, or stages of history into types, I argue, following Rix, that the dynamics of social life in the East End simultaneously include unusually powerful upwards and downwards vectors. Rags may indeed become riches but others spiral downwards into destitution. This model suggests that the chiaroscuro effect in the East End has, in all probability, always been a matter of juxtaposed contrast and dynamic tension rather than a temporal sequence of static states. This goes some way to answering Cohen's lack of resolution about contradictory East End identities. Bearing in mind Rix's dynamic model, the relevant factual data can be summarised as a contemporary socio-economic profile of the area.

Because her remit includes the outer as well as the inner boroughs of East London, Rix reveals that not only is Tower Hamlets affected by proximity to the wealthy districts of the City of London and Docklands, but it is also markedly different from the neighbouring outer London boroughs of Redbridge and Waltham Forest, Barking and Dagenham. As such, these ethnically 'white' areas are a 'refuge' for those residents of the East End who can afford to emigrate eastwards (Rix 1996: 23).

Rix's demographic summary shows that inner East London boroughs have a high and increasing proportion of young people, high fertility rates and a high proportion of households with dependent children compared with Greater London and the country as a whole. Hence the area has above average numbers of families with three or more children compared with London as a whole (ibid: 36). Nearly half of all births in Tower Hamlets are to women who were born in New Commonwealth states, double that of London as a whole (ibid: 31). Immigration and settlement are much greater in London compared with Great Britain as a whole; in 1991 it contained almost half of Britain's minority populations (Ratcliffe 1996: 18). In the mid 1990s Rix estimates that over 30% of Tower Hamlets residents were non-white (Rix 1996: 27).

With regard to housing, Rix notes that although there has been an increase in owner-occupation in Tower Hamlets, this has had a detrimental effect on the availability of accommodation for the poorest residents: in 1981 Tower Hamlets had the largest percentage of council housing in the country. The council reduced building from over 400 new dwellings between 1981 and 1985, to 90 between 1986 and 1991. Owner-occupation increased steeply from approximately 5% to 23% between 1981 and 1991 because of the Docklands development and the 'right to buy' policy of a Conservative government. The proportion of local housing stock that was in the hands of the council authority thus declined from 82% to 58% between 1981 and 1991. In terms of housing, then, polarisation has increased throughout the 1980s and 1990s with increasing dependence by minorities, single families, the unemployed and insecurely employed sectors of the population on a declining stock of council housing. Homelessness has consequently increased (ibid: 41-4).

In a section devoted to education, Rix notes that whereas the region has hitherto been 'well known' for its low academic achievement, this picture is now changing. In 1993 the percentages of 15-16 year olds achieving five or more GSCE qualifications, and those aged 18 and over with a diploma, degree or higher degree were still below the national average. Hackney and Tower Hamlets, however, had the largest *increase* in higher qualifications within East London. The increase is probably accounted for in part by the settlement of new middle-class residents as well as the increasing student population who attend Guildhall, Queen Mary and East London Universities and need low-cost local accommodation (ibid: 45-47, see also Albury and Smee 1996).

The figures for economic activity tell a similar story: the decline in economically active men in London has been particularly marked in Tower Hamlets so that by 1991 less than half of all men in Tower Hamlets were working full-time, and nearly 20% of men aged between 16 and 64 were economically inactive compared with 10% ten years earlier. There has been a similar decline for women: in 1991, Tower Hamlets had the lowest percentage of women in the labour force of all London boroughs and 43% of women aged between 16 and 59 were economically inactive. Despite the rhetoric that launched the project, the Docklands development has not enhanced the economic opportunities for local residents equally. A decline in manufacturing employment and an increase in professional and service sectors has led to an overall decline in working-class occupations within Tower Hamlets. The average wage for full-time employees remains above that for the country as a whole only because of significant inward migration of people from the professional and managerial classes (Rix 1996: 47-58). The economic polarisation is regarded by Rix as almost wholly because of ethnic diversity (ibid: 58), an important point that is echoed by the census analysts discussed below.

Rix, in conclusion, finds that East London has remained throughout the 1980s (and in all probability the 1990s[2]) a heterogeneous locality and continues to be a 'back region' of complexity and diversity (Rix 1996: 58-9). Although the history of the contemporary Bengali population in Bethnal Green goes back several centuries, the time of maximum immigration in the latter half of the twentieth century coincides with an acceleration in the perennial cycle of East End polarisation. This acceleration began with economic recession in the 1980s as well as longer-term changes in inner city areas consequent on globalisation. Robertson is careful to point out the poverty of arguments which make a simple

---

[2] The Chantry Vellacott DFK report shows increasing distance between rich and poor in Britain during Blair's first Labour government. (M. Woolf, The Independent 28/4/01 p9).

16

opposition between 'global' and 'local' effects. His use of the jargon word 'glocalisation' captures the interconnected and mutually implicated processes which link global and local tendencies in contemporary life (Robertson 1995). Inner-city post-industrial areas become so-called 'metropolarities' (Soja 1997: 26) because their novel reconfigurations of socio-economic inequalities are no longer aligned with traditional social stratification based on class or racial categories.

2.4 Migration history of the Bengali population in East London

The present day Bengali population of Bethnal Green are descendants of the seamen (*lascars*) who worked on ships of the East India Company, British merchant and Royal Navies. *Lascar* (a word of uncertain etymology) was used to refer to any oriental seaman. They feature in romantic literature of the Victorian era as exotic servants and denizens of the East End (for example, Conan Doyle, Dickens, Hodgson-Burnett). They were recruited throughout the eighteenth and nineteenth centuries from East Bengal, the Punjab and the West coast of India (Visram 1986: 53). It is likely that Sylheti men were always numerically significant in the *lascar* workforce because of influential middle men or *sarengs* who acted as brokers between would-be *lascars* and ship owners in the port of Calcutta (later in Chittagong). They chose preferentially from among their networks of connections in land-locked Sylhet (Adams 1987: 13).

As well as *lascars*, Indian servants and *ayahs* (female Indian servants for children) were brought into Britain from the early 18th century onward as trusted, fashionable or ornamental and certainly cheap servants for those who had worked in the East India company and were accustomed to their oriental retinue (Visram 1986: 11). They were used to accompany children to school in England from India and they were expendable. If they were lucky they were recycled to travel with families going out to India for the first time, but more often they were badly treated and cast off at will to fend for themselves and could be found begging and destitute in London (ibid: 16-8 et seq. to 30). This inhumane treatment, graphically recorded by Visram, was also found in the systematic brutality meted out on ship by senior officers who singled out *lascars* for degrading exercises in arbitrary punishment (ibid: 35, Adams 1987: 15-28)

The need for ship-hands during and after the Napoleonic wars led to upwards of 1000 *lascars* a year arriving in British ports and approximately 3000 a year by 1842 (Visram 1986: 34-48). They lived in appalling conditions in the East End while awaiting a place on outgoing vessels. If they had survived the passage to Britain, on arrival they were frequently short-changed on pay, robbed by locals and herded into filthy and overcrowded barracks. The excessively high mortality rate mortality of *lascars* led to a parliamentary enquiry in 1814-5 and the founding of welfare institutions. Given such harsh conditions, many *lascars* left their ships and tried to eke out an impoverished life on the streets, often exchanging one form of slow death for another. Brief accounts of the *lascars'* history which mention their propensity to 'jump ship' do not always qualify the statement with information about the tradition of ill-treatment aboard English ships. This presumably lessened by the mid-twentieth century when settlement in Britain began.

From the 1920s onward, *lascars* who left their ships usually headed for Aldgate and its environs where Ayub Ali Master's coffee shop in Commercial Street and nearby hostel provided informal welfare assistance. This was formalised in 1943 when he set up the Indian Seamen's Welfare League (Adams 1987: 41-3). Other men adopted the role of *sareng* in London, finding places for those who looked for places on out-going ships, or they opened sociable coffee houses which formed the nucleus of contacts from which work in the restaurant and rag trades developed. By 1946 there were twenty Indian restaurants in London, in 1960 three hundred in Britain and three thousand by 1980 (Adams 1987: 47-49).

The political turmoil of the sub-continent influenced the settlement pattern of Sylheti men in London during the 1940s and 1950s. In 1947 a referendum in Sylhet brought it out of Assamese polity and into East Bengal which became East Pakistan in the same year. East Pakistani men at home and abroad at the time experienced discrimination from the Pakistan government and its High Commission in London through selective restriction of passports. In response to this, as well as the growing need for a Bengali social infrastructure, the Pakistan Welfare Association (PWA) was formed in 1952 for a community of about 300 Sylheti men in London (Adams 1987: 54-55). As well as providing welfare, the PWA followed political events in Pakistan closely and supported the nascent movement for autonomy that began after the death of language martyrs resisting the imposition of Urdu on Bengali-speaking East Pakistan on the 21st of February 1952 (ibid: 55). Aftab Ali, the General Secretary of the Indian's Seamen's Union, lobbied successfully to bring about legislative change in Pakistan after visiting East London. A steady stream of Sylheti migrants to Britain continued throughout the 1950s and by 1962 the community was perhaps 5000 strong (ibid: 60-64). Subsequently, Acts of Parliament imposed a voucher system restricting immigration to those who had already gained a job prior to entry, and so once again those already settled in Britain took on the role of *sarengs*, giving vouchers for jobs to those within their networks (ibid: 66, Gardner and Shukur 1994: 148). During the 1950s and early 1960s the demand for labour in Britain came mainly from factories in northern cities such as Birmingham, Manchester and Newcastle (Gardner 1993a: 3). By the end of the 1960s these industries declined in economic importance and East London became, once again, the focus of migration for Bengali migrants within Britain as well as directly from Bangladesh (ibid: 3). As immigration laws tightened and the social infrastructure for Bengali people became more established, the wives and children of migrant labourers travelled to join their husbands, reaching a peak in the early 1980s (Gardner & Shukur 1994: 150). The 1991 census counted 171,500 people of Bangladeshi origin in Britain, approximately half living in Greater London and a quarter in Tower Hamlets (Rees & Phillips 1996: 29-33). The current total is estimated at 200,000 (Gregory & Williams 2000: 37). Local estimates put the current Tower Hamlets Bengali population at 54,000 (LBTH 2001).

What were the original reasons for large-scale and enduring patterns of migration from Sylhet? The appalling conditions for *lascars* have been described not just for historical veracity but also to mitigate any tendency to see those *lascars* who jumped ship merely as opportunists and to raise the question as to why migration to Britain continued at all after the eighteenth century in the face of such hardships. Bengal has a long tradition of extensive population movements, initially to other parts of India and subsequently to Britain, the Gulf States and the Far East (Gardner 1995: 36, King 1994: 43). From 1961 onwards a net 150,000 people left Bengal each year, mostly from Sylhet. The singularity of Sylhet district in the numbers of migrants sent abroad is sometimes related to the area escaping the *zamindari* system of land tenure when the British administratively linked the district to Assam. It is suggested that Sylhet became a society of atomised, independent-minded, peasant land-owners, preferring to emigrate rather than labour on another person's land (Gardner 1995: 37-9). Land tenure systems in India do influence differential migration rates but the relationship is not simple and is only one among many factors for each historical and geographical location (Chandavarkar 1994 133ff., Holmstrom 1984: 33).

Migration cannot be attributed solely to the push factor of poverty (Carey & Shukur 1985: 406) because the migrants were not predominantly from the poorest sections of the population in Sylhet, the landless labourers, but from small land-owning families (Gardner 1995: 40). Nor can the lure of profit and adventure alone be the deciding factor although the poverty of Sylhet as a region and available wealth abroad forms an understandable *post hoc* rationalisation (Gardner & Shukur 1994: 146). Adams' elderly Sylheti informants give a variety of plausible answers to her questions as to why they decided to migrate. It was part of their 'Arab' genetic heritage (Adams 1987: 145) or an expression of their characteristically dare-devil mentality (ibid: 153) or an escape from political corruption in Bangladesh (ibid: 174), an explanation I have often heard. If each *lascar* had his own reason for leaving Sylhet, the well established *lascar-sareng* network can be interpreted minimally as an entrepreneurial enabling mechanism (Ballard 1994a: 9) for turning any one person's idea about migration (whether away from something bad or towards something good) into a fact. Elsewhere in India the role of middle-men (*jobbers*) in negotiating between labourers and factory management was eclipsed by contractors (Holmstrom 1984: 46-54). The role of Sylheti *sareng*-type middle-men continued, however, in Georgian and Victorian London through to the twentieth century and the masculine networks which they facilitate will be described as a significant feature in present day Bengali social connections.

The London Bengali population is thus made up of four cohorts in terms of immigration history: the original male migrants, their dependents arriving in the 1970s and 1980s, those who are born here and, lastly, the relatively few numbers of recent adult immigrants. The 1991 census shows that the Bengali population is more segregated, residentially, than any other minority ethnic population in Britain, dubbed by some 'the encapsulated population' (Eade, Vamplew & Peach 1996, Peach & Rossiter 1996: 123). As Rix indicates, the 1991 census also finds that Bengali households are particularly likely to be overcrowded, and are at the worst end of the scale for unemployment and long term illness. For Bengali people, occupational segregation is marked and the unemployment rates is three times that of the white population (Wrench & Qureshi 1996: 15-17). These problems appear to be caused almost wholly by material inequalities and racism. Peach and Rossiter (1996: 123) suggest that the magnitude of the order of difference in this social geography is such that it must be partly accounted for by the 'internal cultural and social features' of that community. At a superficial level the operation of an 'internal cultural factor' must be part of the explanation for 'culture', however defined cannot be negligible. The exact meaning and operation of 'culture' is unexamined by these authors although it is implicitly an operator of choice and preference. It is, however, risky to use the abstraction 'culture' alone to explain social segregation and inequality if this obscures other dimensions of social relations (Back 1996: 1-6, Farmer 1999, Knauft 1996: 251 and passim, Kuper 1999, Lawrence 1982). The use of 'culture' as an independent explanatory source, I argue here and elsewhere in this thesis, too easily leads to the simplistic and patronising notions of a 'close-knit ethnic minority community' or a 'defensive, introspective community' and an illusion of homogeneity (Gardner 1995: 7). Moreover, analyses of particular attempts to reverse discrimination by targeting resources at specific minority ethnic groups do not always, if ever, have the desired effect (Ratcliffe 1996: 21). The implication is that available models of how 'culture' and 'ethnicity' work in relation to diverse population groups are insufficient, or at least lacking in specificity (see also Jeffers, Hoggett & Harrison 1996: 124).

The social model of bounded communities, internal 'cultures' and external social facts may be wrong but it retains a hold over the popular imagination at least, and those of policy makers (Keith 1995: 557, Wright 1998: 7). It is important, therefore, to clarify the arguments concerning issues of ethnicity, racism and the politics of 'culture' and community in order to achieve a more accurate analysis of British Bengali social segregation and disadvantage. This work of clarification is addressed explicitly in Chapter 7. Until then inverted commas denote contingent meaning for abstract concepts such as 'culture'.

2.5 A walk in the street

Moving away from statistics, social geography can be illustrated with a description of the streets of Bethnal Green. The town is transected by East-West-oriented long streets, aligned with old Roman roads and river courses connecting the centre of London to Colchester in Essex (formerly a Roman garrison). The central street, Bethnal Green Road, is the principal shopping area of the district. This is flanked by small green spaces created by bomb-sites and slum clearance. The residential landscape forms a visible history of the successive styles of charitable and regenerative architecture in 'Estate' layout from the Victorian era to the present day (Riseboro 1996: 218). At the westernmost end is the junction with an urban clearway that runs North-South from the North Circular Road to the City of London. Eastwards from here the street is flanked by industrial buildings lying between Bethnal Green Road and the Boundary Estate (Morrison's (1982 [1896]) fictionalised 'Jago'), until the junction with Brick Lane, the heart of British Bengali commercial life. Wholesale leather businesses have large and glamorous showrooms in Brick Lane and Bethnal Green Road. After prayer times on Fridays large numbers of Bengali men can be seen walking northwards home or back to their workplaces from the mosque in Brick Lane. Residential blocks flanking Bethnal Green Road give way eastwards to shops and small businesses. Here, pedestrians increase and alter from mere traffic going from A to B to shoppers, idlers and general perambulation. From the Post Office to the junction with Vallance Road there is a preponderance of Bengali shops selling food, *saris*, videos, music and wedding goods. Many small outlets change their tenancies frequently[3]. The Bethnal Green Rights shop has mostly minority ethnic population clients waiting in its reception area. From Vallance road eastwards to the underground station, where another North-South main road transects Bethnal Green, the area appears to be a typical 'multicultural-globalised urban zone'. The shops are mixed, including English clothes boutiques, a gold jewellery pawn shop, numerous chemists, Bengali *sari* and general goods stores, as well as large commercial chain outlets such as Tesco's supermarket, Woolworth's and Boots. There are plenty of cafés among the shops of every variety including a traditional East End pie and mash shop to the west of Vallance Road and Pellicci's Italian 1950s-style café in the more mixed section.

This part of the street has space for market stalls as well as two-way traffic. It is unthinkable that Bethnal Green residents would allow wholesale removal of this street-market to a purpose-built setting as happened in parts of nearby Roman Road and Chrisp Street in Poplar. On market-day the street is very busy

---

[3] What was once my predecessor's surgery was later a tanning shop, a courier service and now sells sound systems. Dr Frederyck Zummers anglicized his name to Summers and sought refuge in London from anti-Semitic persecution in Poland. He worked in Bethnal Green until his death in 1983.

and to any observer freely multicultural. Most, but not all of the stalls are owned by Cockney traders selling food, general goods and clothes at cut-price. Bengali vegetable stalls are much more numerous in the nearby Whitechapel Road market but one or two have been trading in Bethnal Green Road recently. Bengali women in small groups choose from the goods on sale alongside white, Somali, Afro-Caribbean, Turkish, former Yugoslavian and South American customers. It is easy to find a significant cluster of people from almost every political state and ethnic background in Bethnal Green Road. As far as can be judged from watching the pedestrian traffic, Bengali groups are never mixed with any other category. On the other hand, white and Afro-Caribbean or other ethnically mixed clusters of shoppers are common. Although I have described the western end of the street as having a greater preponderance of shops selling Bengali goods, the entire street is a 'mixed area' and no one section can be described as an enclave. Within shops there is a more noticeable segregation. It is rare to find a white person in a *sari* shop or in a shop selling only Bengali food, but the Bengali shops which sell myriad small household objects are mixed and the larger chain shops are as mixed as the streets, both in their customers and their staff. Anyone might be found in McDonald's but only East End Cockneys are in the pie and mash shop and no traditionally-dressed Bengali people in Pellicci's. Islamic rules concerning *halal* meat dictates what sort of food should be avoided by Muslims, but it is possible to be selective from the menu and not infringe the rules. On the other hand some families are strict enough to avoid buying any foodstuffs if that shop also sells non-*halal* meat.

Away from the main street, the parallel thoroughfare to the north, Old Bethnal Green Road has few shops and so acts as a rapid pedestrian transit route without the distractions of window-shopping between home and school for parents and children. Again the segregation pattern seen in the shopping street is reproduced. Clusters of teenagers around the gates of secondary schools show that Bengali children are almost always separate from others although white and Afro-Caribbean or South-East Asian children mix more freely. Bengali parents of primary school children chat together waiting for their charges, a little apart from parents of other ethnic backgrounds. Some of these women are young enough to have been schooled here and need not be excluded from conversation in English.

The census analysts' findings of residential segregation are thus easily observed in the tableau presented by the streets of Bethnal Green. Segregation may be more marked for the Bengali population than for other ethnic groups, but they do not live in a separate enclave or ghetto. People shop elsewhere of course: in the corner shops near to their homes, in the Roman Road, in other East End street-markets and in the West End. The reason for segregation is not obvious from the street view and it will be interesting to see if the forthcoming analysis of the 2001 census shows a similar index of Bengali residential segregation. If the explanation is to do with 'internal cultural factors' then the question arises as to why an enclave has not appeared. Of course it is unlikely that the centripetal force of any such factors would be such as to prevent ordinary families from shopping at Tesco's or Woolworth's, but if it is significant enough to put the Bengali population of Tower Hamlets 'off the scale' in terms of segregation indices at ward and enumeration district level, then it might be thought to exert enough force to discourage Bengali women dressed in black *burqas* from picking and choosing in as relaxed a manner as anybody else from among the variety of underwear on the stalls of white Cockney traders. The segregating process cannot, therefore, be solely an internal 'cultural' centripetal force, nor only an extrusion process engendered by systematic racism, for either would be likely to lead to the formation of an enclave given the length of time of settlement of the Bengali population. The evolving relationship between different ethnic groups, I argue, has led to a particular *configuration* of segregation in Bethnal Green and cannot be simplified to push or pull. 'Race relations' analysis is the subject of another chapter, but these street observations serve as context for the following chapters where public spaces are left behind and the ethnography moves 'within the community'.

2.6 Urban anthropology and methodology

From the background data given, several issues arise as to the problems likely to beset an anthropological study in Bethnal Green. In summary these are threefold: firstly, the genre tradition of a chiaroscuro trope in representations of Bethnal Green alongside the reality of socio-economic polarisation; secondly, the need to consider the urban geography of Bethnal Green as well as its historical legacy of poor social amenities and lack of economic opportunities; lastly, the particularities of the migration history and current demographic and sociological features of the Bengali population must be incorporated within any ethnography. With regard to the latter, this study has had to contend with a remarkable degree of change in the time immediately before and during the fieldwork as the local Bengali population has only recently become established. Family reunions and second-generation families are relatively new phenomena; the social infrastructure of religious institutions, specialised shops and services such as those for travel, transnational finances, immigration legal assistance and weddings that are particularly aimed at the Bengali population have developed visibly during the period of my fieldwork (1997-2000). During that time, some informants have grown from being school-age teenagers to adults with children of their own. To reiterate a previous point, in such a changeable field there is no possibility of using generalised interpretations of abstracted phenomena such as 'culture', 'identity' or 'community', alone or in combination, as anchors, grids or matrices for the analysis of the ethnographic case material. Given the setting, what kind of urban ethnographic approach is most appropriate to a study of Bethnal Green?

Urban ethnography can be thought of as being only an extension of traditional village studies, at least in the fundamentals of its methodology (Hannerz 1980: 304ff.). Anthropology is more readily distinguished from other social science disciplines by its methodology and scale rather than the content of its theory (Gupta & Ferguson 1997b, Knauft 1996: 35, Gell 1998: 10). Any field site may be complex and confusing for an individual participant-observant researcher, but urban settings are less likely to be clearly defined, spatially at least, than most rural villages and are more likely to contain a greater density, diversity and complexity of social relations than other research settings (Ferguson 1999: 18). The basic fieldwork methodology, however, remains the same in any setting with its reliance on participant-observation, usually by a single researcher within a population of informants numbering tens or at the most hundreds of people. Moreover, informants are selected or contacted without any intention that they should be a statistically representative sample of the population under study. The particularities of my fieldwork setting have already been described with regard to how I went about collecting data. My approach to collating such data into ethnographic text, and my choice of the notion of social predicaments as a structuring device, was formed by consideration of the particular features of Bethnal Green, as given above, in the context of social science literature of 'the city'.

Wirth's minimum definition of the city as a 'relatively large, dense, and permanent settlement of socially heterogeneous individuals' (Wirth 1938: 8) may not be unique to urban places but the characteristically urban way of life does find its most pronounced expression in metropolitan cities (ibid: 7). The heterogeneity of a city is, in his view, more than just a function of achieving a critical mass of each sub-population, consisting of a spatial ecology leading to segregated mosaics of micro-environments. In turn, although intensive local relationships can give rise to 'urban villages', city life, Wirth argues, is also likely to include a greater number of interactions or traffic with strangers (Wirth 1938: 12, Hannerz 1980: 11). While early twentieth-century Chicago sociologists are to be celebrated for the power of their detailed ethnography, the ecological theory that such work often entails has led some writers to criticise them for a general bias towards spatial determinism (Rogers & Vertovec 1995: 16, 18, Keith 1995: 558). The theoretical essays of the Chicago school certainly favour a deterministic view of the city, with an emphasis on anomie, the superficiality of social encounters and a tendency to moral disorder (Park et al. 1968), themes which endure throughout urban studies and the media (Hannerz 1980: 59ff). Wirth places greater stress on social relations and his essay, *Urbanism as a Way of Life* (Wirth 1938), justifiably continues to attract critical acclaim. Hannerz (1980), and Rogers and Vertovec (1995) emphasise social relations, favouring a methodology which includes network and situational analysis derived from the ethnography of Mitchell, Gluckman and others in the Rhodes Livingstone Institute.

Replacing so-called spatial determinism with an approach that attempts to humanise the city (Cohen 1993) by placing the individual centre-stage may also suffer in its explanatory potential if the effects of urban geography and political economy are too radically displaced (Soja 1997: 21). The proximity of Bethnal Green to the rich commercial districts and suburban Essex may not have an inevitable deterministic effect on the social lives of all its residents but this topography is not without effect. If Rix typifies the area as a 'back region' (Rix 1996: 59), it is certainly not a backwater outside the flow of cosmopolitan life. Barrow boys from Bethnal Green market-stalls can walk to the nearby City of London and get jobs cleaning the floors of the commodity and currency trading rooms. In time, given ease of travel and proficiency with figures and trading acquired from working on family market-stalls, some become international currency dealers with large incomes and expensive acquisitions, remaining all the while living in council blocks of Bethnal Green. Industrious working-class families can acquire sufficient resources over time to move to Essex and in this way may retain their jobs and family connections within Bethnal Green while living in suburbia. Others aspire to make large fortunes through illegal trading in drugs, bank-note forgery or stolen goods, economic activities which are particularly suited to the material resources and layout of urban environments. Such life histories are visible models for others whose imaginations are excited by proximity to such dramatic trajectories out of the limitations of manual work or unemployment and welfare dependency; alternatively the hopeless are further depressed.

The ambitious do not only fight their way out of Bethnal Green through the boxing-ring at York Hall in the clichéd mode of ghetto life-stories (for example, 'Dutch' Sam - inventor of the upper cut); ex-residents also become famous through careers in science (Elizabeth Garrett Anderson, Jacob Bronowski) the arts (David Bomberg, Solomon), entertainment (Bud Flanagan, Jack Warner) and business (Lord Grade, Sir Charles Clore). In this way it takes little imagination to see that the spatial or topographical relations of the area do go some way to contributing to the social polarisation and the dynamics of upward and downward social mobility. Soja's notion of 'metropolarity', the urban form found in older inner-city towns which have been emptied of manufacturing and other working-class industries and patchily transformed by pockets of residential gentrification, immigrant populations and enterprise zones, applies to Bethnal Green (Soja1997: 26). Without resorting to spatial determinism, this finding of simultaneous cosmopolitan as well as village characteristics goes some way to explaining why the social landscape in Bethnal Green is polarised.

Unravelling the multiple qualities of any such 'postmetropolis' must be followed by some measure of reconstruction in ethnography. In Bethnal Green, fluidity, diversity and change are found in extreme measure, but so are very hard formations of socially distinct groups with agonistic boundaries. Wirth's mosaic city may be subject to deconstruction *as a theoretical model* by anti-essentialist discourses, but city life in Bethnal Green is observably both hard like a ceramic mosaic and in constant flux. Paradoxically, then, in areas where social and cultural change, degeneration and regeneration are all prominent concerns, notions of fixed, separate and essential cultures and societies, now thoroughly out-moded in academia, remain evident in practice (cf. Gupta & Ferguson 1997a: 39, Gilroy 2000: 103). Whilst diasporic populations may be used rhetorically to deconstruct theories of bounded cultures and societies (Gilroy 2000: 123) they can also provide telling ethnographic examples of how apparently solid social formations emerge out of highly differentiated social environments.

In order to include such differentiation as well as whole social formations I pay attention to recurrent social predicaments which appear to be salient and particular to Bengali people *in the context of* the mixed society of Bethnal Green. I do not isolate the Bengali population in Bethnal Green in order to conduct a survey. The cross-cultural setting is my basic research tool and may well exclude certain social facts that could only be revealed by a researcher from within that population. By fixing on people caught up in events in particular places and times, I felt comfortable leaving the models and theories of peoples, cultures and places to one side until the empirical data had been exhausted. Among the early Chicago sociologists, Burgess (1968 [1925]) cautioned against those (social workers) who collected data without fixing a theoretical framework in advance since he saw this as unscientific[4]. As my research setting comes perilously close to such 'social work' without prior theory among the settlements of a multicultural city, I take issue with what seems to me an unnecessarily lofty and deductive stance. A scientific study is defined by its practice rather than theory (Durkheim 1966 [1938]).

The use of social predicament as a methodological tool has some resemblance, not only to Durkheim's distribution of social phenomena, but also to the situational analysis and extended case study methodology of the Rhodes Livingstone Institute (RLI) anthropologists, and with Hannerz' model of urban 'situations' and typology of urban lives (Hannerz 1980: 100, 255, Hannerz 1992). Ferguson's criticisms of the RLI notwithstanding, his response to them in the light of his own fieldwork has parallels with my approach,

---

[4] Sibley quotes the memoirs of a Chicago student in 1919, 'I heard little about the social services. However, there were occasional rumblings about "the old maids downtown who were wet-nursing social reformers."' (Sibley 1995: 168)

'I am less interested in a succession of typical forms over time than in an understanding of the whole spread..... of diverse modes of getting by that may exist at any one moment....'(Ferguson 1999: 20).

Ferguson translates 'diverse modes of getting by' into performative 'cultural styles', whereas my experience of Bethnal Green suggests that 'getting by' means strategic actions prompted by the exigencies of predicaments. The notion of a distribution of social predicaments also resonates with Sperber's epidemiology of cultural representations (Sperber 1996). An epidemiological perspective, Sperber argues, allows anthropological interpretations to be situated in the context of myriad contextual observations and avoids the fruitless search for a 'macro-mechanism' which explains cultural facts (ibid: 54). Replacing 'representation' with 'predicament' makes the argument in his essays cogent to my research. Looking for predicaments, and working outwards until a pattern is discerned, rather than looking for illustrations to a programmatic theme, need not be read as pathologising the lives of the people in the study (although I prefer 'distribution' to 'epidemiology' to avoid such connotation). A bias towards trouble-cases, I argue, may be used heuristically to unravel the workings of culture (or any other matter of interest) in relation to other social effects (cf. Addams 1917).

As my fieldwork progressed, recording diversity remained more prominent than notes about commonalities, yet certain regularities of predicaments emerged. If my informants have humdrum concerns with health, employment, social resources and the conduct of family life, nevertheless a particularly Bengali flavour to recurrent ordinary problems is discernible. Almost predictable configurations of family members, neighbours and institutional personnel make their appearance in similar circumstances, whether it is a household negotiating with welfare officers, the dispute of a young woman with her parents over issues of education and marriage, young men troubled by peer group relations, conjugal relationships, anxieties over spiritual maladies or neighbours gossiping about the behaviour of others.

During fieldwork this patterning of predicaments fostered thoughtfulness about the interplay of factors such as custom, gender, class, migration history, education and racism, without the risk of theory constraining field data. New material could be brought in, from the bottom so to speak, increasing the range of observable predicaments, while from the top, to continue this rather hydraulic metaphor, the collated data, with their regularities and exceptions, were a fund for thought about kinship, racism, spirituality and gossip in Bethnal Green as well as about general and abstract concepts of culture, the individual and society. The pattern of predicaments is thus not only a useful device for stabilising highly differentiated data, but also allows the delineation of whole formations ('cultures', 'communities' and 'societies', and their inter-relationships.

The idea of writing about a diversity of cultural expressions in one field area is hardly novel. Other regions are rich in ethnographic analyses of plural and contested cultural meanings within the context of power and gender relations. Knauft, a Melanesianist, has consistently advocated a critical approach to ethnography and this is particularly well argued in his broad review of theory (Knauft 1996). His argument is echoed by Kuper's review of culture and ethnography (Kuper 1999). Both authors perceive the limits of deconstruction and the tensions inherent in writing about cultural diversity and social inequality in one text. My fieldwork and ethnographic approach is aligned with these authors' views. Anthropological methodology can, I argue, be inclusive with an economy of resources, allowing political, historical and sociological data to be contextualised by the collated analyses of a series of anthropologist-informant relationships.

The next chapter goes to the heart of this methodology and is remote from the broader data summarised here. The bulk of my fieldwork notes form a doctor's case-book and a selection from that casework follows.

CHAPTER 3 SOCIAL PREDICAMENTS

3.1 Plight and Predicament

A consultant writes to me after an out-patient consultation with one of my patients:

"Thank you for referring this young Bengali housewife (Aliya). She has had four or five months of epigastric pain with some associated vomiting. Since you referred her, this seems to have come under control with Rabeprazole and she is not really getting very much trouble any more. Pathology in a young woman of this age, particularly someone who looks so well, is unlikely and I think that she had a bout of non-ulcer dyspepsia which now seems to be resolving.

She lives with her husband and three small children in a one-bedroom flat. He works as a chef in a restaurant and is away for six evenings a week from 6pm to midnight. Although there is some support from his family, she has no relatives in the UK and is clearly homesick for her parents. She would like to visit them but, at the moment, they cannot afford the fare.

Stress-induced illness is common among these young Bengali housewives who live in cramped conditions, often alone with small children for much of the day and who feel cut off from their home and families in Bangladesh. It seems a pity that this period of looking after pre-school children, which should be very rewarding, is so often one of stress and functional illness. I am sure that her problems will ease when her children go to school and that things will get better if she and her husband could be persuaded to refrain from enlarging their family for the time being."

The consultant is without doubt sympathetic. His diagnosis is of stress-induced illness caused by what is now to him a familiar constellation of social problems. He frequently sees Bengali families who endure substandard housing conditions and limited employment opportunities (the Indian restaurant trade) with poor pay and conditions (the unsociable hours). His enquiry as to her family support confirms his assumption that, being a migrant, she has the additional ('natural') distress of separation from her natal family in Bangladesh. Finally he makes a comment which suggests that there is a cultural element compounding their problems - excessive fertility.

He sees her as being not so much in a predicament from which she may take action or form a strategy to ameliorate her distress but as a woman in a pitiable plight which is shared, sadly, by many other young Bengali housewives. The facts of migration, local economics and what are to his mind, 'fixed cultural beliefs' about fertility lead to the image of a family locked into a situation of hardship. Leaving aside for the moment a more detailed analysis of this case history, his account of their social difficulties as part of a medical opinion is adequate for the purpose of pointing the GP back in the direction of psycho-

29

social care rather than instituting further unnecessary and potentially harmful investigations.

My point of view as a GP is not so particular as that of the consultant. I see all kinds of people, well and sick, happy and sad, from all sorts of backgrounds rather than the selective population of referred patients in his out-patient clinic where he sees recurrent similar problems. I have the advantage of knowing about patient's circumstances in greater detail through our personal-list system of family medicine. Diversity and disparity are as prominent as 'typical cases'. It is easy for me to find counter examples which undermine the logical chain of causality of socio-economic deprivation and racist practices leading inevitably to victimhood. Not all women who share Aliya's predicament are as unhappy or as apparently helpless as his summary of her life's problems leads him to conclude.

Why some people cope better than others 'given the circumstances' needs to be explained if anything is to be said that goes beyond the depressing generalisations which are all too easily made about minority ethnic families' lives in Britain. Statistics, well annotated, give an overall picture of what we might expect to find for any one population group (Modood & Berthoud 1997) and life-histories can illustrate both what is typical as well as variations from the usual situation (Adams 1987, Centre for Bangladeshi Studies 1994). Taken together, the bare facts and illustrative detail still do not give a systematic account of the reasons and chains of causality for variability within any one particular population.

The selected stories in this chapter are given not just so that the more conventionally aggregated generalisations in subsequent chapters will be inhabited in the reader's memory by 'real' people, although this is one purpose. It is also intended that they should pose more questions than they answer and that the route to the answers should be discernible through the detail of the methodology even at this stage. They are illustrative in a limited way but they are not an exhaustive set of cultural types within local Bengali society. They are, in fact, somewhat jumbled as to social categories and are far from being neat expositions of particular aspects of Bengali 'identity' or 'culture' in Bethnal Green. Taken, as they are, from a doctor's case-book, they focus largely but not exclusively on trouble cases. It is when trouble strikes that contextual issues come sharply into focus and apparently effortless 'normality' is shown up in contrast as being the product of effort and action. I note the effort required to think analytically about those whose lives runs smoothly and also about the exclusion of certain women through this mode of research.

Apart from trouble, I have emphasised the cross-cultural nature of these encounters rather than exclusively Bengali cultural practices. If there are many different positions within the Bengali population of Bethnal Green there is also a variety of cross-cultural interfaces. This is the confounding factor in mixed society research: no cultural isolate is discernible except by artificial construction, which means that the analysis of cross-cultural relationships threatens to become impossibly complex and elusive. If there is no singular community boundary or cultural interface between Bengali and non-Bengali people in Bethnal Green, there is still *an* interface in almost any context susceptible to research. Against all this difficulty, there is one cross-cultural encounter which is uniquely available for analysis, and is, in my research position at least, the most basic tool of enquiry. There may be no singular way that Bengali people interact with 'outsiders', but from the point of view of one outsider, myself (who, it must be assumed, works in more or less the same way from day to day), thoughtfulness about the variety of ways in which cultural matters intrude or are suppressed or deemed irrelevant to the doctor-patient relationship is my primary research tool.

Doctors cannot be expected to have time to become conversant with all the customs of the many different transnational families who seek their care. There is, for anyone, an opportunity to reflect on the reasons why some cross-cultural encounters in any setting go badly, or do not allow resolution of the matter in hand, or leave a feeling of bafflement and dissatisfaction. If a religious or cultural issue comes to the fore in these reflections, the question arises as to whether this was because of what the patient did or said, or whether in fact it was raised by the doctor, in which case why did it intrude on their normal style of practice? The same process of analysis can be applied to encounters between teachers and pupils or shop-keepers and customers or between neighbours. Explanations which focus on communication difficulties are usually given as the most immediate cause of the difficulty in comments such as, "Isn't it hard when people can't speak English", or, "I never really know if Muslim women mind seeing a male doctor or not" or "I never know if her husband is really translating what she says" but they do not really get to the nub of the question (Smaje 1995: 104). It is possible to become self-conscious of the circumstances which lead to *inappropriate* interposition of 'culture' in any relationship and to develop strategies for removing blocks to good medical or educational or neighbourly relationships, without being an anthropologist. The corollary is that such analyses can also be used as a research tool.

There is yet no direct answer to the questions of the pattern and reasons for a particular distribution of social predicaments for the Bengali population of Bethnal Green. I will mention where further information is needed to contextualise the material presented here. To begin with, observable difference in social position gives a loose organising structure for this chapter which moves from young housewives and their husbands to single men of a similar age and then to older parents and their unmarried children. The encounters described are anonymised by disguising certain personal details and conflating some aspects of similar stories without compromising veracity. Any of the quotations and circumstances that are given here have been said by, or could be attributed to, at least one other person. A reader who feels they have identified themselves in any of these narratives is more likely than not to be reading about someone else.

Returning to Aliya, one aspect of this couple's predicament is that a kind English specialist read their problems as a pitiable *plight*, not amenable to change except by persuasion, "... if they could be persuaded to refrain from enlarging their family". This plight is seen as contingent on their minority ethnic status and cultural beliefs. We can imagine how an English patient might have been 'read' within a different paradigm where psychosomatic illness is usually thought to be caused by difficulties within the patient's psychological make-up or their immediate social relationships rather than cultural beliefs and so might be susceptible to some sort of psychological therapy; this was not suggested in this particular case.

What is central to this family's difficulties is in fact a series of mis-readings by others, both Bengali and non-Bengali. The reason that the consultant letter struck me as inaccurate was that my recollection of this couple was not so much one of pathos and victimhood as of a pair who frequently got on the wrong side of the very people whom they expected to be able to help them with their difficulties. The trouble usually arose because they sought to extend their social network in an active and sometimes risky manner.

Although it is true that Aliya's parents are in Bangladesh and are missed, she would have left them far away had she married and stayed within Bangladesh as some of her village age-mates must have done. This is not the most immediate cause of her difficulty. When her husband Mohammed said to the consultant that 'his family' gave some support he actually meant his brother-in-law, Aliya's sister's husband, who lives in a neighbouring borough. Mohammed's parents are also in Bangladesh and he only has distant kin in the UK, living outside London. Mohammed and Aliya's practical difficulties arise from debt, homelessness and problems with benefits rather than being a direct consequence of migration from Bangladesh. Several moves occasioned by their economic difficulties have disrupted their children's schooling. Aliya reached a point where she could not see any way out of this chain of dismal events. The last straw came when Bengali neighbours were rude to her because they thought she was a gossip, and by inference, lower class. In my consulting room she almost fainted with emotional exhaustion on one occasion.

Before recent events they were a glamorous, personable couple who wore stylish clothes, more fashionable than mainstream local Bengali dress, but not in the modern Islamic styles worn by others of similar age. They are unsettled, never established at one address, their manner lurching from confident affability and a well-to-do presentation to a tableau of wilting despair. A long holiday to Bangladesh was much enjoyed, (although it curtailed social security and housing benefits) and Mohammed brought his brother-in-law to see me soon after their return with the children who had troublesome mosquito bites. The room was filled with a noisy happy family group on that occasion. The two young fathers were noticeably companionable and at ease managing lively toddlers with no hint of the sort of embarrassment that I expect from most English fathers managing small children in public. Aliya once brought a younger female friend with her to another consultation, and her pleasure at showing her friend how her doctor spoke Sylheti was evident. They were, on these occasions, very unlike the stereotypical lonely immigrant family of the consultant's letter.

Mohammed is keen to make more money than a restaurant worker's wages, but his ambition to be a head chef made him an irritable junior kitchen hand and he fell out with his employers. He now does some mini-cab driving while looking for a better job, but this still leaves Aliya and the children alone at night and if they are ill or worried he has to break his shift and come home. Breaks in employment mean a trip to the social security office and as Aliya is now feeling ill, he would rather take a certificate from me for stress-related illness than find another job at present. The social security staff argue about whether he really is ill or not but in the end they prefer the label of invalidity as he otherwise refuses job interviews or training schemes on the grounds that he is needed at home too often to be able to apply himself consistently to work. Mohammed and Aliya are eagerly dependent on my services as an advocate to help with their social problems and such dependency can make me ill at ease. At times the flattering language Mohammed uses makes me embarrassed as it sounds craven, sometimes almost sacrilegious and implies I am susceptible to flattery, "You are very good doctor, please can you help me; next to Allah you are good to me, I will pray for you doctor". Their contraceptive care broke down not through ignorance or religious belief, but because they were temporarily far from my surgery and could not trust another clinic. Against the potential inference that I am a doctor who fosters dependency, my explanation that serious disease was unlikely to be the cause of her stomach pains, in Sylheti[5], was insufficient, hence the visit to a more powerful person, the specialist.

In social terms, anticipating some of the general data in later chapters, Aliya and her husband enjoy the relative freedom of being distant from the authoritarian gaze of the older generation. There is no-one in their immediate sphere checking on the propriety of their behaviour. They are not obviously lonely as they do have some local family and friends, nor are they overly anxious about custom *per se*, for unlike others, they do not give religious or cultural reasons for refusing certain kinds of medical care. They are, in summary, a sociable couple who go out of their way to build a network of contacts. It is probable that the friends and relatives who occasionally accompanied them were meant to witness how successfully they and myself got on. The efforts they make to engage the help of those they judge to be useful like myself or their neighbours or social security clerks can be successful but can also misfire. I have described my own discomfort and it is not going too far to extrapolate from this to others whom they come across in institutionalised settings.

Their problems are not primarily cultural in origin: there are no specific customs which block a rational course of action to take them out of their difficulties, but cultural or 'culturalised' aspects of certain *relationships* do hinder their progress. Their predicament is that of a young couple with little in the way of 'traditional' support and meagre socio-economic resources. They have got onto the wrong side of neighbours through Aliya's stretching of customary neighbourly chatting which labelled her as a gossip. They have at times also found themselves on the wrong side of what should be relatively straightforward arrangements - paying rent, finding employment, schooling, medical and welfare support. In short Aliya and Mohammed push the boundaries of what can be expected out of, say, a family doctor, but given their circumstances they are not unreasonable in their demands. They are successful and skilled in family relationships but currently in a mesh of difficulties which cannot be attributed to one single cause. This is compounded by inappropriate cultural readings of their predicament by others when they are seen to be 'a typical Bengali couple'.

Other couples who share a similar position, having few or no local relatives, live more contained and orderly, if persistently isolated lives. Rahena and Muffasir are a couple whose relatives are all living in Bangladesh. When Muffasir's father was ill they could only afford one air-fare to Bangladesh; Rahena's life became precarious as she was left in charge of their three young children and neither she nor they spoke adequate English. Other Bengali mothers have had to use social services on occasion to care for their children if they went to hospital while their husbands were away, having formed no close relationships with neighbours who could provide child-care even for a few days. Despite their isolation, Rahena and Muffasir are happy with their life: the marital relationship is harmonious and they enjoy making a home for their children in Bethnal Green. One night Muffasir was attacked walking home from work and was taken to hospital only when someone in a late-night shop noticed him lying bleeding in the street and called an ambulance. He recovered and went back to work. I expressed sympathy and was prepared to hear justified condemnation of mindless racist violence in 'my' country. The group of youths were apparently mixed, some white, some black, he wasn't sure, "It happened so quickly, but what can you do? This happens everywhere, it could have been anyone, thank God I am still alive anyway." Perhaps this was a rationalisation or a wish to be polite in my company, but his attitude is consistent with the way

---

[5] I speak sufficient Sylheti for consultations; interpreters are not freely available.

that he and his family exhibit a momentum of carrying on whatever the circumstances.

Whereas Aliya and her husband take risks and get into difficulties for the trouble they take to enlarge their social world, Muffasir and his wife, remain isolated without feeling particularly at a loss, like many inner-city residents. These examples suggest that similar placement within a social network may have different outcomes in a mixed urban society.

3.2 Dynastic Success

When there is nothing pressing in terms of immediate social needs, the notion of predicament recedes, but with effort and reflection apparently unremarkable encounters can act as a useful counterpoint to those who present more obviously in difficulties. Unlike Aliya and Mohammed's isolation from the older generation, young Bengali couples usually have older kin in this country and are meshed in with a large number of relatives who, if not resident in Bethnal Green, are within East London. This allows them to be read by others as fitting in with the (historically) local pattern of kin networks which emphasises certain relationships such as that between mother and married daughter (Young & Wilmott 1957).

Continuing with the examination of my relationship with young Bengali women, I notice that with Fatima I am often seeking to soothe, to approve of her judgement and be supportive of her point of view in matters slightly peripheral to medical care, such as toddler eating problems or school difficulties. I am rarely challenging and find myself giving advice and seeking to reassure more than is usual in my practice. I am aware that reassurance alone can be a misplaced kindness in a professional setting since it signals to the patient both that their anxiety was groundless and that they lack the resources to find solutions independently of authoritative others. Fatima, however, is always so pleasant, grateful and polite that I am not always immediately aware of the direction taken by our doctor-patient relationship until I reflect on it outside our face-to-face encounters. She evokes in me a tender regard, and in this way the hierarchical difference between us from time to time is emphasised. When the hierarchy is sharply defined she is like a dutiful married daughter and I inhabit the role of an older motherly woman; the pattern is not consistently asymmetrical for at other times the atmosphere is more egalitarian, like that of two mothers discussing common daily family problems.

She is the eldest daughter of a family that has been established here since she and her mother joined her father in Bethnal Green in the early 1980s. I have known her since she was a child; her younger brothers and sisters were born here. Her father is energetic and has managed to sustain a series of factory jobs (leather work and tailoring) from the 1960s until late in his fifties which is relatively rare given the prevalence of chronic heart disease in middle-aged

South Asian men living in Britain. The family managed to move ten years ago from a small flat in a very dilapidated block to one that is roomier and in better condition through perseverance with the housing office. Fatima and her husband were able to obtain a council tenancy nearby because her parents put in an application as soon as she was old enough and they were willing to accept whatever the council offered. Fatima now has three children and is often at her mother's house when her husband leaves for work as a waiter in South London.

Fatima married her husband, Tahir, in Bangladesh and he obtained his visa to live with her in Britain 18 months later. Custom, as will be discussed in the next chapter, has been reversed here, for virilocal marriage is preferred by Bengali families. The rule is overlooked when the groom comes from Bangladesh and an independent, neolocal household, although near to the bride's parents house, is not technically an uxorilocal arrangement.

Fatima and Tahir get on well; he has accepted what is, in effect, a demotion from white-collar work in Bangladesh to waitering here as a consequence of his marriage, "When he is established, when his English is better, he can do another college course here, just for now he is doing a waiter's job", Fatima says. Tahir does not remain monolingual for long, nor out of work although his lack of British qualifications reduces his present opportunities to that of the Bengali restaurant network or factory work. Fatima jokes about his helpless state to me without cruelty, "I have to show him *everything*; he gets lost even when he's not far from our street and I feel like a tourist guide sometimes." This light-hearted exchange betrays something of a predicament: although custom dictates that she is junior to her husband, in practice she is the person of action and he is dependent on her. This relationship must be carefully managed if she is not to frustrate or humiliate him or engender hopelessness in a man who is, if only because of his position, susceptible to loneliness and anxiety about his standing both at home and abroad. His younger brothers-in-law are much further ahead in socio-economic terms as well as being socially at ease in London. One brother has started his own take-away business while another is an undergraduate at London University. Part of Fatima's management strategy is to ensure that she herself is not anxious about domestic headaches, hence the seeking out of a reassuring, advice-giving doctor.

Consultations with any of this extended family, including Fatima's husband run smoothly: they do not trouble me for home visits unless essential, nor do they ask for assistance with letters to social services or the housing or immigration services. They manage perfectly well without using persuasion or flattery to engage my attention when it is needed. They present their problems in a straightforward manner; they are polite and deferential, always open and ready to be themselves. We are, in short, always professional together, but the professional distance does not shade into chilly reserve, far from it. In a crisis some years ago my advice was sought on an intimate matter, the older couple and I in a triangular huddle together with hushed voices and serious faces going back and forth over the best solution to an emotionally demanding medico-ethical problem.

Fatima's style and manner fit in with this straightforward theme and could be described as mainstream traditional Bengali. She always wears a *sari* and her long hair is coiled up neatly in a knot. In cold weather she wears a cardigan or ordinary coat and a loose triangular headscarf that drapes casually over her shoulders when indoors. Other Bengali women of her age and status may wear formal Islamic *hijab*, *burqa* and face veil or fashionably styled coats and head scarves with elegant and elaborate make-up. Fatima's jewellery and make-up are minimal, her hair plainly styled but her choice of *sari* colours is pretty and far from being dull. In fact there is little or no difference between herself and her mother in dress style so that she therefore looks almost 'old-fashioned', if such an word can be used in an area of such diversity.

Pleasantness, deference and a noticeable lack of complaint mark our relationship. In particular, the doctor-patient relationship is not, at first sight, affected by cultural difference. It is worth repeating that the smooth running of our consultations means that the exact nature of the relationship requires some effort of reflection to bring into focus. Giving the matter thought I notice that I recurrently tend to reinforce her pre-existing beliefs, customs and mode of life without challenge although I am accustomed to avoid harmful collusion. As health advisors we are habituated to our role in encouraging lifestyle changes where it is needed but with Fatima I am more inclined to concur than to question. Since her medical problems are no more than common self-limiting illnesses it is interesting that my role with her has become noticeably that of the soothing protective advisor.

In summary, this extended family has sought out and retained geographical, economic, educational and institutional stability. Their 'groundedness' is evident in the unchanging fashions of dress, and a theme of reproduction of custom without anxiety. They have managed to avoid a lot of moves and dispersal of the family which is otherwise not uncommon among local families of all backgrounds. They have improved their housing, retained good relations with a doctor-advisor and strongly encouraged and supported their children's development and education (at the expense of extra income in the short-term). The whole is more than the sum of its parts: they may have had good fortune in the father's good health, energies and robust personality but a particular strategy is discernible that has 'brought out the best' so to speak, so that their goals and strategies are well matched.

3.3 Irregular Marriage

Salena has followed an unorthodox nuptial path in contrast to Fatima. Originally promised to a cousin in Bangladesh while her boyfriend in London was betrothed to a bride (also in Bangladesh) they bucked the system and 'married' each other in an informal mosque blessing ceremony without the state registrar. A Christian minister who worked in a youth club took pity on the runaways and acted as a negotiator between the two families as well as assisting them with housing and social services while the couple hid outside the immediate area for a while. The two sets of parents cut their losses and Salena moved in with her husband's parents. This was, after all proper in fulfilling the norm of virilocality although her mother's house was roomier. Her mother being divorced, her household was 'irregular' and a place of dispute between Salena, her mother and siblings. Salena glowed with pleasure at achieving 'normal' family life, but not for long. Her change of clothes from trousers and denim jackets to a *sari* and *burqa* was physically uncomfortable, demonstrating the difficulties of adopting unfamiliar body practices (Mauss 1973). This was made worse when she and her two sisters-in-law who were similarly dressed were jeered at in the street by a white stranger, "Its like Macbeth here - three witches." The expected duties of a daughter-in-law were especially irksome for someone like she who, although from a broken home, had, as a consequence, enjoyed considerable autonomy in a fatherless household. She had felt free to jokingly criticise her older brother as "stupid", rather than according him customary respect as "*borrobhai*" (respected elder brother).

Salena's attitude did not please her in-laws although she tried to do what was required within limits. The difference in outlook could not be hidden. Her father-in-law sought to exert control and she found his behaviour threatening and aggressive (recalling her own father's behaviour). Her husband, too, became abusive in his own parents' home. By now a baby had been born and this concentrated Salena's mind on where her responsibilities lay. In this she was pushed by the Health Visitor as well as pulled by her own maternal feelings, since a mother who puts up with domestic violence has her own parental responsibility called into question if she does not seek a safer domestic environment. Social advisors will make this point to any woman in a similar position although with Muslim families, the tendency to emphasise this message is a measure of how intractable Muslim husbands are deemed to be in their eyes. Salena sought the help of the housing department[6] and social services again and a flat was found near to her mother's house for herself and her child. Another child was born and her husband was gradually 'prised' away from his parents and taken back by Salena over a period of time on sufferance. In a short space of time she had altered from being an independent if emotionally overwrought school leaver, with hopes of becoming a teacher, to becoming a young mother, subjected for a second time to domestic violence, trying to manage two young

---

[6] These compressed biographies under-emphasise details such as the protracted and difficult process of negotiating a housing transfer which is harder in Bethnal Green than in most other parts of the borough.

children and a flat needing extensive redecoration on minimal welfare income. The consequences of all these upheavals inevitably took their toll. A self-confessed seeker of relief in pouring out her difficulties with a combination of melodrama and self-deprecating humour, Salena gave me turbulent disquisition on the relative merits and demerits of married life Bengali-style, compared with her idea of the general norms of the area. Her use of expletives and a strong Cockney accent enlarged the space for informal discussion, and could be read as an attempt to prevent anyone seeing her as a typical Bengali housewife.

Salena has drawn freely on both 'systems', seeking help from the state welfare system, Christian charity, and also, when she was psychologically unwell, from traditional Bengali healers, "I know it's probably rubbish, but if it works? Well I don't care then, whatever it takes". Before she was married, she got into trouble with a previous boyfriend and could almost be described as someone who revelled in the cloak and dagger melodrama of her secret double life. Now the pain and suffering that she has endured has modified her discourse to an earthier pragmatism. She accepts the lion's share of responsibility for managing their affairs (although her husband grew up in London he is not fluent in English and left school early). She can be overwhelmed at times by the unremitting burden that she carries and the limited help given by family and statutory agencies. Her broken early family life exposed her extensively to the problematic ways that such agencies operate, and at the same time made her cynical about the hypocritical attitudes she found among Bengali people who could, in her opinion, have been more supportive and less prone to gossip. Having made her bed, however, she will lie on it and at times she has literally laid down incapable. In crisis moments she can evoke sympathy but also irritation when there is a sense of manipulation afoot. The so-called manipulative and contradictory behaviour in her case speaks of her frustrations and intermittent social paralysis. Despite marginal benefits there is a rational necessity to her strategic manoeuvres.

Her best support comes from a married sister: together they can happily "slag off" the men in their lives and band together as independent women against the way of the world. Her admission of being "hopeless" in domestic duties can be read as a protest against submission. Interestingly, however, she sided with her mother and uncles when it came to persuading her sister against divorce and she advocated patience in the face of suffering much as her mother did to her, and presumably her grandparents did to her mother. "*Sullai lou*" such parents say, (Carry on), "*Kunno surrot, sullai lou*" (Use any means to carry on).

The differences between Salena and Fatima suggest that the social meaning of divorce and marriage in Bengali families needs further examination, not just in itself but also in the context of local society as a whole and the factors that mitigate or accelerate the negative effects of divorce or the positive effects of marital stability. It might be guessed that Bengali social disapproval of divorce might be attenuated in Bethnal Green by the plurality of local discourse, statutory agencies support for single mothers and so on. The question arises as to why, as will be shown to be the case, Bengali women suffer particularly badly through divorce compared with other local women. As for women of all backgrounds, Bengali women who enjoy marital stability will have greater socio-economic security than divorcees as well as fulfilling a culturally approved family norm. Bengali divorcees' problems are exaggerated in comparison with other local women because of a negative vicious cycle whereby the low cultural status of divorcees is compounded not only by economic hardship but also by potential loss of citizenship, loss of the family advocate (where the husband has greater fluency in English than his wife) and an uncomfortable exposure to inappropriately culturalised interpretations of their predicaments by statutory agencies and others from the non-Bengali population.

The contrast between Fatima and Salena's doctor-patient relationships are illustrative of the way that cultural readings of any one situation or predicament are emphasised or suppressed. I am aware of 'culture' with Fatima only on reflection afterwards, but with Salena it is an uncomfortable part of our relationship. Fatima's 'predicament' is hardly noticeable as such for any detrimental consequences of her minority ethnic status are lightly worn. Securely and happily married, she found in me an older supportive advisor. A closer look at an apparently unremarkable doctor-patient relationship reveals a theme which arose more from her needs than my habitual style of practice. I frame my advice to her carefully because she is junior and orthodox in her relation with me, thus tacitly and unquestioningly supporting her customary practices, against my better judgement that reassurance alone may be unhelpful. In the context of medical care, as she is not often ill, this does not matter too much in itself, but it is revealing of how relationships of this nature act to reinforce the reproduction of (virtuously perceived) custom. Salena, by contrast will comment on my relative cultural 'freedom' and I am called upon to discuss or even advise on the rights and wrongs of 'Bengali marriage' and must judge carefully how far I might be drawn into being authoritative beyond my expertise. Salena's emphasis on 'culture' works rhetorically to recruit my support by highlighting differences between Bengali and British family customs.

3.4 Marital difficulty

Rukshana, like Salena, has a problem husband because he drinks and through drink loses his job frequently and becomes abusive. When this comes to light she neither asks me to condemn him as a 'typical Bengali man' as Salena might have done, nor does she quote the ennobling effects of a wife's suffering like Salena's mother.

Rukshana displays a quiet confidence and enjoys many aspects of her life, taking pride in her appearance which is rather individual among local fashions.

She is religious, intellectual, and demonstrates a breadth of tolerance and understanding which makes her an engaging and likeable person. She gets on well with her in-laws who are sympathetic and do what they can to improve their son in his role as a husband. She embarked on marriage with energy, accepts a traditional division of labour in the home and does not give up in the face of adversity. Trained as a pharmacy assistant, she intends to return to work when the children are at school and her mother-in-law will mind them. In the meantime she is not resentful of staying at home. One day she came to see me with one of her children, who was not very ill and then in a diffident way, her voice light, a slight smile fading as she turned to release our mutual attentive gaze, she said that she had a problem with her husband. The story came out hesitantly in bits and pieces, with prompting, about his drinking, his addiction to card games and his violence to her but not the children. She was near to tears but did not break down. She repeated without conviction that he had explained it as something he could not help, "...because he loses his temper - but that's not right is it?"

After lengthy discussion I pressed her to go to the domestic violence unit of the local police. She felt this was out of the question because they would make her leave and she was worried about being alone as she needs his help, "It's so much work alone." She was pensive and said "Oh" and "Mm", openly pondering the things I said about the predictable behaviour of alcoholics and the effect it could have on the children if nothing was done. She is upset about his slackness in religious observance but not condemnatory; she thinks that he is probably ill and has a weak personality. She is also fearful that others will gossip about her although there is no specific person whom she can think of who might do this. The last straw came when the council refused to make essential repairs to her damp and infested home. If I notice that I feel sorrier for her than for others in similar circumstances it is because of the doubly unjust position of women who are able to put custom, cultural difference and racism into a coherent perspective in order to get on with the practical business of improving their family life against the odds, but are finally undone when they are pushed just one bit too far by the officiousness of a clerk. The temporary mental or emotional crisis that frequently ensues from such eventualities is poignant rather than simply pitiable.

An historically ordered presentation would begin with the original migrants, and their wives and children. This chapter, which is about the variety and particularity of social predicaments, gives prominence to young British-born wives and mothers because it is often they who evince the richest material on the immediacy of the trials and tribulations of inner-city multicultural life. The facts of maternity obviously bring them into contact with nurses, doctors and teachers. They are also the focus of attention because a variety of relationships condense and converge upon their lives within and across identifiable 'cultures' or communities. They are closely engaged with all other generations, their anxious parents and in-laws in London or Bangladesh, their younger siblings, whose own marriages and careers depend on them, their husbands, their children, and the many institutional professionals who have statutory or other interests in their household.

Consideration of the young Bengali men of similar age forms a counterpoint to these embattled housewives.

3.5 Troubled young men

Fatima's brothers are eager, personable and keen, already making rapid progress in their chosen careers. Rukshana's brother, although probably clever enough to go to university, has a reasonably well paid job as a warehouse foreman. Salena's unmarried brothers have had more mixed and dispersed fortunes. The eldest has a clerical job in local government in another city and is not yet married although in his early thirties. According to Salena he prefers to keep his distance from their parents. The next brother stayed with his father and is not known to me but is disliked by Salena. At home with their mother is a younger brother still at school and an older unmarried brother, Jahangir.

I am aware of the powerful physical presence of groups of certain kinds of Bengali boys on the street locally, but when one of them is in my consulting room asking for help, they are understandably diminished, and in Jahangir's case, forlorn. Most Bengali boys do not join such gangs, or not for long, but Jahangir has been in trouble frequently because of a continuing on-off involvement with street violence. More than one of his friends have died or been seriously wounded in this way. I find myself thinking of him as a rebel without a cause because of the lack of resolution to any of his problems.

Characteristically he often makes appointments to see me and then does not turn up. When he does come to see me and discuss his difficulties he defaults on follow-up appointments and we go back again to square one. We revolve around the same problems of being unhappy with his life but somehow being unable to move on. The doctor-patient relationship is fragmented as time spent trying to break the cycle of rumination and depression is interspersed with long intervals where we do not meet. He mostly needs me for practical help with certificates and letters for college or employers. He will allow himself to be involved to a limited extent with a psychotherapeutic relationship but then absents himself and remains uncommitted. He is reluctant to reflect on how he tends to use my services for immediate practical help without making use of the insights he could gain on why his plans often go awry. Nevertheless he does not go to see other doctors and the glimmers of hope that he sometimes shows helps to maintain some sort of a relationship of trust. When I try to pursue particular details of his current problems I am recurrently made to feel as if I could not understand his world, "No, its not like that really, you know, I don't let anyone say things to me or I'll put them in hospital, I just get so angry" but this stance of romantic honour defended whatever the cost contrasts with his poor performance in the world of work, his continuing dependence on my (apparently useless) help and the poverty of his social connections, "People are always letting me down, and they look down on me - I want respect."

The diffident and irregular doctor-patient relationship has parallels with his mixed feelings about other British institutions as well as his unsettled position in the local Bengali social world, both with his fragmented family and with friends. The hospital follow-up of Jahangir's chronic asthma is less than adequate and we waste time re-booking appointments that he cannot keep because he is on the run at the time, or trying to help a friend who is in a crisis. His accounts of relationships with girlfriends are romantically tragic stories. He rarely makes eye-contact when he is talking about himself but listens intently when I talk about him. One sister is happily married and settled, and he could take advantage of his brother's position outside London to move away and make a fresh start; his mother would be glad to be rid of the trouble he brings on the household. Instead he alternates between casual work in restaurants locally and restarting college courses.

Jahangir seems to be drawn to trouble. He is antagonistic towards the police and his unwise intervention in a street scene recently earned him yet another police caution. He has been involved in fights between Bengali and white boys in the past but nowadays some sort of a general truce obtains and he has been attacked more often by Bengali boys from rival groups than by white boys. The event that sparked off a fight which led to a near-fatal stabbing was, in fact, when he was seen with a white girlfriend in the park. The person who saw him 'informed' a Bengali vigilante group who punish such boundary transgressions, even going so far as to pursue him for further abuse in the local hospital.

He shares the same background as many other young Bengali men: arrival in London after early childhood in Bangladesh, the transition to nuclear family life in London, secondary schooling, college and then work, business or unemployment. Jahangir has ground to a halt on the threshold of maturity. Now in his late twenties he wants to put trouble behind him, go back to college and get on with his life but something he perceives as being outside his control always gets in the way. Our discussion revolve around his own body image and his relationships with others who let him down or read him the wrong way or episodes of mistaken identity and tragic dramas. He might be said to suffer from being destined to perpetually act out the stereotype given to him by society. Other young Bengali men are similarly misread, but while they manage to retain their composure, with Jahangir it almost inevitably spirals into a drama.

Jahangir's story could be interpreted in terms of family psychology, for he and his siblings were at an impressionable age when there was domestic violence at home ending in divorce. They were left behind while the three older children made off for an independent life, or went with their father. It is true that the children of divorced Bengali parents feature prevalently in stories of adolescent delinquency, but a poor outcome is by no means inevitable and in fact the majority of such youths find some sort of stability in work and marriage, as did his older brother. Although the narrative of leaving behind a misspent youth for an adult life of probity through religion, work or marriage is a common enough theme for young men of any background, negotiating the transition obviously requires that one's efforts and resources are directed towards the particularities of each predicament. Jahangir remains engaged with the one group where he can earn respect, the gang, but this also risks trouble.

Indeed, Jahangir could be replaced in this story by one of his Cockney skin-head enemies with a very similar narrative of 'masculinity-in-crisis'. What is distinctively Bengali about his predicament is that although he often seems to be in a liminal state, he does retain strong links with a Bengali 'cultural system' of respect. He sees this as being irreconcilably opposed to British institutions and attitudes with which he has an antagonistic relationship. He has, like Salena, been unable to leave the extended family entirely whereas their older brother has essentially 'left the community'. On the other hand they have not resolved their position through retreat into orthodoxy. Salena has tried this strategy or rather has been more or less forced to do so by the responsibilities of marriage and motherhood which intervene at a younger age for women than men in this population.

3.6 Boundaries

3.6.1 FAZLUL AHMED

Fazlul Ahmed is one of the men from Sylhet who, because of the changing political geography of the sub-continent, were born in British India, migrated from East Pakistan and married in Bangladesh. Older Bengali men who have young unmarried children still at home are of course in a very different social position to the young people described thus far. Their histories and typical biographies, which will be described more fully later on, are unique compared with all earlier generations of male migrants from Sylhet in that they are the first cohort to have established families in Britain in significant numbers.

Ill health caused Fazlul Ahmed to retire early. Unlike Fatima's father, who is usually to be found in ordinary trousers and shirtsleeves, he is formal in his appearance, conforming with the traditions of senior Bengali Muslim men: a long shirt, woollen waistcoat and hat. His wife is always chaperoned and wears a full black *burqa* with head and face coverings when outside the home whereas Fatima's mother, who is just as 'respectable' in every other way, never wears a *burqa*. Fazlul Ahmed's health needs are many. Our relationship is marked by formal politeness both in language and deportment (we shake hands after each consultation). This can abruptly change into joking and banter which is never uncomfortable. His English is stilted but adequate, eased by a sprinkling of my recently acquired Sylheti. I have become habituated to his peremptory manner and direct requests. I have seen him in the street with a knot of other men of a similar age leading a spirited harangue that appeared to be about morals. He maintains a powerfully controlled demeanour with which I can work comfortably enough.

I am taken aback one day when, without any preamble, and with evident nervousness he interrupts a routine discussion about his medication with a peremptory demand, "You must talk to my daughter, she is doing something wrong, she sees some boy, you must tell her to stop." I hesitate, feeling uncertain, but before thinking about it much further I blurt out "But why don't you talk to her?" He looks down, "For us it is shameful." "*Shorrom*?" I return (shame, modesty), lowering my voice to match his, and he nods in mute assent. There is an awkward pause as he is unable to elaborate further and his unexpected emotional presentation of blushing shyness inhibits the previously easy to and fro of our conversation. The admission that you cannot talk to your teenage daughter in any way at all about such (alleged) behaviour strikes my British ears as a yawning gap in 'normal' family relationships. I do not think quickly enough to comment that his 'for us' implies that for *me* and my like it is not *shorrom*, nor do I think to ask what he thinks such a discussion would be like should it occur, although the request itself implies trust in the advice I might give.

It becomes clear that although there is the appearance of self-contained traditional Bengali family life with which his daughter, Bushra, outwardly conforms, and a pragmatic use of local services, something is lacking. The request is not presented as a last resort in the way that many parents will come to a doctor saying something like, "You talk to her doctor, she might listen to you, God knows we've tried." The implication is, that from the moment such a problem came to light, there was only one course of action to be taken, to find the person who could breach the *shorrom* modality and talk to her frankly about romance and sexuality. Despite evidence of a wide network of social connections, there is a piece missing in the family jigsaw, at least here in Bethnal Green, and Fazlul Ahmed must co-opt someone else, in this case a female English doctor, to fill the gap.

Bushra has, in fact, already been to see me, and unlike her father she is not so certain I can be trusted. Her symptoms of stomach pains lead to no obvious diagnosis and only with much hesitation in the face of pressure from me to say more about other problems, together with reassurances about confidentiality, does she open up and tell me about a relationship that sounds quite exploitative. Her life is governed by a strict regime in that she is expected to account for any time outside school and home in detail; all telephone calls and visitors are closely monitored. This means that meetings with friends who do not gain parental approval must take place during school hours. The locations for these must be the street or the flats of other young women who are married (this is how Salena courted her future husband) or those of older sons left alone while their parents are in Bangladesh. By missing a lesson here and there Bushra has gone further in this relationship than she finds comfortable. She is out of her depth but has literally no-one, neither school friends nor sisters in whom she can confide. I pressed her to give the details, because when the affair started she was younger than the legal age for consent. The notion of habitual *shorrom* for her in such matters is, however quite invisible. The gap between parental and childhood attitudes towards traditional values is thus emphasised.

Surprisingly, her father and mother did not follow up what happened by cross-examining me at later consultations and I was fearful of the strain on medical confidentiality that might have ensued. I was given full trust and the situation continued for some time and settled only because the relationship itself came to an end for other reasons. Given the degree of distress evident in her awkward struggling to hide what was going on I thought it unusual that the parents did not know more about the extent of her misdemeanours. In my general experience, teenagers' troubles come to light one way or another, but she and others like her have told me of 'double' and even 'triple' lives carried on for some time, extensively as well as intensively without their parents having any inkling of the real nature of events beyond the general suspicion that something irregular was afoot. This does not imply that they are necessarily naive about what might be going on: some parents all too readily assume the worst.

3.6.2 RAHMAT KHAN

Rahmat Khan monitors his daughter even more closely than does Fazlul Ahmed. With almost no grounds for suspicion other than a lively personality he has accused his daughter of immoral behaviour, fitted locks to her bedroom windows while removing the same from her door and forbidden her to answer the telephone. When she complained, he and his eldest sons threatened her with a beating. Undeterred, she continues to make efforts to avoid sequestration and to see her friends from school. She has been sent to see me by her parents, not for advice, but for me to prescribe medication to alter her behaviour. Some leeway must be given to what is only her version of events since she was allowed to see me without a chaperone and she tells her story with skilled eloquence and a wry humour that is likely to recruit sympathy. Listening to her I am struck by the way that her direct and forthright manner mirrors that of her father. She is scornful of the way in which I have been obliquely co-opted to assist her family. She has taken on the might of parental disapproval with courage and confidence and I anticipate that the battle of wills is likely to end in a stalemate. Unlike Salena, she does not implore me through drama and bathos to take her side, but is in fact rather superior, controlled and powerful. I am not surprised to discover that she is more often an advisor among her peers than one to need advice and help. She accepts the interpretation that there is a family similarity in strength of personality. On the other hand she distances herself from them because she sees herself as someone who was liberal and democratic in her choice of friends. They, by contrast, are reportedly so nervous about social status as their fortunes have prospered that they have progressively cut themselves off from most of their neighbours and from junior kin relations. She mocks their fear of neighbourly gossip, and hints that they are superstitious about black magic. Having stayed with me for just as long as it takes to explain matters, she apologises for taking up my time unnecessarily, thus effectively closing the matter on her terms, and leaves.

Fazlul Ahmed needed an advisor for his daughter. In every other way he was self-sufficient in matters of family custom and religion. Rahmat Khan, who is always self-confident, asked me indirectly to bolster up his authority over his daughter. Both were more or less confounded by their daughters' social skills at managing, or rather evading the doctor as surrogate parent as well as the control of their real parents. This suggests that there is something more specific than just a generation gap between parents and daughters. Authority thins out suddenly and advice and guardianship for teenagers is attenuated. The urgency of Rahmat Khan's problem, according to his daughter, has something to do with the immediate neighbourly world being gossip-ridden.

Fazlul Ahmed's politeness with me is in fact no more than a formality and he is fully able to cross what he sees as a boundary in a pragmatic way when needs dictate. Others, Bengali or non-Bengali, make much of the fact that such boundaries are never to be crossed and are explicit about territory that is acceptable for mutual discussion (i.e. medical expertise) and that which is unacceptable (any discussion about the conduct of their personal and family life). The ways in which boundaries are marked are not always obvious but on the whole the problem is most evident when it is expressed as religious difference rather than what may be glossed as 'Bengali culture'. This does not, however, imply that it is only through issues relating to Islam that differences are made explicit between myself and Bengali informants.

3.6.3 MAMUN

Mamun has come to see me to ask for a second opinion. He has a large birthmark on his neck but has been told by one plastic surgeon that if it is removed he will need a graft of skin taken from his leg. Aged twenty two, he is old enough to decide for himself what should be done but he mentions that his parents do not approve of the idea of the graft, "They said to me, this is not right, a skin graft, you know so can I see a private doctor?" His cheerfulness is a little nervous and edgy. I hesitate for three reasons: I want to know if he agrees with his parents or is following their suggestions while harbouring private doubts. Secondly, I find that I am already interpreting what he said about his parents to mean that they may have religious objections to grafting ("it is not right") rather than anxieties about the best medical treatment. Lastly, I am worried that the family might have unrealistic views about private doctors being uniformly better than NHS doctors. The consultation has already become quite complicated.

Is it just his appearance that shifts the discussion into something more like a stand-off than a straightforward negotiation? Unlike most Bengali men of his age (but increasing in prevalence) he has a beard and wears a long Islamic shirt and pyjama trousers. His hat (*toki*) is richly embroidered and spectacles give him a studious air; he works for a local Bengali community organisation. The discussion becomes more uncomfortable after my question as to his feelings draws only a non-committal response. Jumping to religious conclusions, I ask him if grafting is not allowed according to the Koran, but he deflects this without hesitation. His answers are short, his lips close tightly and little giggles cut short attempts at discussion. I feel embattled and struggle unwisely to think up better questions but still he does not open up or satisfy my need to know what he really feels about the problem. His nervous laughter works like a sort of shutter and makes my questioning seem clumsy. He has, after all, asked for referral to a more powerful, private doctor, and I am now aware that I appear to be an irritating woman blocking his way. Discomfited, I force a compromise by making a referral to another NHS specialist but mark this consultation down in communication terms as a failure.

Similar stand-offs crop up during Ramadan as we advise ill patients or pregnant women not to become dehydrated especially when Ramadan is in the hot summer months and the fasting time, which is widely and strictly observed by Bengali adults, is prolonged. I am sometimes bold enough to quote the Islamic rule, as I understand it, whereby fast days may be broken if they are made up by fasting outside Ramadan and if extra almsgiving is undertaken. Since menstruating women cannot fast this is not an uncommon event for women at least. At times patients do specifically ask for advice relating to their religion, for example if they enquire as to whether certain medicines and cosmetics are acceptable to a Muslim if they contain medicinal alcohols. Without such a specific request, the strategy of quoting personal knowledge of Islamic practice does not usually work. More often than not, the response is a cool and polite acknowledgement that I may be 'correct' but they do not choose to follow my advice.

Why do I suddenly choose to adopt a cultural or religious modality with some patients rather than using, for example, more powerfully formulated medical and scientific data to back up my position? With Mamun I tried to outflank an obstruction because I thought that I had detected a subtle religious confrontation simmering beneath the surface of the doctor-patient relationship. Somehow a straightforward doctor's visit has taken an unanticipated 'cultural' turn to the detriment of good medical care. In the short time that we have for consultations for minor illness I have made a quick guess as to his viewpoint, and he has seen me as someone whose opinion on these matters cannot be trusted. The prickly atmosphere de-professionalises our relationship and the basis for giving advice has foundered. This does not occur if patients just say simply, "No, doctor, this is our religion" and the matter is put aside without offence.

Consultations which turn out badly point to the ways in which wariness of cross-cultural conjunctures and an anxiety to mark boundaries can unnerve those who think that they are neutral whether they are in receipt or delivery of services or, by analogy in other kinds of relationships. In this way, two cultures form camps (Gilroy 2000) and the possibilities for mutuality become limited (Yuval-Davies 1997: 203-6). This is commonly occasioned by liberal and racist non-Bengali people alike when faced with what they perceive as Islamic fundamentalism.

3.7 Sequestered women

In this set of notes, who has been overlooked in terms of social position? Apart from the younger children, there are some wives and mothers who have so far featured little in this set of case-histories. Often hidden from direct view and conversation as they remain for the most part within the home, physically covered in public, and do not often speak English, their lives and predicaments are not easily observed through this method of research. Grandmothers, aunts and older siblings, rather than mother herself, bring small children to the surgery more often among Bengali families than those of different backgrounds. The habitual contours of family relationships are then not so easy for the doctor to interpret when she is used to building up a picture of family dynamics through a Western model of mother being closest to young children. Young brides who live in extended-family households are similarly brought to the doctor in the company of her mother-in-law or sister-in-law rather than with her husband more often than those from non-Bengali populations. Doctor's visits to the home and time spent outside my practice in the homes of informants who are not patients are more revealing. A Bengali woman seen at home, wearing a loose cotton dress while she nurses a sick husband or child, her hair loose, her body casually exposed, appears strikingly different from the person who attends surgery heavily swathed in layers of clothing. These coverings and sequestrations need not, of course, hide anything. My inability to 'see' women more easily when dressed one way or another is echoed by my Bengali friend who feels she cannot 'see' me because I do not wear a *sari*. Likewise my inability to 'know' someone because I could not speak directly to her did not mean that she was hidden from me, only that our *mutual* observations and rapport were limited.

Before I learned any Sylheti, women such as Rena, who has lived here since the 1980s, always came to the surgery accompanied by a bilingual relative, usually a child. There was little in the way of eye contact or any sense of rapport between us as all conversation was directed through, and constrained by the translation skills of her children. As my Sylheti has improved she has sometimes come to see me alone, or, if accompanied, we can talk to each other directly for the most part, and only turn to her child when we cannot translate a particular word. What is noticeable is that she has become more authoritative and assertive, or, to be more precise, the relationship has become one of two women of a similar age and stage in life discussing a medical problem on a more equal basis. Previously, whatever I actually thought of her as a person, the stereotyped minority ethnic woman in receipt of institutionalised services interfered with the appropriate conduct of our relationship.

3.8 Discussion

The detailed description of doctor-patient or anthropologist-informant relationships is, I argue, revealing of the strategies that the same people use outside that relationship to solve the problems of everyday life. Muffasir and his wife kept themselves to themselves but Salena was involved with many different people with a view to obtaining assistance; Aliya and her husband fell foul of many of their social connections. These patterned modes of behaviour may be productive, perennially useless against adversity or just habitual in the circumstances in which people find themselves. Moving away from the detail of these episodes there are suggestive pointers here to further research into the regularities of the observable contexts to these predicaments.

Out of the detail of individual case-histories, what can be pulled out in a systematic way that marks off the likelihood of the occurrence of one type of predicament rather than another? If this can be done then some analytical purchase on the data can be gained which moves towards an understanding as to why, even within the variety of positions given by generation, gender, marital status and occupation, lives may take very different turns and have different outcomes. From the case-histories given here, relationships of kinship and social support, family roles, gossip and relations of difference are suggestive areas for further examination. The ethnographic material in the following chapters is organised according to these issues. Household life, kinship, negativity and relations of difference are examined in turn. The more usual social categories of gender, class and socio-economic status are subsumed within these chapter headings rather than being allotted separated sections because I found that issues of household life, kinship and negativity, as well as racism, came to the fore in the course of fieldwork, rather than gender, class and socio-economic status. If the sequence suggests autonomous cultural 'domains', this is purposefully undermined by reference to the cross-cultural method of research as well as observations of Bengali views of British family and social life as a form of reverse ethnography.

CHAPTER 4 HOUSEHOLDS

4.1 Introduction

In the last thirty years the Bengali population in Tower Hamlets has changed dramatically from a minority group of mostly male migrant workers to a society of families which has settled here and whose children are now the majority ethnic group among their generation in the borough. Within any one Bengali household there may be several different early life histories, for although three generations can be found, there is as yet little or no repetition of biography: father and mother were both born and brought up in Sylhet but they started family life apart, she with her mother-in-law in Sylhet and he with other separated men in London. Some of their children were born in Bangladesh who then came here at school age or older and some were born in London. Daughters-in-law and sons-in-law may have only recently come from Sylhet. Different pasts herald different futures and while mother and father might appear outwardly to have changed little, the children diverge. The eldest daughter may have been married as a teenager and never thought of having a job, but her younger sisters may be university students or in full time work. Mother may wear ordinary village style *saris* but her daughter is in full Islamic *hijab* or a leather jacket and trousers. Being a recently settled migrant population in Bethnal Green, there is, as yet, no typical development cycle of the Bengali domestic group.

For current purposes I leave relationships between Bengali and non-Bengali households in the background. This is in order to clarify what is happening to Bengali families before adding another layer of analysis. A brief glance at non-Bengali views of the evolution of the Bengali population, however, serves as an introduction to the questions that a household analysis might be expected to answer. The expansion of the Bengali population and the evolution of their family life in Bethnal Green has been a startling phenomenon for all residents of Bethnal Green in the scale, speed and diversity of change. As already indicated, there has been no time for reproduction in the sense that each generation differs from the former in distinctive biographical ways, quite apart from any consideration of the attitudes or 'identities' of individuals. Local ideas about what that change means are often overly concise, betraying the subjective bias of the speaker. This is quite understandable: there has been little time to build a body of common knowledge that explains what the precise social effects have been or continue to operate because of this expansion of one ethnic group in the area.

A school teacher has recently been exasperated by parents who keep their children off school too frequently because of minor illness and he feels that this is more common among Bengali families than those from other backgrounds. We discuss a particular case and without prompting he gives his own explanation, "Well I can understand it - Bangladeshis worry more because *in*

Bangladesh they think even a little scratch might mean the child will die, but it doesn't *here*, only they don't realise it". He may be right at a general level of understanding about health beliefs, and while I am sure, from the rest of his conversation, that he is politically liberal, he shows that in a short-hand way he thinks of Bengali adults not just as if they belonged to a separate 'community', with or without a new 'identity' here, but as if they have been simply transposed from another place and still maintain an outlook that belongs entirely in Bangladesh. I reflect afterwards that the mother in question has spent most of her life here and that all her children are British-born. Her anxiety derives from the death of one of her children in infancy in London from a rare disease rather than from any 'culture-bound' health beliefs (Littlewood 1998: 239), rooted in Bangladesh and unaltered by the experience of bringing up children in Britain.

A youth worker looks through the other end of the telescope: he and I discuss the problems of young men in the area but we disagree about the extent to which the Bengali and white populations in Tower Hamlets are segregated and whether or not this is a perpetual problem without satisfactory explanation. He thinks that the problem is likely to "go away on its own" because the younger generation have adapted so fast to life here, "They're not like their parents and so *traditional* any more, it's really changing." When pressed, it is hard for him to think of many examples of mixed-ethnicity friendships among the young people he knows. Sympathetic to the needs of the young Bengali men in his care, he is projecting on to them a strong notion of progressive liberal modernisation where hidebound tradition inevitably gives way to enlightened tolerance and 'multiculturalism'[7].

Neither the teacher nor the youth worker, who both have close everyday contact with many local people, are wrong, but only partial in their views. Both display anxiety about inflexible traditions that in my local experience is found typically among the middle classes especially in relation to Muslims, and is in contrast to white working-class anxiety about loss of their own (timeless) British traditions because of immigrants moving into the neighbourhood (Cohen 1996). The question that the disparity of these views raises here is this: are we dealing mostly with a traditional group in a modern urban setting or is a rapid acculturation process unfolding that will soon render the traditions of the older immigrants negligible?

This chapter presents a description of that time of change, and of the development of Bengali families locally through an examination of their households in Bethnal Green. If the inter-subjective analysis of the anthropologist-informant relationship is the smallest dimension of ethnographic research, as given in the previous chapter, and background historical, social

---

[7] As with many other terms, inverted commas denote contingent meaning given by the context, the voice of the youth worker in this instance. The issue of multiculturalism as a political position will be discussed in Chapter 7.

geographic and sociological statistics, as given in Chapter 1, the largest dimension, then a location such as the household is a middle-range format for ethnography. There are other middle-range locations that are equally fertile ground for analyses of individuals in relation to social categories such as class, gender, 'culture', economics and relations of power and inequality. These are locations such as the body (Csordas 1994, Mauss 1973), workplaces (Ong 1987, Parry 1999, Wolf 1992), houses as distinct from households (Carsten & Hugh-Jones 1995), the neighbourhood in itself (Baumann 1996, Whyte 1943) as well as biographical and narrative devices (Finnegan 1998). The household, which although it defies universal definition remains a useful 'odd job' concept (Yanagisako 1979), is particularly appropriate where demography and transnationalism need to be included with the categories already mentioned (Hannerz 1992).

Yanagisako warns against approaching the household as a unit without prior inspection of the kinds of activities that are central to domestic relationships in the population as a whole.

'If we start by identifying the important productive, ritual, political, and exchange transactions in a society and only then proceed to ask what kinds of kinship or locality-based units engage in these activities, and in what manner, we decrease the likelihood of overlooking some of these salient units, particularly those that do not fit our conventional notion of a household' (Yanagisako 1979: 186).

To begin with the household itself and then work outwards too readily leads to a 'building-block' model of social reproduction and a bounded view of the domestic domain. Moore acknowledges that the mutually constitutive two-way working of the relationships between the household and the social processes outside them is something that is 'extremely easy to hint at but difficult to analyse in practice' (Moore 1994: 88). Following Yanagisako's methodology in broad outline, this middle ground of my ethnography moves back and forth between the inner life of households and the world outside. I do not aim to encompass all that an analysis of Bengali households could yield. An overly inclusive view of household analysis threatens to become an ethnography without bounds, but instead I retain the simple question that was raised by the polarised view of two concerned and engaged local people earlier, namely is this population following an assimilative or a segregated trajectory? If, as we might expect, there is heterogeneity of biographical trajectories within this population, what are the key factors that govern this diversity?

To structure this lengthy but necessarily unified chapter, four sections follow. The first is an extended descriptive section which includes an account of the biographical diversity of Bengali households and observations made at wedding parties. The second is devoted to an analysis of the development cycle of the Bengali domestic group. The third section is a brief examination of household economics with a particular focus on the changing economic behaviour of young women. The last section is again descriptive of the roles, practices and opportunities of Bengali married couples. Rather than being an exhaustive catalogue of all categories within households, marriage is the recurring theme and focus of this chapter. The bride and recently married women are found to be public monuments to any family's achievement, and so any examination of household life is pulled towards the subject of weddings and marriages. This aspect of household life is therefore the most revealing of the ways in which individual family problems may develop into recurring patterns of Bengali social predicaments.

4.2 Preliminary ethnographic description

4.2.1 CONTRASTING FAMILY BIOGRAPHIES

The London Bengali population is made up of four cohorts in terms of immigration history: the original male migrants, their dependents who joined them more recently, the children born here and lastly, the relatively few numbers of recent adult immigrants. The first cohort is sometimes referred to as *'furani Londoni'* ('old Londoners'), the men who came on their own to work in Britain but established their family households in Bangladesh (or, formerly, East Pakistan) and until about 1970, did not think to bring their families here (see Anwar 1979 for discussion of the myth of return). Their history has already been given in Chapter 1. Elderly English patients still on occasion talk about *'lascars'* although it has been decades since any Bengali seamen worked in the now defunct London docks. The second and third cohorts are self explanatory: these wives and Bangladesh-born children of migrants arrived in greatest numbers in the late 1970s and early 1980s as British immigration law tightened (Gavron 1998: 55).

The last cohort, contemporary adult immigrants, are brides and grooms of British residents, or men who have an opportunity to join brothers or uncles or other kin here for work. Although they leave Bangladesh in the same fashion, they join a very different social world in Britain from that encountered by their *furani Londoni* antecedents. In an attenuated form, however, they represent continuing evidence of the chain migration system through the brokerage of *sareng*-style middle-men in Dacca and London (Gardner 1995: 45). Occasionally whole families arrive more or less at the same time, usually middle-class professionals who are taking up specific jobs in education or religious work or journalism and do not have to undergo the separation typical of older migrant workers' families. A few elderly dependents gain permission to join their children and grandchildren.

When I first came to work in Bethnal Green in 1984, medical consultations frequently involved the whole of the newly arrived Bengali family attending together for one person's illness. The children of that time, now grown up, recollect the fact that it was easy to get lost and panic in the unfamiliar streets of London only a short distance away from their homes when they were recent arrivals in Britain. Their physical appearance at that time expressed a strong sense of dislocation, anxiety, chronic illness and poverty in the forlorn manner of the smaller children and their drab clothes that carried the smell of damp housing into the surgery. Only the father would be able to speak some English in a limited and formulaic manner. Visits to family homes, especially to privately rented flats in the Brick Lane area revealed alarmingly dilapidated accommodation. Very old buildings that had never been maintained or repaired were infested with mice and rats. Damaged front doors, filthy common staircases, gaps between walls and floors, dangerous wiring, faulty plumbing and overcrowding were commonplace. Mayhew and his colleagues in the nineteenth century were unlikely to be exaggerating in their descriptions even if their stylistic genre encouraged a sense of the exotic and lurid to the exclusion of more analytical expositions of East End sociology. It may be that the tradition of 'Victorian' or 'Dickensian' poverty, like the mice and rats, will never be eradicated from the East End; even now it is not difficult to find families who live in conditions that can only be described as degrading. What has changed is the consistency of the dreariness and subdued homogeneity of the poor life of Bengali migrants of the 1980s which has been replaced by a marked diversity both within and between households.

Fifteen years later these children have grown up into teenagers, young adults, parents and some are even grandparents (thus four-generation British-Bengali families do exist in small numbers). Physically they are often taller than their parents, better nourished and better dressed, stylish, assertive and vocal in two languages. Marriages have been made, children born and grandparents have died or returned to Bangladesh. New arrivals from Bangladesh, having successfully negotiated stringent immigration rules (Menski 1999), are usually incorporated into established households. The old flats have been redecorated and new households have been set up by young couples no longer living with the older generation. The myth of return has apparently evaporated. Differentiation in clothing styles alone appears to denote an explosion in the possible life-styles that these people can now pursue, ranging from a continuation of Bangladeshi village traditions, smart modern 'Asian' looks, international styles or Islamic orthodoxy (cf. Ferguson 1999: 97).

A regular story unfolds thus:

Abdul Choudhury was born just before World War II in a village in the Sylhet district of Bengal in British India which became part of East Pakistan while he was a small child. He came to Britain on his own in the early 1960s when in his mid-twenties and for fifteen years lived with other Bengali men and worked in a variety of garment factories. Every time he made a visit home he gave up his job and had to find another on his return to Britain. When he was forty his first child was born in Bangladesh, soon after his marriage to Monowara Nessa who was not yet twenty. By now, East Pakistan had become Bangladesh after the war of independence. Three years later his second son was conceived and then there was an interval of almost ten years before another longer visit could be made to Bangladesh. During this time his children were cared for in his home village by his mother and his wife. Village songs in the category *'dukhor gan'* (sad songs) reiterate themes of separation and loss in love and marriage (cf. Gardner 1995: 1). London Bengali housewives listening to recordings of these songs find them redolent with painful memories of years as a wife alone waiting for their husbands who were abroad. The letters in Abdul Choudhury's medical file show that during those years when he was alone in London, hospital specialists related most of his symptoms to 'stress' and felt that a physician could offer little help. Another child was born during his last, longer visit home before his wife with their infant and the older children returned with him to settle permanently in London. Another three children have been born since then.

The age difference of twenty years between this couple is much greater than that of younger contemporary Bengali couples, and the spacing of the children's births has been determined by the infrequency of the visits father could make to Bangladesh. The age range of their children now spans seventeen years but while Abdul Choudhury considers himself to be an old man, his wife remains young enough to have more children. By British standards he has married late in life and the couple have had to manage more or less continuous bachelorhood or very intermittent family life until late middle age. The biographical sequence just described is unique to this cohort of immigrant families, for although Bengali men continue to work away from home (discussed below), such lengthy separations no longer occur among the next generation. Because of the wide age range of the children, parents must think about young in-laws and grandchildren as well as teenage sons and daughters while the youngest may still be in primary school and continuing fertility remains an important consideration. The family has not come together under one roof as a settled household until father was in his late fifties. They have a small council flat in a post-war tower block with only three bedrooms typically dividing its sleeping arrangements into parents', sons' and daughters' shared bedrooms leaving no private space for the older children to study.

Abdul Choudhury is now in his sixties and has retired from many years in factory employment. He has a fixed demeanour with surgery staff and myself allowing little rapport. He finds it difficult to respond to my newly learned Sylheti preferring the fixed formulations that he has found serviceable over the years, "She is suffering from too much cough (or fever or pain) for three weeks now, please give medicine". Having delivered the message he busies himself with papers in his pockets and rejoins the consultation only as the prescription is delivered despite my attempts to involve him in the intervening stages of examination, diagnosis and management decisions. His wife, Monowara Nessa is cheerful, eager and attentive, but whereas other monolingual Bengali women of her generation show relief and appreciation with my language efforts, she can never get used to my speaking Sylheti and fails, despite some effort, to suppress giggling embarrassment when I speak. She repeats the Sylheti words that I have used, nodding vigorously, and then turns to her husband for him to translate. Both are modestly dressed in cheap Bengali clothes. Abdul Choudhury has only lately grown a beard, something that most Bengali men will have already assumed at a younger age as a mark of seniority and full maturity. For Monowara Nessa, an ordinary English knitted neck scarf serves as a head covering so that she looks like a Victorian toothache sufferer, and a plain long raincoat takes the place of the Islamic *burqa* that many other women wear. The surgery staff feel sorry for her. She does not work and speaks no English at all. The children are serious, studious and have almost unaccented sophisticated English in contrast to some of the Cockney accents of Bengali children from other families. The younger children still wear old clothes that smell of a damp house that I have never been called upon to visit in fifteen years although they have been ill enough on more than one occasion to justify such a service. I notice that their chronic eczema is regarded by better off Bengali patients as a disease of the poor who live in damp overcrowded houses.

All in all the parents display a theme of almost stereotypical minority ethnic family sequestration with extremely limited expectations of health care and no hope, or perhaps desire, for a personal involvement with health workers. If their relationship with me is narrow, although enduring, this has not hindered their opportunities for making social progress elsewhere:

The children in this family are remarkable achievers, steadily going through local secondary schools to University courses in academic subjects. Cultural issues are never brought into the conversation by anyone in the family although other Bengali patients will at times recruit a cultural argument to explain their particular attitudes towards certain illnesses or treatments. This family does not talk about personal matters or their extended family. The children are loyal to their parents and work hard to improve themselves without causing a fuss about the lack of study space or the restrictions that father places on their social life. Their teachers like them enormously and there is a noticeable lack of anxiety on their part about the girls' future because they appear to have so much self-determination about them that it is impossible to imagine that they would be pressured into an early marriage or that their brothers would be pushed into a job just for a wage. The siblings talk of each other in a friendly respectful way showing appropriate concern. They never complain about their parents but their quietness and reticence is not of a melancholic or depressed quality: they can be animated and discursive as appropriate but they do not become over-involved with the doctor in the way that teenagers commonly use the doctor-patient relationship as an arena for exploring alternative parenting or for sounding off about problems at home.

This family is an exemplary model of how rational modest strategies can reap rich rewards, and how hard work and thrift can result in high achievement. It is a simple story and as such the family might be described as lucky, for Monowara Nessa's resilient cheerfulness combined with Abdul Choudhury's rather rigid but not tyrannical attitude have paid off in a complex world. They are not so strict as to prevent their daughters going out into mixed society, but a strong sense of the distance between 'us' and 'them' has allowed the children to use local educational opportunities without becoming confused about the place of custom or 'culture' in relation to their pragmatic conduct of daily life.

The reunion of divided families was not so easy for all. The added responsibilities of protecting and providing for vulnerable dependents at a time when the National Front's racist action was very prominent in the area (CRE 1979) as well as sexual anxieties after prolonged separation unsurprisingly caused strain, and for some, a rupture in the marriage. A family with similar beginnings to that of Abdul Choudhury has not done so well in Bethnal Green and now seems to be mired in chronic, insoluble problems:

Rahmat Miah, came to Britain in the 1960s, his wife, Malika Khanom and their six children in the 1970s and two more children were born after that. The eldest son now owns a restaurant in America and another is an accountant there. The eldest daughter married and settled with her in-laws in Bangladesh and the next daughter married in Britain and lives with her husband's family in north London. The remaining children have not enjoyed such success since the time when their father took to being violent towards his wife; eventually he left home and re-married. Malika Khanom never remarried, nor did she seek employment although her household was now entirely welfare dependent. She is depressed and ill. The younger children have been educated entirely in Bethnal Green, achieving good examination results, and at the time of leaving school were socially outgoing and assertive. Since leaving school they have been unable to settle themselves in higher education, work or marriage although they have tried each in turn. The daughters arranged marriages for themselves through cousins after suffering abusive relationships with boyfriends. Subsequently they both divorced their husbands because of their dissatisfaction with "lazy Asian men" and were furious when the extended family tried to force them to continue with the marriages. They subsequently have aspired to jobs such as nursery nurses, social workers or teachers, but have themselves been often sick with stress-related illnesses and the momentum seems to have gone out of their career ambitions that were strikingly biased towards being carers of other needy people. Their brothers would like to get involved with business but somehow family connections do not seem to amount to any material support and they drift between restaurant jobs, unemployment and sickness benefit. The sisters think that one of them is probably using drugs because he has become secretive and moody lately.

The children feel that their mother constantly criticises them but at the same time they feel very sorry for what they would describe as her helpless victim status. For that reason they find it hard to leave home. "Bengali culture", and the iniquities of "Asian men" are often quoted as explanations for their problems. External issues such as the limited economic opportunities for minority ethnic women in Britain, for example, do not feature in conversations about their problems. The daughters frequently blame "Bengali people" for the way they gossip about divorced women and the way that "our culture" degrades them as if British 'culture' never could or did do so. Even worse than slander, they have heard that their father's associates have used black magic to harm his ex-wife and children, "That's all rubbish isn't it?" one of them said, "I don't know what to believe, my brother said he saw a ghost in his bedroom and we all heard a noise but its just superstition really." I acknowledge her suggestion of superstition but add that the ill-feelings behind her father's alleged behaviour were significant and she had rightly felt that they could not be discounted or completely ignored.

These intelligent and thoughtful young adults have a strong sense of how difficult it is to resist the influence of other people's thoughts, feelings and the particular cast of animosity towards them from close relatives whether expressed in emotional or spiritual terms. They are ambiguous, as many children are, about their parents' divorce even though their father was violent. From their own perspective on cultural matters they still think a "good Bengali marriage" is a worthwhile goal although they have found it in practice to be inimical and objectively it is the one social norm that has done them most harm. They maintain a close, if non-conformist, relation with Bengali 'culture' with a comparative perspective. They can explicitly state that Bengali 'culture' has not done them any favours, and can make astute comparisons with families of different cultural backgrounds. They continue to try to make progress with dogged determination and a leavening of ironic deprecating humour to try and pull off the trick of being Bengali marginals as divorced women, fatherless daughters or unsuccessful Bengali men without being merely passive victims of social malice. There does not appear to be any question of them repudiating their background wholesale and living independently. They continue to feel meshed with Bengali social appraisal and judgement and they try to work with this, rather than running away from it, in conjunction with help from 'outside the community'

The children in Abdul Choudhury's family would appear to be well adapted to life in a mixed society. Some would describe them as adept code-switchers (Ballard 1994a: 30), pleasing their teachers at school and their parents at home and enjoying the benefits offered by both. This model of switching between codes does not accord with my experience of their integrated outlook. They are on an accommodative rather than an assimilative trajectory, one that fits with mainstream versions of multiculturalism. Why cannot their counterparts in the second family use similar strategies, and, despite the distress caused by a broken home, make the most of what British society can offer in terms of training, work, higher education and other types of long term adult relationships? The daughters correctly see their problem as arising from the way that the harmful effects of what they call 'Bengali culture' compound the generic inequalities of gender and socio-economic statuses that exist in Bethnal Green. A more complete analysis must be postponed until later chapters, but a third brief case illustrates the more limited issue addressed here of assimilation versus segregation:

Alea has just returned from Bangladesh. She left her job as a nursery nurse in London to marry in Bangladesh and it is her first antenatal appointment with me. She feels ill, dizzy and light-headed. Medically speaking all is normal and so I say that I think she is worried and use the Sylheti word for serious anxiety, 'sintha' to emphasise the point although she is a fluent English speaker. She smiles wryly and talks of her fears about her husband's immigration visa which will take time to obtain and so he may not be here for the birth. In fact the family is well connected and has several useful strategies that are likely to short-circuit immigration law, and in any case she can afford to return to Bangladesh to see her husband whenever she wants. She speaks with warmth and animation about her time there with his family. "Would you like to live there?" I ask incautiously, since her husband has a good business there and she obviously got on well with her in-laws, "Oh no..." her face falls (as my suggestion feels out of place, at odds with the sense of the preceding conversation) and she cannot at first find the words to explain a fact so obviously out of the question, "I am used to life here since I was little..... I couldn't live there".

In one sense, then, life in Britain does take you over, and the idea of a negotiable attitude towards where and how you live does not seem realistic. Only a very few people in Alea's position set up permanent homes in

Bangladesh. The compelling momentum of London life does not, however, imply that rapid acculturation is thoughtlessly embraced by the younger generation. The vigorous criticism by some of Bengali 'culture' may use, rhetorically, the so-called freedom of British 'culture' to make a point but significantly does *not* include the idea of becoming like British people. Moreover, there is evidence that despite the critical attitude of some younger Bengali people, the customs and rituals of daily life, religious holidays and weddings are often carried out with enthusiasm and feelings of close identification with the meanings expressed in such rituals.

4.2.2 WEDDING PARTIES

At large gatherings such as weddings, the general categories and customs of Bengali family life can be seen more intensively in a setting where British society can largely and temporarily be excluded. Gender and generation are the most obvious divisions: men sit apart from women and older women prefer not to be even within sight of the men, and grumble a little if the arrangement of the tables for the wedding meal in the school hall or restaurant does not allow for that degree of seclusion. Women may discreetly observe the men if the layout allows, but are mildly irritated by the glances of men who come in briefly to fetch a small child or to give a message to their wives. Nevertheless such minor incursions are tolerated without fuss in the pleasantly informal party. Styles of dress in both rooms vary, the older men in traditional long shirts and waistcoats, some with an Islamic cap or a loose head scarf. Younger married men wear smart lounge suits with an almost indefinable 'Asian' style of detailing that is reminiscent of, or informed by Indian films. Unmarried men wear modern styles of smart casuals that appear to be indistinguishable from clothes worn by their non-Bengali contemporaries but again there is a subtle 'Asian' aspect to the styles. Schoolboys usually wear clothes universal for this age group locally but some of the youngest, who stay with the women, are in fancy suits from Bengali wedding shops like their female counterparts.

In the women's room the eye is drawn first to the teenage girls by their self-conscious movements and postures, clustering on the edges of the crowd, hesitating to sit here or there, usually finally settling together in a gang. They are overtly glamorous in gauzy embroidered trouser suits (*shalwar kameez*) or other Asian costumes with plenty of jewellery and make-up. Their head scarves may be flimsy, heels high, but their demeanour is demure at first and then playful as the meal progresses and the atmosphere relaxes. Their older married sisters and sisters-in-law have the richest appearance of all, wearing heavily embroidered *saris* with some or all of the gold jewellery that has been given to them at marriage, and perfectly applied elegant make-up. No *burqa* covers such beauty unless they have chosen to wear the formal Islamic *hijab*. Their appearance can risk being within a hairsbreadth of eclipsing the bride's finery but the red colour of her *sari* should be unique at her wedding and only the bride will have her face elaborately painted with traditional designs in red and white and gold. The jewellery is measured in Indian weights or *'tullas'* of gold and speaks of a gravitas and weighty ostentatiousness that juniors cannot imitate. A group of such as these, sitting together, presents a powerful and not always very approachable tableau of nuptial achievement. Their looks are no longer self-consciously excited or timid like the younger women, whom they do not often condescend to notice, but is confident, knowing and superior. Outside these clusters, other young married women break with tradition wearing denim jackets and long skirts or trousers with a token headscarf, "I don't really like wearing all that stuff" one woman commented, "But if my mother-in-law was here (i.e. she is in Bangladesh) she'd probably make me". Their own mothers may or may not wear special *saris* but many put on an everyday cardigan or *burqa* on top of the *sari* and their make-up and jewellery is not so conspicuous as that of their daughters and daughters-in-law. Some of the older women wear the white *sari* that denotes retirement from the grubbier jobs of cooking and cleaning in the house. Within each style a subtle hierarchy of styles is discernible, for the *hijab* can be worn ostentatiously or with humble simplicity and western clothes can be designer-label style or very plain.

The interesting developments in Bengali women's clothing styles in Bethnal Green over the last thirty years could occupy an entire thesis in itself. New fashions within the many varieties of head coverings emerge at least twice a year. There are probably a dozen basic categories ranging from using the end of a *sari* alone, a woollen scarf worn wrapped around the head, simple lengths of fabric of various styles, Indian wool shawls, scarves that are part of a matching costume, whether *shalwar kameez* or *burqa*, scarves which could be generic and not specifically Islamic, smart black Islamic scarves and then all the variations of formal *hijab*. Currently I have noticed that Calvin Klein and Yves Saint-Laurent have manufactured discreetly monogrammed black Muslim headscarves which are competing with a devoré style of fabric that is more intricately elaborate than that of last year. Likewise coats, shawls and *burqas* are changeable in style and connotation of religiosity and social status. Muslim head and body coverings (*purdah*) for Bengali women in Bethnal Green are a continuously elaborated and important communicative bodily practice, whether in the breach or its observance, in the discourses of religion, gender, status and cultural difference (Jeffery 1976: 110ff., Jeffery 1979).

At a social occasion such as a wedding, where it is common to gather up all family connections, the humble as well as those of high social status, no particular style of dress in the women's room seems to attract attention. Public behaviour is discreet, but it is not difficult for outsiders like myself to overhear or elicit comments from one sub-section or another on how *"they"* dress. This attention to fine discrimination of status as well as anxiety about loss of status will be seen to be a theme which recurs throughout the descriptive ethnography of this and following chapters. At the same time it has proved impossible to pin down any kind of schedule of statuses of the Bengali population through differences in occupation, educational achievement, economic standing, style of dress, religiosity or 'jat' (glossed here as 'Muslim caste'). All these categories are important and necessary to classify a person's status, but none are sufficient in themselves. Moreover, the transition from Bangladesh to Bethnal Green and the transnational position of many families makes it difficult to 'read' any person's status through knowledge of these categories alone. There are, of course, a few households which are typically 'middle-class' in that all or most family members have had a higher education and a professional career and are, relatively speaking, economically well-off, but the majority of the Bengali population in Bethnal Green does not have such a background. In fact the variety of occupations of a group of brothers of the older generation appears to follow the pattern of minor, landed, English families from over a hundred years ago: one brother stays in Bangladesh to manage property, another is a cleric and another a doctor or teacher; other brothers become adventurers abroad, some of them keen entrepreneurs and some remain factory workers or waiters for all their working life.

To excel in one category may compensate for deficiencies in another: poor families may not be condemned to low status if they are recognised as being of a good 'jat' or lineage. Status is shored up or even enhanced by 'good' marriages or other kinds of social connections, but the authenticity of such connections and any apparently fixed attributes of status are always open to question, particularly in the changeable world of a migrant or transnational population. This latter point should not be over-stressed: Gardner (1995: 128ff.) paints a very similar picture to that of Bethnal Green in her ethnography of Bangladesh where she found status and hierarchy to be fluid, dynamic and constantly re-negotiated multidimensional categories. In Bangladesh, 'money talks' and polarisation of status appears to be increasingly dependent on economic capital growth through investment in migration alone. In Bethnal Green there is a greater variety of opportunity for upward mobility through education, altered religious practice and women's economic activity as well as the more traditional emblems of status placed in Bangladesh such as a large house in Sylhet town. The changing practices of *purdah* and the finely nuanced and contingent assessment and discrimination of status through social networks is illustrated further in this and the following two chapters.

Clusters of wedding guests congregate loosely into same generation groups broken up by small children, the youngest boys being managed by mother or grandmother rather than by their fathers or grandfathers. Little girls are also often to be found sitting with grandmothers or older siblings and not exclusively with their own mothers. Soon after the food is eaten the younger ones move away and play outside if there is space, and the teenagers move away from their elders taking photos and chatting while the older women are given trays of *paan* (a combination of *paan* leaf, betel nut with or without lime paste and tobacco, chewed by men and women throughout the sub-continent) and settle and regroup at tables to talk. Some sit in little quiet knots alone, and presumably there are some absences. There is no fixed order of service or ritual for the two public meals that are the *bia* (wedding) and *walima* (the meal given by the groom's family), sometimes combined into one meal for the sake of economy as the guest list may be the same for both. There may be a prayer beforehand at the mosque for the men or briefly in the wedding room just before the meal to bless the couple, but mostly it is just a sociable and relaxed public meal. Earlier in the sequence of marriage ceremonies (of which the registry office ceremony is the least marked by ritual, and the engagement (*akht*) is the most formal) the bride and groom have separate parties at their own homes using *hollood* (turmeric) and *mendi* (henna). These are more or less gender specific except for close cross-sex relatives. The homely setting and the conduct of a fixed, if still simple, ritual sequence brings us closer to the domestic setting of the household.

The bride's family work hard to decorate the house and prepare food and special effects for a series of wedding parties. The gate to the house is replaced with an archway thickly decorated with artificial flowers and decorative banners hang over the front door. The living room is crammed with women in yellow or green *saris*. The younger brothers play outside eagerly greeting new guests. "Thank you for coming Pollen, go in, go in and see, everyone is in there". Smaller boys and girls mill in and out of the house excited and bewildered by turns. Father stays back in the kitchen after his presentation of food and *hollood* to the bride, occasionally intervening to assist the hired video cameraman. The room is elaborately decorated and the bride herself is enclosed in a tent of embroidered cloth hung with flowers with two young women attendants standing behind her in matching yellow *saris*. Before her is a large platter of fruit, a wedding *mendi* tray shaped like a heart or a winnowing-basket holding the ingredients for henna decorations and a dish of *hollood* paste. The room is hot and the glare of the video lighting makes it easy for her to sit with downcast eyes and a solemn expression. Her veil is maroon for this day and her *sari* yellow; it was gold for the *akht* and will be red for the wedding. Guests come up to her in pairs, women of similar age together or a mother and little children. They proffer a piece of fruit on cocktail sticks to her lips; she makes a minute gesture of refusal turning slightly then accepts and eats the fruit. They rub *hollood* paste on her folded hands and the attendants wipe it off. Some kiss her and hold a pose for cameras. Mother enjoys this party and there are no tears as there were at the more solemn *akht* ceremony. The bride at times is unable to eat so much fruit and the attendants take it from her, or she smiles at friends or whispers to one and this excites no comment of disapproval. The ceremony takes some time and one male relative offers refreshments to the guests who stand and wait. Slowly the crowd thins out and many leave after they have given fruit to the bride, stopping for a short while in the kitchen to talk to her parents and the knot of older women who have been helping with the preparations and chatting throughout the evening. Now there are only young women and the few non-Bengali guests in the living room who have held back partly out of awkwardness and unfamiliarity and partly in deference to more obviously senior-looking women.

The bride's closest female relatives and friends wear matching *saris* and look almost like an official entertainment troupe. The atmosphere relaxes as the remaining guests chat with the bride who talks more freely and enjoys herself in their company in the absence of the older women. There is no sense of naughtiness or of rebellion or cheek; if anything the young women are more urgent than the older generation in making sure that everything is done properly, "Who hasn't been? why haven't you? Go on, you go *now*" they say, encouraging laggards and shy guests to go ahead. They fuss over the home video now that the official cameraman has left, and the lights and ceiling fan with busy, self-conscious pleasure, proud to be in charge of things. They check for absentees among little brothers and sisters ensuring that nothing is left out. The contrast with the older generation lies in their language, their use of English rather than Sylheti, and changes in the way that they address each other. When all the guests were present they would use the correct title, *afa* (older sister) or name-plus-title, e.g. Rasia-*afa*, but now they use their own everyday casual (non-family) nicknames like 'Razz' and 'Mo', but they are not rebellious nor openly resentful of being part of a 'traditional' ritual.

Matrons perform their part in this ritual comfortably, with assurance and deftness. They do not hesitate or demur or show any awkwardness, nor any playful hilarity: it is just so and they are satisfied. *Mendi* parties in Bangladesh, I am told, include more joking and fun than those in Bethnal Green. A video of a Londoni groom's *mendi* party in Sylhet town was similar to London parties I attended, and only a little more joking in style but the contrast in overall atmosphere experienced by informants is unlikely to be captured by video film. In London, few of the younger, English-speaking women, when put on the spot could say specifically what the *hollood* paste was for: "I don't know, they just put some on, - you know - its what you use in cooking - what's it called? - oh yes, turmeric, *hollood*? well it means yellow, yes[8]". Only the older generation could explain that in fact the bride should be covered all over in *hollood* paste which is then washed off in a ritual bath to make her skin beautiful and golden. This is what women say when teaching you how to cook, the *hollood* is for its beautiful colour rather than flavour which in excess is unpleasant.

Reflecting on the variety of ways in which women participated in this *mendi* party, the generation that were brought up in Bangladesh are the most familiar with the conduct of the ritual but their demeanour is straightforward and not emotional. The contrast with the more excitable younger women could be said to be just the simple contrast of youth and (time-weary) maturity. However, the younger women who were born or brought up in Britain can be examined more closely. They speak with confidence about matters of taste in dress and cosmetics and answer to no-one but themselves about personal conduct, distancing themselves from what they regard as the less sophisticated traits of the men and older women, but they nevertheless comply generally with correctness in dress and styling. It is worthy of note that they do not rebel against the ritual, certainly not openly, nor is it detectable in semi-concealed cheek, or sullen resistance. It is also noteworthy that they are not fanatical revivalists of a cultural 'heritage' which could denote a distinctive 'identity'. Instead, their generally cheerful but concerned behaviour speaks of how they are striving to make the ritual personal for their friend. They grasp key points and ensure that things are done properly; they feel their way through to the meaning of the ritual, building it up where they can by looking intently for information, "Which finger is right for the ring? shall I ask *bhabi*?" (the classificatory older brother's wife and formal adviser to the bride). In the event, *bhabi* is not sure, and another 'aunty' comes to the rescue because when I am asked the question I hesitate to generalise from the English rule and risk making an error.

There is no feeling of fixed attitudes here, and although each generation is keenly aware of differences between them, there is no charter for older people and another for youngsters' behaviour. Mother cooks the party food with traditional utensils while the daughters are in charge of the video, but the whole family made the decorated tray for the groom's family together. There is a noticeable absence of parents pontificating except in the matter of the general structure of the ritual: the attitudes and behaviour of youngsters are not corrected by the older generation and the young neither rebel nor do they copy slavishly. The impression given is that the ritual is re-created with the right sort of enthusiasm and is not reproduced from a 'cultural arts-group' formula, nor under strict instruction from elders. In fact the least at ease are the younger wives from Bangladesh, who, while too young to be part of the older generation's groups, are not suited to the company of young bilingual women. As the odd one out I am useful for mopping up awkward guests and we make an in-between group, speaking in mixed English-Sylheti, closely observed by our seniors.

The sort of person who shows a more scrupulous attitude to the rituals of her 'culture' is likely to be found among the well-to-do. A young woman met at another wedding party is married to a man with a good career in the local civil

---

[8] In Sylheti *hollood* means both the colour yellow and turmeric powder.

service. They are comfortably well-off and she enjoys her work as a home-maker as well as socialising with her husband's English colleagues without any difficulty. She talks to me of her regret that Bengali teenagers and young adults have changed so much in the few years since she got married. She especially dislikes the way that they are less careful about their 'culture', language and religion. She would like to be more religious in her dress and daily practice but her husband thinks this would not look well in public, being aware of British attitudes to covered women. I become aware as she is talking that the increasing distance she feels between herself and other young Bengali women may be as much to do with her own rising status and ability to recruit the asset of 'cultural' distinctiveness in Britain as with the apparent decline in the 'cultural' integrity of her juniors. She celebrates both Bengali 'culture' and Islam although the two are not always compatible. Like many other religious Bengali people, she deplores what she sees as Indian Hindu influence as much as Western lifestyles on Bengali 'culture', particularly with regard to corruption of language, and what are seen as inauthentic street festivals (*melas*) sponsored by the local council, Bengali businesses and arts foundations. I notice that she speaks English with her sister in between chatting with myself; this observation is made not to discredit her integrity, nor does it show that she is unaware of the ways in which she differs from her more traditional forbears. She is demonstrating that the difference between herself and others is that can she can afford to choose when to be distinguished in a 'cultural' sense and so has become very aware and self-conscious about the relationship of the 'domain' of 'culture' to that of social status.

It is obviously unsatisfactory to present cultural heterogeneity as if it were merely a set of variations from a fixed rule, normative discourse, or from an assumed prior and fixed state of affairs such as so-called typical village life in Bangladesh. The women at these wedding parties are not simply aligning themselves each with one of a given set of normative types that could be labelled as 'the Islamic woman', 'the village Bengali wife', 'the modern progressive liberal woman'. What comes to the surface at these gatherings where all 'types' are juxtaposed, is the hope and desire for felicitous relationships which include the possibilities of several, if not all, these traditions at once in the context of many other issues not yet described.

It now seems that the teacher quoted at the beginning of this chapter is wrong to think that most Bengali people in London situate their belief systems wholly in Bangladesh with or without taking account of alternative notions that are available here, but the youth worker is also incorrect if he thinks that all will be swept away by inescapable 'Westernisation'. It is difficult to analyse and theorise the most important and affective themes through 'situational analysis' of events like *mendi* parties (Gluckman 1958 [1940]) although it is easier to have a feel for what is going on. A closer look at the household itself brings out the different strands of social facts and influences which may be permissive or obstructive in relation to the continuity of Bengali traditions or Westernising tendencies.

4.3 The Developmental Cycle of the Bengali Domestic Group

4.3.1 INTRODUCTION

After the wedding, the couple spend a few days at the bride's home before settling in the groom's parental house. The stream of daily guests finally dries up and the house returns to normal quiet domesticity. The effort has been tremendous. Given that there are so many guests, one might assume that there would be plenty of help for the preparations; in practice, active support from local family is reckoned to be thin. The invitations are spread quite far and those who are considered close kin, few. The Bethnal Green Bengali household in its normal daily existence is more isolated than it would seem if only visited for special parties.

At first sight the domestic unit of Bengali families differs little from that of the general population locally. Most Bengali households in Bethnal Green are nuclear, comprising parent(s) and their unmarried children. Of the non-nuclear households there is a predominance of the three generational, lineal-joint type. A similar pattern of co-residence does not mean that Bengali households are thought of by their non-Bengali neighbours as being like themselves and so a brief excursion into the perspective of non-Bengali local residents is appropriate. Identifiably different by their styles of dress and skin colour, cooking smells and naming systems, but otherwise living alongside local families, going to the same schools and shops, Bengali households are seen by the local population as evincing different styles rather than radically different sorts of families. Their lives are thus judged as a variation on, or deviation from, 'universal' normative family life. They are seen as ordinary folk who have 'Asian' customs like curry (which is popular), and arranged marriage (which is not). Family relationships are read as if the nuclear household were a natural phenomenon, and the differences between Bengali and other British families are discounted so as to fit in with this notion. The large number of children within Bengali nuclear families is thought of as a 'cultural' phenomenon, especially if the parents have been explicit about their religious beliefs, but the idea merges with one that typifies such parents as just ignorant or backward. Two generations ago East End families were of a similar size and English families of seven or more children nowadays are seen as old-fashioned.

Upwards of ten adults and teenagers, not counting small children, may be registered as living at one address in Bethnal Green and this is much more common among Bengali than non-Bengali households (Murphy 1996: 219). Households comprising three generations are read by outsiders as being determined by the scarcity of housing for new families rather than as a 'cultural' phenomenon. This notion is reinforced by the frequency of requests from young Bengali couples who, like anyone else, ask for doctor's letters to help with rehousing. Overcrowding and the limited availability of vacant housing for new families in the area are important local issue (Gavron 1998: 65) and household arrangements for all local residents are severely constrained by the local housing stock. Bengali families use whatever choices they have to shape the pattern of residence where possible. This point takes the argument into the multiplicity of issues that affects the development cycle of the domestic group.

4.3.2 DATA

Typologies of households and the Development Cycle of the Domestic Group is a matter of interest in Indian ethnography in relation to ideologies of kinship as well as gender, caste and issues such as demography, urbanisation and economics (Gould 1968, Kolenda 1968, Parry 1979, Singer 1968). The conceptual usefulness of 'odd jobs' words like 'family' and 'household' has already been noted but care must be taken over any naturalised assumptions about these institutions, especially on the basis of genealogical ties alone:

'[This] conveys the implicit notion that there is a fundamental similarity in structures of the units which share the same label...... The structure of a family, household or any social unit is not merely the sum of its genealogical ties, but the total configuration of social relationships among its members'. (Yanagisako 1979: 185, see also Harris 1984).

Kolenda's meta-analysis project avoids this error and I start with her classification for approximately 400 persons living in 80 households in Bethnal Green (Table 1). These are households of both patient- and non-patient-informants for whom I have sufficient data about household composition, occupation, health and other social data (see page 10).

A census analyst describes those one in eight of British households that are neither nuclear nor single-person as 'unconventional' (Murphy 1996: 228) in comparison to the majority of the population who live in nuclear or sub-nuclear households. If, following this view for the moment, we take the notion of joint household *in Britain* to mean co-residence of any persons in addition to the 'conventional' nuclear family, then classes II and V-XII combined, contain approximately 20% of the study population. The equivalent rate for the whole British population is 12.5% (Murphy 1996: 228). Kolenda notes that it is not until about 30% of households are joint (in her more restricted terminology) that the majority of the population lives in such households; this rarely obtains even in the Indian sub-continent. On the other hand, nuclear families in India are hardly ever 'perpetual structures but always part of a cycle' and thus the proportion of a population that has ever had experience of joint household life will always be greater than current prevalence (Kolenda 1968: 350). In Britain most (non-Asian) nuclear families cycle between the subnuclear and nuclear types without entering the phases that include additional adults, let alone more than one married couple (Creed 2000: 344).

Type of Family		Number	%	Description (Kolenda 1968)
Nuclear family	I	56	70%	A couple with or without unmarried children.
Supplemented nuclear family	II	8	10%	A nuclear family plus one or more unmarried, separated or widowed relatives of the parents, other than their unmarried children.
Subnuclear family	III	5	6.25%	A fragment of a former nuclear family. Typical examples are the widow with unmarried children, or the widower with unmarried children, or siblings—whether unmarried, or widowed, separated, or divorced—living together.
Single-person household	IV	0	0	
Supplemented subnuclear	V	0	0	A group of relatives, members of a formerly complete nuclear family, plus some other unmarried, divorced, or widowed relative who was not a member of the nuclear family. For example, a widow and her unmarried children plus her widowed mother-in-law.
Collateral joint family	VI	1	1.25%	Two or more married couples between whom there is a sibling bond—usually a brother-brother relationship—plus unmarried children.
Supplemented collateral joint family	VII	0	0	A collateral joint family plus unmarried, divorced, or widowed relatives. Typically, such supplemental relatives are the widowed mother of the married brothers, or the widower father, or an unmarried sibling.
Lineal joint family	VIII	10	12.5%	Two couples between whom there is a lineal link, usually between parents and married son, sometimes between parents and married daughter.
Supplemented lineal joint family	IX	0	0	A lineal joint family plus unmarried, divorced, or widowed relatives who do not belong to either of the lineally linked nuclear families; for example, the father's widower brother or the son's wife's unmarried brother.
Lineal-collateral joint family	X	0	0	Three or more couples linked lineally and collaterally. Typically, parents and their two or more married sons, plus the unmarried children of the three or more couples.
Supplemented	XI	0	0	A lineal-collateral joint family plus

lineal-collateral joint family				*unmarried, widowed, separated relatives who belong to none of the nuclear families lineally and collaterally linked; for example, the father's widowed sister or brother, or an unmarried nephew of the father.*
Other	XII	0	0	
Totals		80	100%	

Table 1: Household types (Kolenda 1968).

The higher than average prevalence of joint households in Britain for Bengali and other South Asian populations in Britain cannot be explained simply as a cultural preference or as being wholly the result of discriminatory practices without a more detailed analysis. Murphy makes the point that the higher prevalence of joint families endures within the longer established South Asian populations of Britain and is not a temporary feature of recent immigrants (Murphy 1996: 233). This supports a 'choice' theory, but must be qualified by his finding that more affluent British South Asian families are less likely to live in joint households.

Several factors affect household composition regardless of the aspirations of its members. These must be sorted out before we can attribute anything in the way of kinship ideals as causal factors in the observed data, let alone a discussion of attitudes and preferences towards joint or nuclear household life. For transnational studies this is complicated because of the greater number of factors affecting the prevalence of any particular household type. I have broken these down into three broad categories, demography, housing resources and transnationalism.

4.3.3 DEMOGRAPHY

The current demography of the Bengali population in Bethnal Green is determined by fertility, mortality and migration. The Bengali population is fertile and households contain above average numbers of young persons. The numbers of Bengali babies born in Britain has steadily risen, so that now about half of the families in this study have mothers who have given birth and brought up all their children in Britain. The proportion of mothers who have had any experience of childbirth and child-rearing in Bangladesh will fall even with continued entry of Bangladesh-born brides. These women rarely give birth in Bangladesh although they may be pregnant on arrival in Britain. At the other end of life, the excess mortality of South Asian men in Britain (measurement of which includes but does not differentiate Bengali from other South Asian men) is much greater than that of the general population, particularly in the younger age-group (20-49 years) where it is 65% greater than the national figure (Smaje 1995: 54). The number of deaths from coronary heart disease (one of the major causes of death for all ethnic groups in Britain) for South Asians in Leicester is predicted to double between 1988 and 2008 (Lowy et al. quoted in Smaje 1995: 54). The number of available grandparents, particularly grandfathers, who could form the upper tier in a joint household is thus reduced by this excess mortality.

Secondly, the original migrants' wives and families arrived in Britain in significant numbers only from the late 1970s onwards. The birth of grandchildren for this cohort of migrants began relatively recently. Moreover, Bengali girls become eligible for marriage from the age of 16, and rarely stay unmarried after the age of 24, whereas Bengali boys mostly marry at a later age, usually in their late twenties or early thirties. Until now, Bengali brides and grooms have preferentially been chosen from Bangladesh rather than from among families based in Britain. The migrants' *sons'* grandchildren have therefore been slower to grow as a population cohort than *daughters'* grandchildren, so the possibility of forming three-generation patrilineal households is also reduced by slowness to provide the bottom tier.

Thirdly, the large age-gap between husbands and wives in the original migrants' generation has been noted (see also Berrington 1996: 182). Constraints imposed by migrant work abroad has affected the timing of the conception of their children so that siblings in any one family may have a very wide age-range. This increases the prevalence of families containing widows and young unmarried adults, with or without older married siblings and their children.

Before adding in any other factors, the household data can be reviewed in the light of demography alone. I found ten lineal joint families derived from an original male migrant and his wife (rather than a married couple taking in elderly parents). Most of the nuclear households, where the married couple are of a comparable age to the oldest couple within joint families, do not yet have a married son, let alone grandchildren. Several of these nuclear households do have married daughters who have moved out on, or soon after their marriage. Daughters, whose husbands are still in Bangladesh awaiting visas, may stay alone with their parents until they can live with their husbands, but none of these grandparents has a son-in-law living with them. In other words, there are no uxorilocal couples except for a short space of time, perhaps for as long as six months or a year while a new house is sought for a married daughter whose husband has achieved entry to Britain.

Few local Bengali households become nuclear as a result of all their sons marrying and moving away. I have not found any elderly Bengali couples who have been abandoned by all their sons after marriage. The few isolated elderly Bengali couples that I have met were either childless or living in temporary accommodation for the homeless after spending excess time in Bangladesh according to the terms of their tenancy with the housing authority. Five married men known to me who are sons of migrants and live apart from their father's household comprise one who is from a very overcrowded household and is wealthy enough to have bought his own house, three who are sons of divorced mothers and one whose wife is from a London family. A widowed mother is rarely abandoned by all her sons; a divorced mother, on the other hand, rarely, if ever, has a married son living with her although unmarried sons do not always leave just because of the break-up of his parents' marriage. Less dramatic disruptions to joint families, disagreements and domestic difficulties are alluded to but not discussed in detail by a number of couples who, after a period of homelessness, have been re-housed at some distance from the husband's parents. As is found elsewhere, it is likely that although disagreement between women is frequently quoted as the immediate reason for the break-up of a joint household, the impetus to move out may come from the son (Aziz 1979: 50, Parry 1979: 177).

The reasons for married sons moving away from their parental homes, thus reducing the proportion of patrilineal joint families, can therefore be summarised as being caused by international migration (the nuclear households of grooms from Bangladesh), economic advancement, parental divorce and other family disruptions. A more extended discussion of preferences and attitudes will be postponed until other material considerations have been dealt with, but the evidence so far is that uxorilocality is avoided and patrilineal joint families containing at least one married son are in evidence where demography allows, with some exceptions.

4.3.4 HOUSING RESOURCES

The population of the borough has grown rapidly in the last decade[9]. Housing resources have not kept pace except at the most expensive end of the property market. The vacancy rate for council-owned properties in Bethnal Green is particularly low compared to the borough average, especially for housing with more than three bedrooms. If more than one married couple live together, sleeping arrangements become severely constrained: whereas a three-bedroomed flat might accommodate up to ten children of a single couple, albeit in overcrowded conditions, if one of them married, there would be no space for both conjugal couples and their children. Housing associations have been busier than the council in building new and more spacious properties, but their rents are higher. Leaving the council property sector entails loss of a whole set of associated benefits and services including repairs and alterations. Although being tied to the council's services is irksome for those with sufficient resources, if any significant alterations need to be made, for example to accommodate disability, then housing association and private sector tenants must bear the full cost themselves or appeal to a charity.

There has as yet been no general exodus of the Bengali population to the cheaper suburbs of East London although some have made such a move. The

---

[9] 168,100 in 1991; the number of locally resident patients registered with family doctors in 1999 was 206,418 (ELCHA 2000 Appx. 5).

wealthy married son referred to earlier bought a house within the more expensive housing market of inner-city Tower Hamlets. Lest this slowness to move outwards be thought of only as 'cultural' wish to stay near to one's 'community' (Anwar 1979: 214, Phillips 1988: 364) or an expression of the 'myth of return', whereby immigrant families invest in property abroad, anticipating a return to the homeland, pragmatic explanations are also applicable. There is an economy of scale if a family remains in the more central district of Bethnal Green where public transport is better and continuity of children's education from nursery to university level is more easily obtained within a smaller geographical space than in the suburbs. Continuity of health resources is also a consideration for families who have frequent recourse to primary and secondary health care. Racism is more frequently experienced the smaller the Bengali population is in relation to other groups (Brimicombe et al 2001). Finally economic considerations are basic to any analysis: almost half the households in this study are wholly dependent on benefits and so have no opportunity to buy property. Households with an annual income of less than £20,000 who are not already home-owners are unlikely to be able to afford to buy any property within Greater London (Hamnett 2001: 83).

It must be borne in mind that any strategies with respect to residence are prosecuted in a setting where the majority population's interpretation of Bengali kinship and household ideals (not yet examined) will have an effect on the success or failure of such strategies, quite apart from such issues as demography and available housing stock. These interpretations will colour the attitudes and actions of city-planners, immigration and housing officers as well as neighbours and co-residents of Bethnal Green. Phillips argues that institutionalised racism was evident in housing allocation practices of the 1980s in Tower Hamlets (Phillips 1988). The lack of larger housing units and the pressure to maintain high acceptance rates led to a dual stereotyping of Bengali families. They were seen as being as suited to the worst accommodation because of assumptions as to a 'cultural' preference for areas with greater numbers of existing Bengali residents, and they were simultaneously classified as unsuitable for predominantly white areas on account of 'cultural' customs deemed to be inappropriate to 'respectable' neighbourhoods (Philips 1988: 364-365, Keith 1995: 555).

While efforts have been made to change housing policies that particularly disadvantage transnational families, there is evidence from informants that housing officers' notions of 'fitness' or 'unfitness' of certain tenants to different kinds of accommodation continues. The higher fertility rate of Bengali families is especially likely to attract comments such as, "Why did you have two more children if you knew you only had a one-bedroomed flat?" Requests for four-bedroomed housing is countered with, "If you insist on asking for four bedrooms you will never be rehoused; if you ask for three bedrooms it will take one to three years." This was said to a homeless couple with five children in substandard temporary accommodation.

I argue that constraint in housing resources is still the main reason for the marked residential segregation of Bengali families in Britain. While it appears that Bengali families do manage to exercise choice in some respects (avoiding uxorilocality and maintaining family proximity), the limited scope of such choice does not affect indices of ethnic segregation. I have found no evidence that 'safety in numbers' translates consistently into a preference for Bengali neighbours for other reasons. Constraint or choice is an important question to resolve since the deleterious effects of poverty in any one locale are compounded by ethnic segregation (Massey and Fischer 2000). The argument has recently been reviewed exhaustively (Phillips 1998, van Kempen & Sule Ozüerkren 1998) but no satisfactory conclusions are drawn which fully explain Bengali indices. Peach continues to argue trenchantly that 'culture' is an independent explanatory factor since he calculates so as to take racism and economics out of geographical equations and still finds marked differences in segregation indices between different minority ethnic groups (Peach 1998, Peach & Rossiter 1996). Recent small-scale research leans towards the constraint side of the argument (Bowes et al. 2000, Cameron and Field 2001). Peach's 'culture factor' is, I suggest, likely to be an expression of inappropriately *culturalised* inter-ethnic relationships in the negotiation between individual housing officers and Bengali families which falls short of overtly racist behaviour. Those with the best 'multiculturalist' intentions may, through acts of omission, hinder access to information about housing and other social resources for minority ethnic families, a matter more fully discussed below (Chapter 7).

4.3.5 TRANSNATIONAL AND INTRA-NATIONAL EXTENDED HOUSEHOLDS

To complicate matters further, migration stretches the notion of the Bengali household across continents so that attitudes towards ideals of co-residence become even harder to observe and analyse. Before trying to discern preferences in Bethnal Green, the homeland traditions must be examined. As Gardner points out, a two-way dialectical process exists whereby migration affects household composition in Bangladeshi villages and this in turn affects households in Bethnal Green. The achievement of sending a family member abroad is symbolic of household success in Sylhet but has had the consequence of reducing, sometimes drastically, the number of joint households in Sylhet, (Gardner 1995: 111, 227-8). Sons who embark on migration rather than settling in joint patrilineal households in Bangladesh increase the proportion of nuclear neolocal households compared with joint patrilineal households in Bethnal Green. The tradition of migration goes back at least a century for Sylhet district and therefore has long exerted a negative effect on the joint phase of Sylheti households (Gardner 1995: 110-127).

Bethnal Green Bengali families with surplus resources invest in property in Bangladesh as well as in British businesses. Whether or not they ever intend to retire to Bangladeshi homes, there is an observable enthusiasm for ownership of a house in Sylhet. The price of land in Sylhet has increased as a direct result of emigration with negative effects on poorer families in these villages (Gardner 1995: 91). Village land and the natal *bari* (homestead) retain the affective and economic interests of those family members who live in Bethnal Green. The exact status of these ties is not clear cut: whereas families in Bethnal Green frequently emphasise the enduring and at times, burdensome duty of remittances to Bangladesh, even after children are born in Britain, Gardner records that most Bangladeshi households said that they did not receive regular money from absent kin (Gardner 1995: 123). The tension lies in the relation between (nuclear) families and (corporate) households rather than a purely geographical divide. The Bangladeshi *bari* typically comprises several homes (*ghor*) which share joint resources such as the fish-tank (*fukhor*), winnowing area and kitchen garden but do not necessarily share a common hearth nor shared land ownership. As the development cycle of the domestic group passes through different phases, the relations of co-residence, sharing of a common hearth and co-ownership of land alter. For example, adult sons and their living parents may share joint land, finances and residence. At the death of the older generation, the surviving brothers usually divide both land and households whilst still living near to each other within the same *bari*. These arrangements are, however, flexible, especially where migration is involved (Gardner 1995). Prosperous Sylheti families may thrive where the *bari* can maintain an economic unit for land management while reducing family conflict over housekeeping chores (see again Creed 2000). The possibility of uncoupling land-ownership from immediate co-residence thus increases the flexibility of a patrilineage with respect to factors such as migration and economic change,

> 'Rather than moving in one direction, forces for change are multiple, and at times contradictory. Clearly households are flexible to different circumstances, and constantly defy easy classification (Gardner 1995: 110).

The same pattern can be observed within Britain. Co-residence is uncoupled from joint land-ownership by international migration. Bengali men who are partners in such holdings will travel back to Bangladesh at intervals to protect their economic interests in land. Apart from (status) investments in Sylheti property, entrepreneurial Bengali businessmen simultaneously invest economic capital in factories and restaurant businesses throughout Britain. The 1991 census shows that the Bengali population is at once concentrated in the conurbations but also widely dispersed (in very small numbers) as far afield as the remote rural regions of Scotland and Wales where at least two Bangladeshi persons are identified in almost every district, in order, it is assumed, to run the local 'Indian'. Restaurant owners can maintain a family home in Bethnal Green and the provincial town, commuting between the two. Eventually, the well to do may move the whole family to a residential property near to the restaurant if it is in a pleasant area. Employees may also leave their families in Bethnal Green, living above the restaurant during the week, or, if the restaurant is in the suburbs they can commute daily. Bengali households thus show a recurrent pattern of men spending relatively long periods of time alone as economic migrants with their families following them at a later stage. Onward migration leaves many Bengali 'households' to be managed solely by women for much of the time. Joint holdings of property and patrilineage members are thus geographically dispersed between the village, Sylhet town and foreign residences and businesses. Efforts to maximise resources in each segment of extended households are evident and no one element is favoured to the detriment of another.

These considerations of demography, housing resources and transnationalism contextualise the bald classification of Bengali households in Bethnal Green and Sylhet according to Kolenda's typology. Attitudes to joint or nuclear households and kinship ideology can now be discussed together with the corollaries of the data already given.

4.3.6 COROLLARIES OF THE DEVELOPMENT CYCLE OF THE BENGALI DOMESTIC GROUP

Housing resources, racism and immigration policies put pressure on Bengali families to become nuclear. Yanagisako emphasises an observation made by several other authors that while wider social pressures may favour nuclear families, the ideology supporting joint family structure may nevertheless remain intact, if attenuated in its expression,

> '[T]here is no inherent contradiction between the view that modern industrial society favours the development of the nuclear family at the expense of the extended family and the view that the extended family remains important.' (Yanagisako 1979: 183).

The patterning of household composition for Bengali families in Bethnal Green is largely nuclear. However almost a fifth of this population live in some kind of non-nuclear household at any one time, and a larger proportion do so for at least part of their lives.

Most young couples of Bangladeshi origin living in Bethnal Green comprise the married daughters of original Bengali migrants living in neo-local nuclear households close to her parents; a small, but increasing number, comprise married sons living jointly with his parents, and a few couples have both sets of parents to hand and may live in nuclear or joint households. Although uxorilocal residence after marriage is avoided, English-speaking young mothers attest to the pleasure and benefit of living near to their mother rather than with their husband's parents, "Well who would *you* prefer, your mother or your mother-in-law?" (cf. Vatuk 1972: 141). Others say that they could trust no-one else with child-care while they work. This all sounds perfectly natural to British ears, but given the short time that families have settled here it would seem that attitudes as well as custom in this matter have changed very fast. Have these young women actually learned so quickly that the rule of living with your mother-in-law after marriage is an entirely arbitrary custom that can simply be side-stepped in mixed society, or have Bengali women always been 'ready' to drop this, aware that it was something that did not suit them or their husbands? They still continue, on the whole, to comply with arranged marriages, so it would seem that some rules are more easily broken, or certain cycles of customary behaviour are more easily accelerated or decelerated than others in a new context.

Demography dictates that there are many more British-born or British-educated Bengali wives who are able to live neolocally and have the opportunity to remain close to their own parents' home after marriage than there are those who live with their parents-in-law, if only because the latter mostly live in Bangladesh (a fact that British immigration officers deploy, quoting the 'known' Bengali norm of virilocality when denying visas to husbands of British-Bangladeshi women (Menski 1999, Brah 1996: 75). Those British-born or educated wives who do live with their husband's family in Bethnal Green will be aware that they are unusual, in the sense that most married women in their peer group, for one reason or another, do not have to live with their in-laws. The personal preferences of these wives, which is not uniform, is tempered by self-awareness of their unusual position. Almost all say that they see this as a temporary stage with neolocal nuclear residence as a desirable and predictable future eventuality.

Continuity of the patrilineal joint household is therefore maintained by sons who marry women from Bangladesh. Bangladeshi wives share a similarity in up-bringing with their mother-in-law unlike a British-born daughter-in-law, but this is sometimes quoted uncritically as the main reason for the preference for Bangladeshi brides by British-Bengali families (Summerfield 1993: 87). By the same token, British-Bengali grooms should be favoured by British-Bengali parents of marriageable daughters as the bride will have some proximity to her mother-in-law, but in practice this is not the case. To return briefly to demography, male migration resulted in Bengali men outnumbering Bengali women in Britain by a ratio of approximately 1·09 in 1991[10]. Bengali boys who migrated as young adults with their fathers before their mothers and younger siblings joined them thus had very few female Bengali age-mates from whom to choose a bride. Once this demographic inequality began to even out and significant numbers of eligible British-Bengali women came of age, the

---

[10] The 1991 demographic analysis is problematic because of bias caused by underestimation of about 1 million people in Britain that was greatest for young people from minority ethnic groups (Wrench & Qureshi 1996: 8).

preference for grooms (as well as brides for British-Bengali sons) from Bangladesh continued although marriages between two British-based families are no longer rare. The desire to send a child to Britain means that there is a 'push' factor from the continuous supply of hopeful spouses offered by Bangladesh-based families. There is also an important 'pull' factor: the family and personal background of Bangladeshi spouses, male or female, is thought to be more readily open to inspection than that of eligible young persons living in Britain. Appropriate knowledge of family background is essential to making a good match and overwhelms consideration of village versus British upbringing. The network of knowledge through Bangladeshi village contacts is thought to be more reliable than the lines of communication in London. It is also thought to be easier to hide family problems in London than to conceal such matters in Bangladesh. I argue that this trust in certain kinds of social networks over others (whatever their reliability in practice) is more influential than demography and the notion of people 'fitting-in'; social networks are discussed more fully in Chapter 5.

Virilocality therefore continues where it is possible but is a negotiable practice. Avoidance of uxorilocality, combined with the workings of the housing market and local attitudes of influential advisors to young women, such as college teachers, health advisors and social workers, make it comfortable for young mothers to live apart from their affines and near to their own family. The most obvious contrast between Bangladesh and Bethnal Green is in the frequency with which grooms live near to their in-laws in a similar position to the inferior 'village husbands' (*ghor jameye*) found among poor families in Bangladesh. The anonymity of a large city mitigates the low status of this position. Ethnography from rural Bangladesh shows that whereas the ideal of virilocal marriage is upheld, joint domestic units split up early on in a significant number of cases; if a joint household maintains unity for the first few years then it is likely to endure (Aziz 1979: 50). In Sylhet, if means allow, a son's new household unit can be built within the same *bari* or village, whereas in London he must find accommodation within hailing distance of his parents to maintain a semblance of virilocality.

With regard to the wives of original migrants, they have now become grandmothers. Some are handing over cooking duties to daughters-in-law while they look after the grandchildren, revealing that for years they performed both tasks without the customary division of labour between mother-in-law and daughter-in-law. One father, whose daughter had just had a baby said, "We are orphans, our children are orphans - here we have no grandmothers". By implication only the father's mother counts as a functional grandmother and even now only sons' children will be brought up in an orthodox patrilineal ambience if most young women continue, as they do, to marry men whose parents are in Bangladesh. These women will bring up their children without sharing household labour with their husband's mothers. The revelation of the discomfort felt by many families because of a specific kinship deficiency, this orphanhood of children without paternal grandmothers, raises the questions as to who else might be missing in the expected scheme of Bengali family life and how the absences might become apparent as the Bengali household undergoes further development. This will be examined in Chapter 5. It should be emphasised that the expectations of Bengali families in Britain do not necessarily reflect the facts of life in Bangladesh where dense co-resident households are depleted by emigration (Gardner 1995) and paternal grandmothers are also, for demographic reasons, uncommon in joint households (Aziz 1979: 50).

The last corollary to be drawn from the analysis of the development cycle of the domestic group concerns unmarried young adults. Bengali men brought up in Bethnal Green who are over the age of 25 have few or no unmarried female age-mates since almost all Bengali women enter marriage early. The consequence is that the longer period of bachelorhood makes a larger cohort of young Bengali men available as boyfriends but not necessarily as husbands for the smaller cohort of younger women who are receiving proposals but are not yet married; this is recognised as a danger by parents of eligible daughters. Education and a career can extend the period between school and marriage for young women as well as elevating their status as potential brides. For this and other reasons, young women represent the vanguard of change in labour patterns for the Bengali population of Bethnal Green. This change in the economic behaviour of young Bengali women helps the analysis of the direction of change for Bengali households in Bethnal Green. An economic overview of Bengali households, with an emphasis on women, forms the final section before roles and attitudes of household members is examined in greater detail.

4.4 Household economics and changing roles for women

Wrench & Qureshi (1996) make a detailed analysis of the economic activity of the British Bangladeshi population from census and Labour Force Survey data. They note that the analysis is statistically complex given the bias from incomplete workings-out of migration demographics and the effects of high local unemployment levels that generally penalise minority ethnic groups. Bengali men and women alike demonstrate occupational segregation, but this is more pronounced for Bengali men than women. Tables 2 - 6 show data for occupation, chronic ill health and sources of income for the same households that were identified for Table 1.

	Male	% (M)	Total	% (T)	Female	% (F)
Adults over 20 years old	70		140		70	
Retired	5 (>65yrs)	7%	7	5%	2 (>60yrs)	3%
Of working age	65	93%	133	95%	68	97%

Table 2: Bengali adults of working age.

	Male	% (M)	Total	% (T)	Female	% (F)
Of working age	65		133		68	
Long term sick of working age	11	17%	38	29%	27	40%
Working age and well	54	83%	95	71%	41	60%

Table 3: Long term sickness among Bengali adults of working age.

	Male	% (M)	Total	% (T)	Female	% (F)
Working age and well	54		95		41	
Occupation not known, not sick	10	18%	10		0	0%
Unemployed, not sick, not home-maker	6	11%	9	9.5%	3	7%
Occupation known	38	71%	76		38	93%

Table 4: Economic activity, working age, not sick

	Male	% (M)	Total	% (T)	Female	% (F)
Occupation known	38		76		38	
Student	4	10.5%	10	13.2%	6	15.8%
Services not restaurant	1	2.6%	5	6.6%	4	10.5%
White collar	8	21%	10	13.2%	2	5.25%
Business self-employed	4	10.5%	4	5.2%	0	0%
Restaurant chef	5	13%	5	6.6%	0	0%
Restaurant waiter	7	18.4%	7	9.2%	0	0%
Mosque	4	10.5%	4	5.2%	0	0%
Homemaker, not sick	0	0%	26	34.2%	26	68.2%
Unskilled waged work	5	13%	5	6.6%	0	0%
Totals within occupations	38	100%	76	100%	38	100%

Table 5: Occupations

Type of Income	Number of Households	Percentage
Multiple	9	14.7
Dual income	6	10
Female income only	1	1.5
Male incomes	17	27.8
Benefits only	28	46
Totals	61	100

Table 6: Sources of household incomes

The category of 'student' is heterogeneous as it contains women who are treading water while awaiting marriage but may not intend to work, as well as young men and women who are likely to gain professional salaries as lawyers and doctors in the near future. These students may also work part-time in shops, contributing some of their wages to a family that is classified as being welfare dependent. The insufficiency of this small-scale data is obvious, but tabulation and enumeration of even small numbers can act as a corrective to the bias inherent in solely anecdotal or narrative collation of household data. In this way some suggestive points and additional remarks can be made, relevant to the question of assimilative or traditional trajectories and preferences for different kinds of households.

These data confirm the high levels of welfare dependency through unemployment and long-term ill health found by the 1991 census for this population. Economic polarisation of families is suggested by the way in which women's waged work occurs mostly in families that already have one income, whereas sick or unemployed men are unlikely to benefit from a wife's or daughter's wages. Some caution is needed here since poorer families may conceal the fact that their daughter has a low-status job, for example, by sending her to work in a shop in a remote district, whereas well-educated women would not conceal white-collar employment. I have also gained the impression that joint families with multiple incomes are able to draw on extra cash resources through family businesses both at home and abroad. This money may be extended as credit to junior connections to finance weddings and new businesses. Illegal but lucrative drug trades also contribute to the lumpiness of the distribution of cash and capital among local Bengali and non-Bengali populations alike. From a masculine perspective, continuity with Sylhet where some men gamble much or all on the risky hope of economic ventures abroad

(Gardner 1993b: 221) is also found in forms of entrepreneurial venture capitalism in Bethnal Green. Gambling with cards, as in Sylhet, also continues in the back rooms of shops in Bethnal Green as a way in which household incomes can be catastrophically depleted, usually for poorer Bengali families.

Whereas very few of their mothers have been wage earners, increasing numbers of young Bengali women enter the job market, at least in the gap between finishing education and embarking on marriage. In Bethnal Green, young Bengali women work at the post office, in chemists shops, *sari* shops or at supermarket tills. Other favoured careers are those of nursery nurses and vocational university training in medicine, pharmacy and law. Unlike Bangladesh (Kabeer 1994) and the rest of the Indian sub-continent (Acharya 1996), female workers in Bethnal Green appear to be drawn predominantly from more prosperous families. There are similarities between Bangladesh and Britain: both nation states profess a wish to promote the cause of women which adds a permissive rhetorical rationalisation for these working women. Secondly, a resurgence in religiosity among Bengali women has encouraged them to be more self-confident as they elaborate their Islamic identity, often in contradistinction to specifically Bengali (conservative and masculine) Islamic practices. In this way, 'an ideological space has...been opened up for them to consider new strategies and opportunities' (Kabeer 1994: 168). In Kabeer's example, most female workers were unmarried, and since only those who successfully negotiated with their male guardians were studied, the most proximate reasons for working in the Bangladeshi factories varied from the need for basic survival, through broader income-earning strategies for households that already had the minimum, to earning to finance increased personal expenditure. The latter two categories correspond with the reasons found in Bethnal Green.

Factory work for women in Bangladesh entails dropping the strict rules of *purdah*, but the justifications given by those interviewed by Kabeer were all elaborated within the cultural norms of female propriety, rather than relying on purely economic argument. None repudiated *purdah* entirely, but narrow views were expanded in the face of new economic realities. Thus the rule became conditional rather than absolute and a sort of situational ethics was adduced, founded on the notion of a woman who carries *purdah* with her. This broadening of interpretation was allowable given the benefits of their labour to families. Many authors attest to the weakness of using *purdah*, (or other cultural practices) as a unitary explanation of limitations to women's economic activity (Acharya 1996: 52, Baumann 1996: 52, Brah 1996: 137, Wolf 1992: 10). Young Bengali working women in Bethnal Green use very similar arguments to Kabeer's informants to rationalise their economic positions. They commonly refer to the narrower views of the older generation. Work uniforms (which generally permit headscarves) reduce the possibility of being read as 'loose women' by others (cf.

Ong 1987: 179ff., Wolf 1992: 209ff.). Progressive, self-assertive women are, the workers say, less likely to be 'victims' both of racism and of what they see as blatant sexism prevalent among Bengali men. Increasing Islamic orthopraxy with respect to body covering allows women to make economic progress without loss of propriety or alignment with Westernising tendencies. In contrast, diversification of masculine Bengali economic activity does not alter household roles or the expression of family values to the same extent as that of working Bengali women.

The relationship between household types, family values and the economy is likely to be complex for a recently settled diasporic population and where women's economic behaviour is changing (Kabeer 1994: 180, Wolf 1992: 10ff., see also Creed 2000 for a review of the literature on households, family values and the economy). Predictions of future outcomes may be uncertain in the absence of sufficient data but from my own knowledge it is likely that the spread of outcomes for Bengali families in Bethnal Green will be polarised as households undergo further development rather than showing a universal trend across the board. As a proxy measure of overall trajectories, supplementary to the economic data already given and using the same households as for Tables 1-6, Table 7 shows the proportions of households which in the next five to ten years will contain a university graduate son *and* daughter, a son with his own business, a salary from one or more white-collar worker, or be reliant only on insecure wages or benefits.

Future trajectories	Number	Percentage
Son and daughter at university	8	13
White-collar career	12	20
Own business	4	6.5
Waged work	21	34.5
Benefits only	16	26
Totals	61	100

Table 7: Future trajectories of Bengali households in Bethnal Green

The table is based on projections and assumes, firstly, that nothing will happen to hinder the courses already set by young adults and, secondly, that those who have been unskilled wage-earners or in receipt of benefits for some time are unlikely to change. The figures are limited in their explanatory potential by the youthful profile of Bengali families which means that in ten years time many will still have no adult children. With these provisos it can be seen that for almost 40%, the future is bright, but, as has become a pattern in this ethnography, the majority will have a precarious socio-economic future. For those who will be at university, it is not only daughters who are ambitious for academic achievement. Four male students come from households which at present are reliant on benefits alone, and three are children of migrant labourers. The likelihood of a polarised future for this population as a whole mirrors Gardner's observations of changes in Sylhet. Differentials in access to, and outcomes of, the risky economic opportunities of migration abroad has caused greater economic polarisation among the households remaining in Bangladesh. Even those who do not undertake the risks of migration may lose in economic terms through rising land prices (Gardner 1995: 271).

4.5 Roles within households

4.5.1 INTRODUCTION

'Household' and 'family' are easily conflated and thus the operations of power are obscured by naturalised discourses (Hertz 1960 [1909]: 3), central to which are those of motherhood (Harris 1984: 138). To extend what was briefly mentioned at the outset, households are not bounded units of production and reproduction but their internal structures and workings both produce and are produced by larger-scale social, economic and political processes. Many other institutions, apart from households (the education system, the job market, the judiciary and so on) are involved in the reproduction of specific sorts of persons and identities. These institutions in turn are part of wider discourses which encode gender ideologies and roles through traditions aligned with household life such as customs of marriage, residence rights and inheritance laws. This permeable model undermines the household as an independent explanatory category (Moore 1994: 86ff.).

The two-way traffic of meanings that converges on transnational households is of a greater degree of complexity than for those with less geographical scope. This complexity is simplified in the discussion that follows by examining the nexus of competing and synergistic roles within the Bengali household from three perspectives. First I present the viewpoint of the older generation and the issue of their children's marriages; secondly, the perspective of the joint household as an institution is used to discuss the issues surrounding young married couples. The perspective then changes to that of young married women who were brought up in Bethnal Green, their marriages to Bangladeshi men and the issues of work and divorce.

4.5.2 OLDER MIGRANTS' GENERATION

4.5.2.1 A woman's view

The wives of older men rarely speak fluent English, although comprehension is harder to quantify. Most have never worked outside the home and have difficulty communicating with non-Bengali people on their own. If father is always the spokesperson and mother is covered up in public then it is not surprising that some non-Bengali observers assume a very dominant and commanding role for father and a submissive, deferential one for mother.

Bengali women of this generation could be described iconographically as the central figures in the reproduction of traditional Bengali domestic customs. They command the domains of kitchen and garden although they are not confined to these shared spaces within the home. They prepare food for twice daily rice and curry meals (*bhatt*) using traditional utensils and ingredients. Food is particularly significant as part of a continuing tradition of Sylheti-Bengali material culture. A bunch of dried, unwinnowed rice (*dan*), sometimes beautified with henna colouring hangs in some Bethnal Green households symbolising the homeland (*desh*). The unsurpassed savour of *desh* food, whether rice, vegetables, fruit or fish is compared to the inferiority of imports from other countries like Africa or Thailand (that nevertheless guarantee almost year-round availability of familiar foodstuffs). This tradition is linked to the significance of Sylheti soil, the land that contains the buried remains of the *pirs* (disciples) of Shah Jalal who brought Islam to the region in the fourteenth century (Gardner 1995: 75). Using traditional implements such as the *dah*[11], *fatta*[12] and *looari*[13] is thought to enhance the quality of the finished dish. Few young married women brought up in Bethnal Green have the expertise to use a *dah* safely although they may work alongside their mother-in-law who continues her work in a traditional manner.

The dress of older women is invariably traditional: *saris* predominate over *shalwar kameez* but a loose dress might be worn at home when there are no visitors. Although unmarried women dress in a variety of fashions there is still a prevalence of 'Asian' styles of one kind or another. An enhanced tradition is seen in respect of *burqas*. A full length, Islamic-styled coat, usually dark in colour was rarely seen in the 1980s in Bethnal Green. Ordinary coats, jackets and cardigans sufficed as outdoor wear combined with a headscarf not intended to match the coat. The increasing prevalence and variety of *burqas* with matching head and, for some, face coverings has spread from the younger to the older generation of Bengali women recently. The practices of the traditions of *purdah* (in Sylheti, *farda*) have altered from physical sequestration within the home (which meant *burqas* were a redundant expense), to physical sequestration of the body outside the home. The range of styles of *purdah* includes the ordinary, the overtly fashionable and those that denote pious international Islam (*hijab*). The changes in women's body coverings is paralleled by the emergence of variety in

---

[11] A floor knife, with a large curved blade for cutting any raw ingredient. A second blade at the end of the footplate is used to hack through bones of fish and meat.

[12] A roughly hewn stone slab for crushing spices with a variety of rollers.

[13] A cast-iron bowl-shaped pan for deep-frying and braising. As a presentation dish in Bengali restaurants it is renamed, ironically perhaps, *balti* which means bucket in Sylheti.

women's religious practices as the number of younger Bengali women has increased in Bethnal Green. Older women perform their five times a day Islamic prayer (*namaz*) in solitude at home and never attend the mosque. The East London mosque in Whitechapel, which looks to the Middle East rather than Bangladesh for Islamic authority (Eade 1996: 219), has a women's room and special sessions for mixed-ethnicity groups of women to pray together. These are attended by young Bengali women; very few older Bengali woman attend any mosque services.

Older Bengali housewives display an enviable deftness and practical efficiency in performing or supervising all household duties including growing vegetables in gardens or on windowsills. They were noticeable at the *mendi* party for being adroit. They are adept at 'multi-tasking' since their husbands' and children's' needs are, for the reasons already discussed, multifarious. Cooking, cleaning, laundry work and gardening are fitted in without losing track of *namaz* time or children's school related needs. In my experience it is nearly always men who are caught short by realising that the 'window' for one *namaz* time is about to close and has to be done in a hurry whereas women have usually thought ahead and planned their activities to include *namaz* without stressful deadlines. Bengali women are commonly aware of this, and complaints about husbands' sloppiness with their prayers are easily found except among those of retirement age who have less demanding schedules. Despatching household tasks (*shongshari*) efficiently leaves time for relaxing, drinking tea with neighbours, watching TV or going shopping. Slovens are rare and in my experience only found among the younger generation where it is not hard to interpret their behaviour as a form of protest. It should not be forgotten, however, that this generalised description obscures the fact that Table 3 (p. 96) shows that 40% of Bengali women of working age classified themselves as chronic invalids (women who have applied for, but not always received, long-term sickness benefit). In such households, husbands and older children supply the missing domestic labour.

With time, older women delegate *shongshari* to junior married-in women and take care of grandchildren, demonstrating the customary role of the paternal grandmother (*dadi*). *Dadi* traditionally shaves the head of her new-born grandchild to remove the polluting fluids of the birth canal (*naffar*). Where there is no *dadi*, babies' heads are shaved by anyone competent, but young mothers give no consistent explanation for the custom when asked, "The hair grows thicker....It's just a custom....I don't really know.....to be clean, I think". For grandmothers, taking on the care of a small child decreases the opportunity or necessity to go out. In the English climate at least, and in a flat with no lift, or one that is unreliable, it is time-consuming and difficult to take a baby out for a walk. Older children help with outdoor tasks such as taking and fetching younger ones to and from school. The outdoor life of little children is therefore more often in the hands of older children and young adults than in *dada's* (paternal grandfather) and *dadi's* company who command their indoor life.

In an ideal setting, the life of older Bengali women can be a dignified form of sequestration in those homes where relationships are harmonious and mutual in their support of all family members. A traditional Bengali mother may be housebound in one sense but her judgement about family matters is respected and not discounted on grounds of her inexperience of the world outside the house. Some sophisticated college students say that they rely on their mothers for guidance with all their educational decisions. Although a significant minority of women confine most of their activities to the family home or family visits to relatives, many others of this generation are freely mobile outside the home. The increased wearing of *burqas*, although not universal, can be related to the increased movement of Bengali women outside the home. House to house visiting and shopping in the company of other women without husbands is commonplace in Bethnal Green and not confined only to Bengali shops. Where husbands are absent at work this is both a necessity as well as a novel pleasure; in Bangladesh, only husbands should go to the bazaar.

To remain mostly at home with little or no language ability in a foreign country (as part of an oppressed minority rather than a colonial elite) can be mis-read as living in an inferior, limited and segregated position. It appears so if the analysis uses standards concerned with equality of opportunity and levels of achievement in the same terms as those of the majority society. It is not necessarily an irrational strategy, nor does it mean that these women have failed to gain access to the English language only through lack of motivation, shyness or because anyone has deliberately put obstacles in their way (all commonly expressed views among non-Bengali people who confront this problem). Their own need for proficiency in English is a lesser concern than the ability to be skilled at managing bilingual children growing up in a plural society. The value of undertaking the tasks of supporting such children as well as their husbands is not limited to the notion of reproducing custom and 'culture' but is work that has an economic value in a long term perspective. In other words the investment required by a family to train such a woman to become a wage-earner (which would include child-care arrangements) may not be economic in comparison to the work of supporting existing and future family wage-earners. Some older women do work, for example as child-minders and crèche-workers or home garment makers, all admittedly within enclosed spaces.

Older Bengali women may be physically sequestered but these practices of the body do not engender a retiring mode of social intercourse. In medical consultations, whether alone or with others, older women say whatever they feel is necessary without embarrassment. On the occasion of a social meal with neighbours, cooking tasks take them to the kitchen while guests sit and chat in the front room, but if the conversation takes an interesting turn they will join in, as far as their work allows. There is no evidence of a rule, custom or etiquette which demands that Bengali women should give way in conversation to anyone else. There are subjects of conversation from which men are excluded: doors close and voices drop when female conversation involves pregnancy, menstruation and childbirth, but in mixed company, these subjects apart, men and women participate equally. Couples laugh and joke together or shout each other down. A Bengali woman's ability to deflate her husband with a sobering admonishment or teasing mock anger is more often observed than the reverse. Likewise a beleaguered housewife can launch into a diatribe about her lazy husband and children with fearsome power and expressivity. The vehemence with which mother upbraids the household may be short-lived but can, especially if her husband is thought to be at fault, blight the whole family for that day and she might retire to bed in fury leaving them to fend for themselves.

For all their sequestration these women appear to be equally astute in social judgement in mixed society as are their husbands. Even women who are illiterate, speaking no English and with few social contacts because of widowhood or divorce, convey a sense of being aware of general current events and the multitudinous ways in which the outside and inside social worlds influence those in her care as anyone else in Bethnal Green. Specific practical knowledge about local services, however, may be lacking not just for these women but for the Bengali household as a whole (see Chapter 5 pages 131ff.).

4.5.2.2 The husband's view

Of all household members, fathers of the older generation (*furani Londoni*) have had the longest experience of life in Bethnal Green and of communicating with officials in public institutions. Many are fluent in English and others can manage with predictable dialogues in limited settings. For those who are less fluent, fixed formulations and consistent slight mis-translations diminish their ability to engage their interlocutor on an equal basis. For example, the Bengali stress words *khub* and *beshi*, which both mean 'very', 'much', or 'a lot', are consistently translated as 'too much', so that all medical symptoms are apparently overly stressed: 'too much headache', 'too much dizziness', 'too much cough' etc. and this lends itself to stereotypes of exaggeration arising from an assumed lack of sophistication about how to behave with the doctor, or with clerks, shop-keepers and neighbours. Opportunities to speak English in the work-place will have been, and continue to be, limited for Bengali men through occupational segregation.

The striking difference between men and women of this age in conversation is that whereas women almost always use a direct and straightforward mode of speech in public, their husbands frequently employ joshing, joking or otherwise artificially impersonal and even manipulative strategies. With senior Bengali men there can be a surprising mix of feelings all at once, so that I can feel belittled and chided by a peremptory manner, and a moment later inappropriately drawn into jocular intimacy. This diverting style of interaction earns them descriptions such as 'this charming old Bengali man' when they visit specialists at the hospital. Witnessing the curt and brusque mode of a Bengali patriarch I can easily empathise with children who have told me that their father is strict and authoritarian. At other times, it is an effort not to patronise someone whose presentation is bathetic. Even those with the most clipped and peremptory demeanour will adopt a joking manner at times and few are consistently formal.

Sometimes this brusqueness of older men seems to protect a fragile persona. These patients become the well known 'funny characters' of the practice, not always taken seriously by all the staff. There are not many of these heads of family (*murubbi*) who do not dissimulate under slight pressure. One such man in his forties, prematurely aged by chronic disease, is often arrogantly rude to the receptionists and quotes the Race Relations Act whenever he wants his own way but he will easily break into wry smile, letting me in on the joke when I suggest that he might be going too far. I find that I let some of his remarks pass rather than taking him to task in an effort to protect his apparently fragile self-esteem. Another man is always uncomfortably polite and overly deferential with me, and has irritated a male colleague. A crisis in his health leads him to reveal the pressure he feels to maintain a correct and smart appearance when he feels excessively old and infirm particularly in relation to his younger, healthier, fertile wife.

These men have had long careers in low-status jobs and, having survived the middle age cull of cardiovascular disease, enjoy senior status, respect and display religious rectitude. Of all the different cohorts of Bengali men they are the most visible as members of a distinctive ethnic group. Their dress is conservative: if not in Islamic attire, most wear semi-formal suits or smart jackets. Beards are *de rigeur* for this age group whereas they are sporadic in the younger generation. An appearance and manner that betrays integrity, benignity and a quiet confidence and authority is admired. Islamic piety and observance of proper Islamic practice becomes more prevalent with increasing age. The proliferation of small local mosques enables the pious to attend for *namaz* on a daily basis and for some, five times a day so that it almost becomes their main occupation. Special religious meetings (*waaz*) with guest speakers from other British cities or from Bangladesh are now staged more frequently than before and provide interesting pious and intellectual nourishment as well as being sociable occasions.

The information needed to contract marriages for your children and nephews and nieces can be got from trusting relationships between men. The drawback is that masculine society can be as much a cause of anxiety as a social pleasure. Family troubles cannot be discussed openly with friends and acquaintances for fear of losing status and allowing others to know of the flaws in the family's reputation. This imposes a constraint on public demeanour. The almost mask-like, set visage of the senior *murubbi* role can be burdensome when there are conflicts at home. Intolerance and inflexibility with regard to the behaviour of his wife and children, outbursts of anger, sexual difficulties, smoking to excess, even when ill, can indicate the severe status anxiety of the *murubbi*.

An older Bengali father embodies self-consciousness, especially when outside the home. He is acutely aware of his responsibility as head of the household. When children become marriageable, their fathers' social standing comes sharply into focus in the public eye and in the gaze of Allah. At this stage, work is less of an issue for many have retired prematurely through ill health, but their reputation among peers is paramount. Bengali parents' religious duty should be accomplished by the time a child is sixteen years old, after which the child carries their own spiritual responsibilities. In practice, fathers continue to try and influence their children's behaviour well beyond that age. These men are now at the threshold of proving their family's worth by the sort of marriage alliances that they can achieve. They are simultaneously made aware of their chances in the afterlife for the high prevalence of heart disease and diabetes in this group means that sudden death is not uncommon and a *memento mori* within an extended family is not hard to find.

His immediate judges are the other men in his extended family, whether locally resident or not. The ranking of male siblings is significant and in the proper order of things he will defer to any of his older brothers (*bhaisab*, respected brother), especially the eldest, (*borrobhaisab*) and he should confer with them over family matters. They will often intervene whether invited to do so or not. He may, by inclination, wish to put his own wife and children's needs first but the opinion of male kin will weigh heavily, urging him to control any wayward behaviour within his family. Father and father's brothers (*sassa*) can become a powerful, even threatening cohort of traditional masculinity, laying down the law for junior kin. Before the arrival of families in Britain, a close camaraderie existed among solitary unrelated migrant men (Adams 1987). At that time the reputations of wives could not be impeached being distant and under the control of their mothers-in-law in Bangladesh, but now the physical visibility of their dependents adds an anxious strain to such friendships.

4.5.2.3 Discussion

The roles of this generation of husbands and wives appear to follow a sharp divide between public and domestic. Symbolically this is so and is emphasised in Muslim households by explicit forms of *purdah*. Bengali fathers of this generation can be seen as searching for power, control and conformity within the households in order to maintain public standing *vis-à-vis* other households, whereas mother's life is directed towards social reproduction within the domestic sphere while remaining cognisant of outside influences. I wish to convey the idea that these women actively maintain continuity of custom and tradition in a way that is not merely conservative, with or without a peppering of self-defeating resistance, nor is it only a by-product of their relative immobility. Their attitude towards custom is intensely personal, social and serious, concerned with the fundamental truths and meanings in relation to the proper conduct, aesthetics and morality of family life and not only with public appearances or the repetition of learned customary practice. These women, although politically weak in the public sphere should not be seen as dependent variables in the lives of Bengali households in Bethnal Green. If anything, the potential for wilful agency of wives and daughters, who may suddenly withdraw their normally reliable domestic co-operation, is the uncontrollable factor, and men's predicament in the face of anxiety with regard to female agency is the dependent variable.

In one sense this older cohort of parents is, literally speaking, a dying breed. Subsequent generations will never share their particular biographical experience. Present-day migrants of all kinds enter a largely settled mixed-ethnicity society. If parents seem outwardly traditional as described by the youth worker, they are by no means blind to the necessary adjustments that must be made because of life in a mixed society. There are many examples of this generation making compromises in their 'cultural' preferences in order to advance the status and economic welfare of their children. In view of this, the question arises as to what kind of legacy they might bequeath to their descendants in terms of traditional customs, material culture and family values.

4.5.3 MARRIAGEABLE CHILDREN

Unsurprisingly, families containing marriageable children are over-represented in the list of trouble cases. Parents whose children are under the age of sixteen are comparable to similar non-Bengali families in their daily concerns viz.: sufficient income, adequate housing and school placements, health, illness and protection of the more vulnerable family members from harm. Although young children are felt to be entirely within the moulding forces of parental influence, television and school are, in some parents' view, already exerting a contrary effect. There is evidence of an unusual degree of enclosure for Bengali pre-school children compared to those from other backgrounds. Teachers find them more difficult than others in the early years at school, unable to concentrate as they find themselves suddenly moved into the unfamiliar mixed world of British schools. Their performance at school entry is consistently worse than children from other ethnic groups but this changes at later stages of primary school and they perform better than other ethnic groups locally at GCSE level (LBTH 2001).

Parents of unmarried daughters are concerned to keep them within the limits of Bengali cultural orthodoxy until they marry in their late teens or early twenties. The task of maintaining sons within what are, for them, broader parameters of culturally acceptable behaviour is longer as they marry in their late twenties or early thirties. All parents worry about children's problems but Bengali parents are aware of contrary influences from non-Bengali quarters. They hope that any difficulty will be resolved equally for daughters as for sons, but whereas for sons there is hope and strategic intent to return them to the norm, for daughters there is the possibility of removal from the family. Just as good daughters move from the natal family home when they marry, so bad daughters can be removed or repudiated if they are wayward. Sons are always part of the chain of masculine family responsibility wherever they live whereas daughters, once they move out, are no longer the responsibility of their parents but their affines. This patrilineal ideology does not depend on co-residence for transnational families. Patrilineal traditions are evident in Bethnal Green in the influence that the older generation seeks to exert over junior kin, and the continuation of joint land-holdings and bank accounts between brothers. Families do not sever ties with well-married daughters but for those girls whose behaviour is considered immoral, patrilineal ideology serves to reinforce isolation of the guilty party. It is possible for male kin to rationalise it this way but their enemies may pressurise them by insulting family honour with a reference to runaways (*bhaggyia*). This can be offset by parents appropriately condemning a sinful daughter and refusing to see or recognise her but their enemies may counter this, saying that a *bhaggyia* will take her kin and entire ancestry to hell (*duzzor*) anyway after her death.

Married daughters become their husband's kin, but parents do talk about how many sons-in-law have been 'recruited' to the patrilineal family, and they are gathered up to be counted, so to speak, at events such as weddings. The bad marriages of daughters, therefore, cannot always be repudiated with impunity. Son's casual and irregular relationships are tolerated because the marriage contract is seen to override previous relationships. In the worst case there is always the possibility of absorbing irregular women into the household: a marrying-in woman can be moulded or coerced to fit with the family's status, but a daughters' irregular relationships will critically and detrimentally recast the status (*izzat*) of her family and the eligibility of her unmarried siblings. Unsuitable Bengali girlfriends and even, on occasion, English women and their babies are sometimes taken on by Bengali paternal grandparents, but unsuitable and especially non-Bengali boys cannot be similarly controlled or incorporated by a girl's parents. This absorption of almost any variety of son's child into Bengali patrilineages may sound surprising, but it illustrates the strength of the role of *dada* and *dadi* whose incorporative behaviour *vis a vis* the patrilineage, can overrule issues of ethnicity, social status and the religion of grandchildren's maternal antecedents as well as the processes of arranging and performing marriage rituals. The contrast with repudiating wayward daughters underscores the gendered ideology of the Bengali patrilineal household.

The parents of marriageable children can therefore be hard pressed, particularly with regard to their eldest daughter on whom all her siblings' marriages depend. In some families the whole period of marriage negotiation for a son or daughter is transposed to Bangladesh where they may stay with relatives for a few weeks, months or even years until the marriage is settled. For some this is a quiet but exciting negotiation between loving parents and a trusting child. For others, near hysterical brinkmanship is shown on either side. How daughters will respond to the pressure of marriage arrangements is unpredictable. Teenage girls whom I have hardly seen throughout their time at secondary school start to come to see me more often, excited or agitated, sometimes at odds with their parents and stressed by the sudden heightening of tension at home. They should not know that their parents have received serious offers of marriage, but little siblings can be sharp-eyed spies. The controls on their behaviour tighten: locked windows, chaperones, and the monitoring of telephone calls constrain their social life. Earlier in their teenage life, many irregularities might have continued undetected.

Fahmeda tells me that her father is very strange, "He's weird really, everyone says so, even my uncles and aunts think so - he's so strict, like I'm not even allowed out for anything. I lied when I came to this appointment, they think I'm somewhere else. I don't go to school any more, I have to have someone come home to teach me. I saw one man and I didn't like him so I said no. Now he wants me to marry an old man, he's nearly thirty - what shall I do?" For years Fahmeda has been seeing and phoning a boyfriend, taking risks by undetected truanting from school. Interestingly the parents do not beat a path to my door to complain about their daughter's agitated behaviour, nor do they try to monitor the sort of advice I might be giving her. In fact when the wedding takes place their daughter is very happy, and soon afterwards is pleased to be having a baby and living with her new in-laws, "My husband is so nice, he really takes care of me, and he can show me how to cook - he worked in a restaurant before." Such apparently rapid adaptive behaviour is, of course the outcome of long consideration of her likely marital future. She, for one, has not questioned her right to choose between a love match or an arranged marriage; she has chosen between the proffered suitors but she has not rejected the notion of parental choice.

Sharmeen's life is different although she is exactly the same age and from a similar family and educational background as Fahmeda.

Sharmeen was attracted to a guest at her cousin's house and began a relationship with him. He is divorced and unacceptable for this and other reasons as the spouse for her parent's eldest daughter. After several months of trying to sustain the relationship with her boyfriend as well as living like an apparently dutiful daughter, Sharmeen makes a decision: she leaves home and finds lodgings with her boyfriend some distance from her parents. When her brothers and uncles try to force her to come home, a social worker offers to negotiate on her behalf but she takes out a solicitor's injunction against her male relatives. Her parents now cannot speak about her. Sharmeen is in tears when talking about her mother and father and her sister who was browbeaten over her older sister's escape even though she truly knew nothing of her plans. Sharmeen wants the family to be united, and feels particularly sad and guilty about leaving her younger siblings (whose lives will henceforth be more narrowly constrained) but she cannot give up her chosen life. In fact her younger sister, while resisting arranged marriage before completing higher education, says she would like her own marriage to be a family arrangement; she admires her older sister's strength of character but recoils from the idea of taking similar action, not because it is un-Islamic, but because of the strength of her emotional ties to her parents and siblings.

Gavron's work in Bethnal Green explores the progress that young Bengali women have made in gaining influence with their marriage arrangements (Gavron 1998). While those such as Fahmeda and Sharmeen's younger sister are illustrations of this progress, the tales of cloak-and-dagger romantic dramas among adventurous teenagers, and the family confrontations that they entail, do not, in my experience, appear to be decreasing in prevalence. Whichever style of conduct is evident, young Bengali women are supported in their enhanced independence by a prominent discourse in the British media and caring professions which denounce what are seen as 'forced' marriages with 'strangers'. A young woman in need will receive greater attention the more her situation appears to be aligned with a narrative of Asian forced marriage. The distinction between arranged and forced marriages may be acknowledged technically in media discourse but is usually blurred by the implicit disapproval given to the former as well as the latter. There is not the space here to discuss this particular issue fully but what needs emphasis is that an overweening attention to the precision with which the notion of a family arrangement may be distinguished from force (psychological, physical or use of deception) obscures the fundamental gender inequalities of British society as a whole in relation to marriage. The predicament of Asian women is better seen as a particular refraction of these inequalities rather than an expression of an alien custom which can be refashioned or suppressed through recourse to legalistic redefinitions of marriage. Even a superficial glance at the available cultural alternatives in the sphere of domestic gender relationships in Bethnal Green would lead most observers to conclude that there was not, in fact, so large a gulf between the virtues and vicissitudes of the two systems, Bengali and British, as is being portrayed by non-Bengali advisors to these young women (cf. Brah 1996: 76ff.).

The other people affected by patterns of marriage and residence are the younger siblings in the household. On the one hand, a sister who marries and moves out will release another bed-space or bedroom for those left behind. On the other hand, an already crammed flat will be even more overcrowded if a spouse moves in; babies can be exciting but also very disruptive to students' work. An older sister-in-law (*bhabi*) can be a useful adviser but if she is from Bangladesh there may be little in common between a *bhabi* and her co-resident younger brothers and sisters-in-law. Younger sisters are anxious about older sisters' marriages because if parents make what is to them a satisfactory arrangement, the heat is off the younger girls once family status has been proved by the eldest's marriage. If, however, the eldest transgresses customary rules the pressure will increase on younger sisters. Brothers are necessarily anxious about their eldest sister's marriage because it will affect their status when it comes to finding brides. They have longer to indulge in romantic attachments prior to marriage whereas for young women there is a race against time for exploring peer relationships before they marry. 'Arranged marriage' is thus truly a household arrangement and is not just the spectacle of a British Asian woman forced into sexual congress and household servitude with a total stranger.

4.5.4. THE INSTITUTION OF THE JOINT HOUSEHOLD

Once a couple has settled down to married life together it should not be thought that an independent nuclear household is sought by all who can obtain the necessary accommodation. Some of the three-generational households in this study have existed as such for more than five years to date. Relationships between mothers-in-law and daughters-in-law are not always as difficult as the almost universal folklore suggests. In the case of a young woman only recently arrived from Bangladesh with none of her own kin living in London it is possible to discern an attitude that is truly that of *in loco parentis*, caring and protective as well as educative on the part of the mother-in-law (*howree* in Sylheti or *shoshuree* in standard Bengali). The harsh and overbearing *howree* makes headline news so to speak, especially among British health and social service workers who have to pick up the pieces when the young woman leaves the affinal home with or without her husband, but harmonious households are less noisome and so can be overlooked.

Although most virilocal couples consist of a London groom and Bangladeshi wife, some British-born wives willingly stay with their husband's family and express appreciation for the positive aspects of mutuality that a shared household should embrace (Brah 1996:76). Three-generational Bengali households are not homogeneously traditional and modern young women of either Western styling or Islamic reformist mode, as well as those who have only recently come to London, can enjoy the sociability that includes affinal relatives of all types. Diversity within a joint household signals a flexibility of attitude that is a good prognostic indicator of durability for patrilineal joint households. This is expressed by an essential core configuration of the paternal grandmother (*dadi*) supervising her son's children, and the paternal grandfather (*dada*) acting as a dignified pious figurehead. As long as this configuration pertains, even marginal mixed-background young women and their children may be absorbed into the household and 'normalised' without undue disturbance.

The risk of break-up of the joint household (whether actually co-resident or living in proximity and co-operatively) comes soon after the marriage of the eldest son. At this stage, an overweening attention to norms, and an overbearing expression of hierarchy is perilous. If the tension between the needs of the patrilineage and those of the new conjugal relationship is not carefully negotiated, the young couple may decamp elsewhere. A bride may return on her own to her parent's home and negotiate with her husband and affines from a distance. Parents therefore put pressure on married sons to remain within their purview. To achieve this structural conformity the older generation may have a wide tolerance of sons' behaviour as already discussed. A love match will be tolerated if the wife agrees to conform but if not, extreme efforts are made to disrupt even legal marriages. Likewise sons who are gamblers, wife-beaters or womanisers but nevertheless maintain the structure of their conjugal household, are sufficient as junior male kin. If his wife or daughters step out of line, older male kin will put intense pressure on the younger man to reform his family. In this, the woman's case is seen as being entirely subsidiary to the primary task of returning to normal structures of hierarchical patrilineal solidarity. Successful joint households are not only aligned with traditional orthodoxies but the arrangement may also work synergistically with economic opportunities.

Arzizur Khan came to London aged fifteen. After leaving school he worked in tailoring factories while still living with his parents. At the time of his marriage he was able to utilise joint family finances generated by his father and uncles to buy a leather jacket factory. His business flourishes and he now contributes considerable sums to his parents as well as caring for the unmarried children of the household while they go through school and college. Rahena Begum, his wife, remains entirely within the home and speaks little English which her husband sees as a redundant skill. She shares the household chores with her mother-in-law, who takes charge of the grandchildren while Rahena is responsible for cooking. Both couples have worked hard to make the household a very solid social and economic base. The younger siblings can use this security to explore different educational and career choices without the anxiety of needing to earn a wage as soon as possible. Also, since the eldest girl is suitably married, they can relax on that front for a while longer. Arzizur is visibly proud of the family's achievements and has no regrets about the choices that his younger siblings now have that were denied him because of economic and social needs.

This comfortable synergy between family ideals and practical economics is disrupted if extreme dogmatism of the former overwhelms the latter. The balance between the two is especially difficult if the family is poor. Excessive zeal for family duties may then compound the ill-effects of welfare dependency and poverty.

Syed Rahman, the eldest son of a widowed mother who lives nearby, has a part-time job as a waiter in a Bengali restaurant. He arrived in the UK aged sixteen, has no British qualifications and speaks little English. He is unable to make any boundaries between his own family's needs and the normative responsibilities he feels for his mother and brothers. As a result his own house is bereft of any but the most meagre furnishings and cheap clothing. His wife, Salema Khanom, complains bitterly about him and tries to involve social services. The strain of twin unanswerable responsibilities leads to depression and outbursts of violence at home. Although his wife's family live locally, they are too fearful of transgressing propriety to intervene effectively. Salema Khanom is better educated than her husband, but she feels that the damage to her children that would result from divorce is a worse evil than the damage to herself while she stays with him. She rails against the 'culture' that dictates such harshness but has enough insight to see that her husband is as much a victim of the system as herself. She is too tired and depressed to put in train any strategy that would ameliorate the situation.

Syed Rahman is unusual in his over-attentiveness to joint family finances, partly precipitated by the death of his father, leaving him as guardian of six younger brothers. Ideally, patrilineally related men demonstrate loyalty by maintenance of a joint financial account that spans continents but it is not uncommon to find married men who no longer contribute to such accounts (cf. p90). Many continue to be pricked with guilt about their derogations, no doubt aggravated by complaints from Bangladesh (Gardner 1995: 123) and give various explanations to rationalise the split. Joint family accounts are generally given approval as a virtuous norm but at some point the needs of your own conjugal family will override those of the joint family (Parry 1979: 178). The moment of separation requires skilled management if a rift in family relationships is to be avoided. Those who earn a good income should be generous within the system, so opting out is harder for the waged than the unwaged. The welfare system's minimum benefits, for all its inadequacies, does nominally reduce economic dependency between relatives; in this way the leverage of the joint account is constrained within extended Bengali families.

4.5.5 THE PARTICULAR PROBLEMS OF LONDON WIVES AND BANGLADESHI HUSBANDS

In marriages between young women brought up in Britain and young men from Bangladesh it might be thought that the husband would be subservient while he is as yet unaccustomed to London life (Gavron 1998: 126). She will be English-speaking, familiar with local society, educated here and perhaps still pursuing a career while he struggles with language and the difficulties of finding work as well as congenial social relationships of his own. Grooms from Sylhet find themselves in a society where other Bengali men of their own age group or younger are already further advanced in work, education and social achievements.

Amina is twenty and has one small child and continues to work in a school while her mother looks after the baby and her husband divides his time between college and working in her cousin's restaurant. "I have to do everything for him, he can't find his way round anywhere and he's really not confident with his English yet. He sees my brothers, they're younger than him but it'll take five years for my husband to catch up and be established."

These Bangladeshi husbands have as yet little social standing other than as a man married to a wife from a good family. With little or poor English initially they must either study hard to get their Bangladeshi qualifications converted to British equivalents, or work for cash in low-status jobs, or do both part-time. In Bangladesh they say, they were used to working flexibly for the family, not strictly according to contract. They find long hours of waged work fatiguing and dispiriting and talk of a 'natural' pace of life on a family farm with servants and labourers or as a junior partner in business where domestic and financial responsibilities were managed for them by others.

Their wives are, as already stated, often the locus of maximal social strain in this population. They take most of the responsibility for the welfare of young children, negotiating their needs with English-speaking doctors, health visitors, social workers, welfare and housing officers and teachers. They are responsible for a husband who is struggling as a migrant and may also take on the care of ageing parents. The multiplicity of problems facing all young men in the area, are aggravated for those from a minority ethnic background and this means that their wives are often trying to support a very frustrated or disoriented young man.

British-born or educated wives are more suited to the labour market than their husbands and often work outside as well as inside the home. They might avoid the irksome supervision of a mother-in-law but also lack her domestic resources of live-in child-care if nothing else. They remain more susceptible to social injustice than their husbands since in addition to a shared vulnerability to British racism these women are at greater risk of social opprobrium through impeachment of their feminine honour by other Bengali people. This sense of injustice is brought home to them because they are made explicitly aware of the relativity of 'cultural' rules having been brought up and educated alongside young women from different backgrounds. Having conformed in the nature of their marriage as well as shouldering the domestic and economic burdens in a difficult environment is rarely a matter for express compliments from their preoccupied beneficiaries. For these reasons a 'good' London husband, although harder to find, can be more helpful, not only in social and economic terms but also because he may be aware of changing norms of gendered domestic roles in the wider society.

The majority of Bengali couples are enduring first-time approved or arranged marriages which to British eyes would make it much harder to achieve conjugal intimacy. Most couples behave in a relaxed good-humoured manner with friendly concern one for the other and often show strong emotional attachment. The relationships within love matches and arranged marriages seem to arrive at similar places after a few years and the arrival of children. Couples who stay together despite marital disharmony can be found among love matches and arranged marriages alike. The increased prominence of a wish for companionate marriage can be seen, however, both at the moment of marriage where young Bengali adults appear to be able to negotiate within the parameters of arranged marriage (Gavron 1998), and in the conduct of established marriages where for some, traditional roles can be re-negotiated.

Divorce in Bengali marriages is still infrequent (although I would estimate that the 2001 census will show an increase from 1991) and is not confined to love matches. The numbers are too small to make any generalisations but it is most likely to occur soon after marriage. Arranged marriages contracted in Britain, through juxtaposition with the diametrically opposite ideal of individual romantic conjugality, contain discursive space for either spouse to say that they *had* to go along with a culturally ordained practice, either cynically or from of a feeling of powerlessness, because of the needs and wishes of others that could not be gainsaid without traumatic emotional wrangling. Having yielded to distraught parents, uncles and aunts, or pity for a young man whose entry visa was at stake (or whose illegal entry might soon come to light), one or other party then finds that they are unable to carry on with the facts of cohabitation, and ends the arrangement after a few weeks or months. The consequences of divorce are, however, quite different for Bengali men and women.

A man who does not consummate his marriage may even carry on as if nothing has happened as his 'bride' will be sequestered in unknown misery in Bangladesh. Those Bangladeshi brides who are abandoned in London (usually after children have been born) are literally *in extremis*, unsupported and vulnerable to the depredations of exploitative men. Any Bengali woman in Bethnal Green who is abandoned by her husband, whatever the circumstances, has to be thick-skinned to withstand the social opprobrium that inevitably follows. Raw feelings of continuing humiliation and hurt wrought by departed husbands are prolonged and damaging even where the union was not consummated. The fact of divorce, and the risk of abandonment certainly adds to the strain of arranged marriage for Bengali women in this country. Going through with an arranged marriage might relieve a young woman of parental pressure, but if the marriage fails through no fault of her own, her parents may be able to do nothing to remedy her fall from grace.

Despite reliance on close-grained village knowledge, from time to time an attractive Bangladeshi or London groom who seemed full of potential at the engagement will turn out to be a disappointing husband. If he is dissatisfied, he can rebel passively by dragging his feet in conjugal matters, or by behaving outrageously until the marriage crashes, for only the bride will lose significantly in such an event. Once married, there is an immense cost to her reputation if divorce ensues, however obvious it may be that the husband was to blame. Moreover the divorced groom may still keep his visa and if he marries again, a second marriage will not affect a family's status so badly, especially if he resides in London, whereas a divorced Bengali woman in London irretrievably besmirches her family's *izzat*. She may find a second husband but this is more difficult than finding a bride for a divorced man.

The Bengali woman who loses her husband may be bereft of her status as a married woman and of social support from her ex-affines who rarely take the daughter-in-law's part, however bad the behaviour of their kinsman. She, or more commonly her children, may lose their residency visas if the marriage had not continued for long enough for all the family to gain British citizenship (Brah 1996: 75). For these reasons, divorce and domestic violence in Bengali families, whatever its estimated prevalence (at present unknown) is felt to be a greater injustice in the Bengali context by abused women. Even if a husband leaves his wife and sets up another household, the extended family's interpretation of events will normalise the new but regular household and may marginalise the now abandoned woman-headed household. It is not hard to imagine that Bengali women in Britain can feel that divorce and abuse is more blameworthy in a system of marriage that is a prescribed religious duty rather than, as they would see it, an entirely voluntary mutual relationship. However much the women in these families criticise the behaviour of Bengali men, evaluations of their own situation remains more closely aligned, albeit in negative terms, with the social mores of Bengali family life. They see themselves as sufferers in the particularities of Bengali 'culture' rather than aligning themselves primarily with divorced and abused women in a wider, cross-cultural context.

Unhappy wives might decamp to their mother's house or that of another relative until their husband's behaviour changes but it is still unusual for them to initiate divorce proceedings. Despite all the risks, some young women take the plunge and decide to take charge of their own futures. This story is commonly heard because it attracts notice but the number of cases is probably few in actual fact. Where they do divorce, young Bengali women can use the rhetorical and practical resources of British social work and housing services to expedite matters and to rationalise their behaviour as illustrated by case histories already given. Summerfield's legal perspective on the effects of divorce for Tower Hamlets' Muslim women is partial, as is my medical one, but her short study is useful (despite somewhat generalised assumptions about Bengali 'ghetto' culture) in showing how Somali Muslim women in Tower Hamlets have greater control over marriage and divorce decisions than do their Bengali counterparts (Summerfield 1993).

Finally, Bengali men still retain the scope for multiple marriages given the geographical distance between Bangladesh and Britain. If a husband's bigamy comes to light by the arrival in Britain of his wife by an earlier marriage in Bangladesh then British law annuls one marriage (not necessarily the earlier one) which may result in deportation of one woman and her children. In Bangladesh, they would be placed in the less economically harmful (if just as uncomfortable in personal terms) position of second wife. Unlike English bigamists, the transnational context usually means that the man is not penalised in law since he did not marry twice in Britain. I am not suggesting that the onus is on British legal institutions to tailor family law to the customs of migrant citizens, for example by imposing divorce rather than annulment on these serial marriages. The mismatch between British juridical policy and Bengali custom is, however, read by Bengali women as yet another example of exaggerated asymmetry in Bengali gender relationships compared to those of other British women.

4.6 Conclusions

I have described the varied and divergent biographies within families and the development and changes in Bengali household life from the time of bachelor migrants to that of the contemporary, settled population. The household analysis has been lengthy and complex in the scope of the material presented but the analytical question posed was relatively simple: what is the detectable tendency as regards the development of Bengali family life in Bethnal Green? Are they reproducing the traditions of the homeland or embracing the norms of household life of Bethnal Green?

4.6.1 CONTINUITY

Continuity of Bengali traditions is found in masculine patterns of behaviour. The ideology of the patrilineage is still evident even without joint co-residence. This is particularly so when the differential treatment of men and women who make irregular marriages is examined. Single or divorced men and their children as well as sons' mixed-ethnicity marriages are linked or absorbed wherever possible into the corpus of patrilineality. Divorced and *bhaggiya* women are objects of repudiation (see Bhopal 1999: 127 and 'deviant' South Asian women). The very few Bengali women who live quite alone, cut off from their families or with non-Bengali, non-Muslim men can be said to have moved out of the sphere of Bengali family traditions altogether. In some sense, the patrilineal mode of family life, rather than shared ethnicity or religion *per se* decides the outer limits of 'The Bengali Community' as a bounded group, if ever such a limit needed to be described.

While patrilineal ideology is seen to continue, joint lineal households are unlikely to increase if only for the scarcity of houses with more than three bedrooms in Bethnal Green. The number of people who have ever had experience of living in a joint household nevertheless remains higher than for non-Bengali populations locally and may increase as more of the original migrants' sons marry. In this I assume that not all will immediately seek a neolocal residence. South Asian households in Britain show a persistently higher prevalence of non-nuclear households compared to Britain as a whole although less than the average for India (Murphy 1996: 223).

Bengali men show strong evidence of continuity with a recurrent pattern of extending the concept of household geographically through migration away from the family home for shorter or longer periods of time in pursuit of work. In Britain this takes place through the restaurant trade. Economic opportunities for men have not been examined in depth here, but Wrench & Qureshi (1996) and the CBS (1994) concur with my descriptive sketches which indicate that a significant cohort of young Bengali men are likely to be upwardly mobile given their engagement with higher education. Entrepreneurship and business success are also likely to continue to be sustained by masculine *sareng*-type networks. The incoming Bangladeshi grooms are particularly needy in respect of this network, emulating the tradition of all Bengali male migrants before them. The ideology of joint (male) family economic interests, although not researched in numerical depth is still evident and can adversely affect the fortunes of those men who are unable to balance the interests of the joint family with those of the conjugal relationship.

In other respects, Bengali men also show continuity in the way that they exert a controlling interest in the sexual and nuptial behaviour of their female relatives. They continue to have superior status in relation to divorce which gives them unfair advantage in the power-balance of the conjugal relationship. The religious practice of the older generation is largely unchanged and is an important component of male networks of social knowledge. Younger men, however, in increasing numbers look to the universal *umma* of Islam in contradistinction to the Bangladesh-aligned religious outlook of their fathers and uncles.

4.6.2 CHANGE

If continuity is found in the basic configuration of Bengali masculine networks of social relations, change in Bengali cultural traditions and social roles is mostly a female affair. An overall household strategy towards upward mobility has allowed young Bengali women access to higher education and work outside the home. These new roles do not radically challenge the ideology of patriliny but soften its controlling boundaries. The roles of older women have also undergone change. While *dadis* return to a traditional role after bringing up a generation of 'orphans', maternal grandmothers (*nani*) are now more closely involved with their daughters' children than in Bangladesh because novel geographical proximity allows enhanced expression of enduring mother-daughter sociability after marriage. This is in line with longer local traditions of mother-daughter mutual support in Bethnal Green (Young & Wilmott 1957).

Material culture, despite its physicality, is often the least durable of customary traditions except in residual 'heritage' form. The daughters of migrants are unlikely to continue the practice of using implements such as the *dah* and *fatta* in small modern kitchens although the *looari* may remain in use being cheap and versatile. Busy young wives are happier using modern gadgets and eating a mixed British-Bengali diet. In other respects, however, they show a continued interest in the vitality of rituals of weddings, Bengali clothing styles and body decoration. Their creative interest in the meaning of such rituals and practices means that customary practices not only endure but also evolve which contrasts with a museum-style practice of preserving (unchanging) heritage. Their success in this sphere is shown in the way that the wider style and fashion world has, with post-modernist eclecticism, almost certainly made a permanent space in Britain for generic 'Asian' styles of material cultural practices of all sorts.

The uniformity of older women's mode of religious practice and dress-style has become elaborated by younger women to include alternative Islamic styles of dress and prayer which marks not only a generational divide but also distinction from the style of Bengali masculinity associated with the Brick Lane mosque. Wearing Western clothes is not part of a general move towards renunciation of the expression of Islam. *Purdah* has in fact become more evident in both generations as women spend more time outside the home, engage with the labour market and become more vocal about their distinctive position vis-à-vis Bengali men and non-Asian society. Paradoxically the practice of importing grooms from Bangladesh has helped to accelerate changes in women's lives: neolocal households, working mothers and closeness of the maternal grandmother are facilitated by the entailments of these marriages. Young wives take up the strain of change but also show a preparedness to adapt strategically to their predicaments. The adaptive behaviour of young London wives who succeed against the odds is distinctively eclectic, insightful and original.

To conclude, continuity of Bengali masculine patterns of behaviour with regard to migration and long-distance households is strongly in evidence. Patrilineal ideology continues but with gendered and religious modulation: changing roles for women and a movement towards World Islam as distinct from Bengali Islam by young men and women alike have both opened up a new discursive space that potentially weakens the ideological basis of traditional networks of Bengali men. Earlier studies of migrant populations in Britain needed to consider the 'myth of return' and the homeland as resources for those who resisted assimilation (Anwar 1979). This has been superseded by the idea of transnational families (Hannerz 1992). A strong commitment to life in Bethnal Green, changes in clothes, food, access to the street for Muslim women and household size cannot be taken as evidence of Westernisation, assimilation or loss of 'culture'. Successful transnational families can manage economic and social commitment over considerable geographic distances. For Bengali families this is not a recent phenomenon, consequent on travel and information technology, but a long-standing tradition founded on the technology of kinship and social networks.

CHAPTER 5: NETWORKS OF SOCIAL RELATIONSHIPS AND KINSHIP

5.1 Introduction

The household as a unit, albeit permeable and mutable, gives way in this chapter to a broader network or landscape imagery of social relationships both within and between Bengali households of Bethnal Green. The inclusion of the particular significance of kinship in this chapter is a consequence of three aspects of the field material.

Firstly, kinship terminology, marriages and genealogical connections figure prominently in the ways that Bengali people in Bethnal Green talk about and conduct their social relationships, especially when talking comparatively about Bengali and British 'cultures'. The plethora of Bengali kin terms, in contrast to the paucity of British ones, is deemed noteworthy and something they take pleasure in discussing. In like manner, Bengali and non-Bengali residents find arranged marriages a diacritical marker of the difference between Asian and British families (Bhopal 1999:125). In this view they are supported by the British media (cf. Sen 1997). Not only does kinship discourse mark 'ethnic' differences, but it also brings out the contrasts between different types of Bengali people. The difference between those who live in Bethnal Green, those in Bangladesh, the older and younger generations and higher and lower status families, are often tellingly portrayed by informants when the discussion is about kinship behaviour. Kinship discourse is thus one of the ways in which Bengali culture emerges as a solid social formation in Bethnal Green

Secondly, the discussion of Bengali household relationships has shown that prominence is given to gendered status-roles within groups of related persons and that marriage is an important issue both for household status and the division of labour within and outside the home. Ideologically loaded and ritually reinforced, Bengali marriages are still arranged between kin groups which extend beyond the nuclear family and have significance for all concerned. An exploration of kinship and the reckoning and conduct of social relationships can be meshed with an understanding of the neighbourhood and household in order to get closer to a description and explanation of the particular distribution of social predicaments for Bengali people in Bethnal Green. The division of labour between chapters that separates kinship and social relatedness from other categories such as neighbourhood, household and social harm is for textual clarity rather than any assumptions about the independence of these categories as social domains (Harris 1984, Moore 1994: 86ff.).

Thirdly, I have described census and observational data which suggest that Bengali populations in Britain are residentially segregated from all other recorded ethnic groups even down to enumeration district level (Peach & Rossiter 1996: 123). These census analysts tentatively suggest that some cohesive internal 'cultural' factor draws Bengali groups together over and above the extruding forces of racism. Although cultural formations such as Bengali kinship can be discerned, this does not allow simplistic extrapolation as to the causes of residential segregation. I therefore resist the naturalising tendency of the argument which suggests that 'ethnic communities' are 'naturally' consequent on culturally determined ways of building social networks (cf. Baumann 1996). Whilst an anthropological readership may see this as an elementary error, Peach and Rossiter (1996) are evidently inclined towards this view (see also Peach 1998) and, in my experience, local residents and institutional personnel frequently exhibit an understanding of this popular model of culture as unquestionably cohesive and based on unqualified notions of 'community' (Bott 1971 [1957]: 99).

The inclusion of 'kinship' might be thought to be an 'Indianist' bias, or to give undue prominence to one kind of ideology rather any other that may govern notions of relatedness. As already stated, the justification for retaining kinship as a rubric arises from the field material and not from a wish to add to the recent revival of interest in formal kinship studies (Augustins 2000, Collard 2000, Godelier et al 1998, Trautmann 2000: 563). This chapter does not have recourse to an analysis that relies on correspondences between the reckoning of social relatedness and the grammar or deep structures of kinship terminology systems. I am cognisant that actual or perceived consanguinity and marriage arrangements alone do not comprise a complete system of social relatedness (Schneider 1984). Kinship is rightly thought of, however, as a significant ingredient in the ideologies and practices of families, households and gendered relationships in any society (Collier & Yanagisako 1987, Creed 2000, Moore 1988), and especially for South Asian societies (Dube 1997).

I will use the way in which I came across kinship, friendships, family structure and social networks during fieldwork to shape the first half of this chapter. My starting position was that of a doctor who had extensive but unreflective knowledge of certain Bengali families in Bethnal Green together with some background knowledge of local sociological data and the anthropological literature on Indian kinship. Learning Sylheti and meeting informants who were not patients allowed me to learn about how Bengali people befriended each other and appraised their social knowledge of other people. I also learned the importance of kin terms of address and the proprieties of kinship behaviour for at least some sections of this population. The second half of the chapter looks at the effects of migration on the formation of social networks both locally and abroad and the experience of living in a mixed society.

During this early part of fieldwork I found the landscape of Bengali relationships to be shaped by an extensive and inclusive networking propensity in concert with the 'corporation' claims of patrilineal families. The altered and changing social atmosphere of Bethnal Green's social landscape in comparison with that of Bangladesh (as a real, remembered or imagined community) was found to be of dramatic concern to some families. By the end of this phase of research I found that although many Bengali people talked of the comparative dilution or thinness of their personal social networks, consequent on migration, they also spoke of certain discomforts caused by living in an area thickly populated with Bengali residents. This chapter, which is an enquiry into positive relationships, leads directly, then, to the next, which is concerned with negative and harmful relationships.

5.2 Learning about kinship

I begin with the issue of segregation, since this was data I had from the census before embarking on fieldwork. The comfort of 'ghettos' (Wirth 1998 [1928]) is a cliché which is too easily repeated where the constraint of racism is thought to need balancing with a 'choice' argument (Carey & Shukur 1985, Hannerz 1980: 41, King 1994, Phillips 1988). Although the notion has internal logic, there is in fact no necessary correlation between residential segregation from other ethnic groups and social cohesion within minority groups. Given such a marked degree of residential segregation it could be inferred that within the population there is also social segregation. Prior to any ethnographic evidence, a close-up view of the Bethnal Green Bengali population might reveal internal fragmentation that could then be expressed externally into a larger picture of social segregation. Sometimes described as an 'atomistic rural society' in Bangladesh (Greenhalgh et al. 1998: 978, Maloney 1979: xiii) where villages are spatially divided and extended (Gardner 1995: 26, 31), these transposed social groups may just as logically disintegrate as cohere through change of place. Indeed my primary experience at the beginning of fieldwork, was that internal segregation, loss of social density and an unwonted social dilution were common and unhappy experiences for many Bengali migrants.

Ordinary medical practice prior to fieldwork did not yield much information about the family connections of Bengali patients. This is not surprising given that General Practice is directed towards individuals and families unlike population-based public health programmes. A specific attention to kinship information from minority ethnic group patients is partly an exercise in removing prejudice and blocks to what should be standard medical practice rather than a separate ethnographic enquiry tacked on to the work of a physician. It is obvious that lack of a shared language limits what can be said, but I also detected a bias in my attitude arising from the feeling that I would not be able to process or contextualise 'foreign' kin data as the information given might not be equivalent to that given by English patients. On reflection I also perceived in my attitude an understandable reluctance to ask about a subject that might reveal yet another negative aspect of these patients' already difficult lives and of underscoring the dependency on the doctor of patients from marginal groups in the absence of 'natural' social support. In retrospect I was, of course, given a lot of kin data indirectly even if the question, 'Do you have any family here?' was usually answered 'No', because cousins, aunts and other family members who are visiting relatives consult me as temporary patients, or as companions to my patients. This information was subconsciously bracketed out, however, and so there remained a persistent impression (shared by colleagues) that most Bengali families had few relatives nearby. We filled this vacuum in kinship knowledge with an assumption that such as they were lived for the most part in Bangladesh.

I moved out of the surgery to visit Bengali homes for the purposes of learning Sylheti one day each week when I was not working at the surgery. I was abruptly introduced to the notion of Bengali kinship as an important system for social rules of etiquette in addressing others, in particular the avoidance of personal first-name terms in favour of kin-terms. An English community teacher introduced me to a middle-aged widow, Jahanara, who agreed to teach me to cook Bengali food and to improve my conversational Sylheti (she speaks no English at all). Within minutes of our meeting she said that I must never use her first name but instead should address her as *afa*, older sister, and she could call me Roseanna as I would be her younger sister. There is in fact only a year's difference between us in age. She suggested that this would be enjoyable, sisterly and was visibly pleased at the arrangement. She looked through the kitchen window, caught sight of her teenage children approaching her front door, and at once her manner changed to one of anxious urgency. She stated emphatically that I must *never, ever* say her name, Jahanara in front of them; I could call them by their names, but they would call me *khala*, mother's sister. Moreover they should say *salaam aleicum* to me by way of greeting and never vice versa because they were my juniors. Kin forms of address were revealed in this context as mandatory, desperately important in order to avoid social embarrassment. As this was more or less the first thing we spoke about, she must have known that non-Bengali acquaintances needed instruction in this basic form of etiquette. I had already learned the basics of Sylheti with a bilingual school teacher; in his house first name terms were used without any embarrassment between us, but he was someone habituated to working in mixed society. In other contexts, with his in-laws for example, I noticed that kin terms were always used. The urgency and all-encompassing dogma of using proper terms of address with Jahanara delivered me into different if differentiated conceptual world, into the field so to speak.

Non-patient informants in this study include people from both large and small households, some long established in this country and others only recently arrived from Bangladesh. As I had found within the practice, my unprompted enquiry early on in relationships, 'Where are your relatives?' ('*Afnar attio kwoi?*')

usually produced the answer, Far away ('*Duroi*') with a regretful expression and the sort of shrug that suggested no further discussion was desired or likely to be forthcoming. Again the asymmetry of the relationship inhibited pressure to pursue this with further direct questions: why pester apparently lonely people about their relatives who are far away and probably sorely missed? The fact of migration does mean of course that most people can say that some or all of their relatives are far away in their family homestead, the *bari*, distant in Bangladesh. The *bari* is the primary location of kinship for Sylheti people, whether they have moved to Sylhet town or to London, so the narrow question, 'Where are your relatives?' can always be answered with, 'My *bari* is in such and such village'.

I had discovered the importance of using the right terms of address in certain contexts but I was clearly not going about collecting quantities of information about Bengali relatedness efficiently, or it might be that there was little significance in collecting kinship data *per se*. I had certainly not taken account of the fact that if specific kinship data was not forthcoming, one explanation might be that divulging close social connections early on in a relationship might be thought impolite, like using a first name with a senior, or even unwise. Among patients, withholding such information could be read as a strategy to ratchet up their self-depiction as needy people to gain my attention, but this can hardly be a practical long-term strategy in family medicine. Some patients did mention high-profile social connections or their relatedness to other patients in the surgery without inhibition.

As further evidence that Bengali people are not reluctant to befriend strangers, my access to informants outside the practice was extremely easy and in fact, setting limits on the number of people with whom I could realistically spend a significant amount of research time was more of a problem. Given my fixed position and part-time status I could not take on a commitment to very many people outside the practice. Invitations (*daiort*) to family meals, were given to me by all and sundry and I met some people by approaching them opportunistically in a shop or the street. My status as a doctor (which I neither advertised nor concealed) was no doubt important in some respects but it would be premature to say that these informants were only status-seekers before knowing very much about what kinds of statuses are important for Bengali people. Instead I initially read this eager behaviour as arising from their social isolation, particularly from non-Bengali people. Apart from using the correct etiquette of address with some people, I did not encounter any other thresholds of difference that operated as inhibitions to entry into Bengali social circles. Following Muslim customs (*sunnot*) such as shoe removal in people's houses and eating with fingers rather than cutlery was appreciated but never requested.

As time went on, relatives appeared in Jahanara's house when I was there, or they telephoned, or we met people in the shops or street whom she would say were related to her, usually through her deceased husband's family, but some were related through her mother. I could then more naturally ask exactly who they were and what would be their correct form of address. This often led to a sort of tutorial where Jahanara or other informants could teach me all the kin terms using an imaginary family: 'If I had an older brother and he was married, what would I call his wife's sister?' and so on. This was clearly enjoyable for Jahanara, since using the notion of educating me in the lore of kin terms as the subject for conversation classes allowed a reversal of what was otherwise an asymmetrical relationship: informants could be authoritative about kinship, good manners and cookery while I was ignorant. On the other hand, in more equal relationships with educated, bilingual, white-collar workers, a conversation about kin terms can provoke nervous laughter. Being habituated to conversing with people such as myself in English, the inappropriate introduction of Bengali kin language (in comparison with 'straightforward' vocabulary and grammar) feels peculiar in mixed company. A further reversal can take place, for example among teenagers who might be in disagreement as to who exactly a person is in kin terms, and if I suggest the right answer, they laugh and say with embarrassment, "Look even *she* knows, probably better than me!" The familiarity and at-home feeling about orthodox Bengali kinship behaviour is therefore seen to be heterogeneous among this population according to context, generation set and migration history.

Improving language skills increased what could be said and learned about social connections among Bengali patients. Some of their relatives asked to join my list when they heard of a female English doctor who could speak some Sylheti. Those who expressed a preference for an English rather than a Bengali doctor (not all of whom, locally are male or from Bangladesh) made comments along the lines that being a patient of someone who is knowledgeable about the Bengali 'way of life' can be felt to be intrusive. Patients have alleged that some Bengali doctors have different but significant prejudices about Sylheti patients in Bethnal Green (cf. Wilce 1998) so an English, Sylheti-speaking doctor can be seen as providing a comfortably balanced service knowing neither too little nor too much about other people's lives.

5.3 Thick and Thin

Invitations to *Eid* parties and weddings allowed me to see Bengali people in their own social setting. Simultaneous social loneliness and uncomfortable social density was brought to light. Two Islamic festivals of Eid are celebrated: the excitement of *Eid-ul-fitr* which comes at the end of the Muslim month of fasting, *Ramadan*, is on a par with Christmas in Bethnal Green. Fasting is widely and strictly observed by Bengali people locally. Schools close for *Eid* and the streets are busy with cars packed with families visiting each other and groups of teenagers on foot, looking glamorous with their hair unusually loose. Although the custom of oiling women's hair is falling away among the younger generation, modest Bengali married women and teenage girls who observe *shorrom* rules of behaviour would at other times avoid being seen in public with long loose hair. *Eid*, although a religious feast, is also seen as a time of social excitement and conviviality. Cars filled with groups of flash young men roar past in style; it is impossible to find a car to hire locally without booking well in advance. Everyone who can afford to do so wears a new outfit after a ritual bath on the morning of *Eid*. Men attend the mosques where a series of prayer sessions is held in the morning; the largest, the East London Mosque, accommodates several thousand people at once.

At one of a number of homes I visited on a particular *Eid* day the telephone rang constantly and a stream of guests came and went. The steamy kitchen was crammed with piles of recently prepared special snacks and saucepans of rice and curry. On the same day I also found women alone or with a solitary visitor, in some cases because their children and husbands had left to visit their own friends rather than going out together on a family visit, in other cases because they had no relations to visit or entertain. Likewise, several hundred guests might be present at a wedding, apparently indicating that the families I knew had a dense network of social relationships, but the small household of the bride containing only two adults had had to make all the arrangements without any outside help at all. In Chapter 3, Aliya and Mohammed suffered from the difficulties caused by a surfeit of connections whereas Muffasir and Rahena were vulnerable in their isolation. The density of the Bengali social world in Bethnal Green has a parallel world of loneliness.

Middle-aged Bengali men, like many other rural to urban migrants of all backgrounds, compare the lonely streets of London with the sociability of a stroll in Bangladesh. For them, the key difference is that Londoners of any description are too busy for the easy to and fro of casual and enjoyable social encounters, and this, they feel, has eroded Bengali social values. A father complains to me about those members of his kin group who were unable to attend a family ritual, "In this country, whatever happens, if your *mother* dies you still have to work." I remonstrate that compassionate leave was usually allowed by most employers, "Yes, in *your* work, but other work, like restaurant, you cannot leave - in Bangladesh you work if you feel like it, if you don't feel like it you don't work." He went on to elaborate how most men in Bangladesh work for themselves and just as much or as little as they needed, so paid employment was unfamiliar to people like himself. It is significant that the example he gave was that of Bengali employers, restaurant owners, who were being strict and uncaring about the important rituals of life here. This man's idealised recollections, which he uses to heighten the comparison between Bengali and non-Bengali social life in conversation with myself, are sometimes qualified, if he sees that he is being overly romantic, by his saying that this is how it *used* to be and that Bangladeshi society has now also deteriorated (cf. Parry 1999: 116ff.).

Bengali women of a similar age do not compare strolls in Bangladesh and Bethnal Green, sociable or otherwise, since they would not for the most part have had the possibility of street social life in Bangladesh. The sociability of life within households, however, is perceived to be attenuated in Bethnal Green compared to these women's (perhaps idealised) memory of life in Bangladesh. I could not at first square this with my observations. Lonely mothers appeared to be exaggerating when they said they were perennially isolated: during a chance visit to one friend I found a pleasant group of women having a tea party. Later she explained this as, "You know, they're just neighbours - you know Bengali people, they like to talk, you know, gossip like". This comment, corroborated by many others, suggests that the density of social contacts does not necessarily entail social support or pleasant intimacy.

Even a family with a healthy quantity of local kin may feel relatively isolated and despondent in London. When it comes to negotiating with housing or Social Security departments, the normally cheerful mother of a well-run traditional large household with many local relatives, feels that no one is around to help in this socially depleted world. Kin might live nearby, but their daily concerns are much too time-consuming in London to allow them to be sufficiently available unlike village life in Bangladesh. British civil servants, in my experience, dislike dealing with large groups and prefer to isolate the individual claimant rather than have a case-conference. Engaging the personal help of a Sylheti-speaking English family friend can make them feel less isolated. To British eyes, numerous bilingual signs and leaflets and the availability (admittedly limited) of advocates and interpreters, seems adequate provision for non-English speakers. For Bengali people, advocates do not necessarily suffice unless they have the interests of the family at heart because of a personal rather than a professional connection. Professional, by-appointment, unknown advocates are treated with caution by some, precisely because they are likely to be connected to other Bengali people and are thereby potential gossips. In this respect, the Bengali receptionists are usually popular as interpreters in a medical setting because patients will have had a chance to find out exactly who they are and can decide whether or not they are likely to be suitably confidential.

A more differentiated set of meanings for the range and intensity of social relationships was coming into view which included the idea of extensive kith and kin on the one hand, who count for ritual occasions but might otherwise be too busy or dispersed to be sociable, and an intensive neighbourly society on the other which may be overly interested in the affairs of others. The latter might be quite variable in utility, support and reliability beyond superficial social intercourse, and even, from some quarters, harmful. This differentiation of social relationships is illustrated by the uneven dissemination of information among Bengali households within and across ethnic boundaries.

Older bilingual Bengali children would appear to be useful interpreters and advocates from their parents' point of view. Apart from the issue of how this is inappropriate from the perspective of the child, at least in a medical context, it is noticeable how needy many young Bengali people are themselves for information. It is understandable that older monolingual migrants might be under-informed as to practical matters but it would be reasonable to assume that bilingual youngsters brought up in Bethnal Green would be sufficiently knowledgeable. I found, however, that once a connection is made as a friend of the family, my assumed knowledge about a variety of matters is eagerly plundered. In such situations I feel disconcerted, being habituated to the attitudes of British teenagers who commonly affect 'cool' and disdain for the opinions of their parents' (boring) friends. Typical questions asked in English like, "Where is the swimming pool?", "Where can I get stationery for my home computer?, What do you think I should do for A-levels? What do I do about my kid-sister's school problem?", betray a narrowness of practical knowledge on the part of these lively teenagers. These are not just random topics brought up to initiate a conversation; it has been a recurrent impression that once a certain level of trust has been established, the flood-gates open and an urgent list of questions pours out. On the other hand these same teenagers are remarkably acute and sophisticated when describing the social world of their colleges and schools. They skilfully relate the motivations and strategies of fellow students and teachers in gossipy stories about who did what and why and how they were undone by unanticipated consequences. These tales commonly have a darker conspiratorial tenor than the lighter gossip-narratives that might be culled from TV soap operas, (which are enjoyed by anyone and everyone in Bethnal Green). Practical, trustworthy resource knowledge, seems to be thinner on the ground than astute judgement about social attitudes and behaviour. This is apparently a bias in Bengali households as casual contact with Turkish, Somali or Chinese families locally does not deliver the same impression of unevenness in gaining access to particular kinds of social knowledge.

It is unsurprising that minority ethnic populations should be particularly sensitive to the attitudes of others given the importance of racism as a local concern. Practical help is consequent on social connections for everyone to a certain extent, Bengali or otherwise, but without a minimum level of confidence in the person who is providing the help, there is little possibility of a productive outcome. Knowing a non-Bengali person who can speak some Sylheti immediately increases the sense of trust, and opens the possibility of tapping into her resources. Moving the argument into another sphere, and as a further example of this unevenness of social knowledge, there are several Bengali doctors locally, and their patients may speak of them as a friend as well as being their doctor. This social closeness does not, however, seem to enable diagnostic and therapeutic processes to run particularly smoothly. "*In Bangladesh*, doctors know at once what is wrong", I have been told, "Without even an examination, but *here* they can't say what is wrong, they don't *know*". The introduction of the idea of a geographic effect on knowledge is telling. The problem is described as being not just a deficiency or dilution of Bengali knowledge in Bethnal Green, but also as an effect of being placed within non-Bengali society where "*They* [the English] know everything." When pushed on this point, older religious-minded Bengali men say of English intellectuals that, having discovered the Koran contains all scientific, religious and moral knowledge, they appropriate it for themselves and obscure its riches from others whom they regard as alien and inferior. Ordinary office clerks are often felt to be obstructive or limited with their information, "If they think you don't know, they don't give" but withholding information is not always seen as deliberate or just a consequence of language difficulties: the transmission of knowledge, and by extension social help and support, is somehow clogged up by a mixed society *per se*. The implication is that the flow of useful knowledge is blocked if the right sort of relationship does not pertain. Transposition from Bangladesh to Britain not only attenuates knowledge by the reduced density of Bengali society, but also by the operative norms of British social intercourse jamming the information channels.

5.4 *Making friends and knowing who people are - the village network*

Moving on in my fieldwork, walking the streets, picking up children from school and going into shops, I observed the formation of acquaintances and the maintenance of neighbourly friendships. By simply walking to a shop with Jahanara I had the prickly experience of exposing to view a white and a Bengali woman together. English people studiously ignored us. In London, where anonymity is the expected norm on the street for someone of my background, it is hard to assert that you were more ignored when you accompanied a Bengali woman to the shops than when you were alone but it felt as if it were so. Bengali people, on the other hand, would nearly always do a double-take of surprise, for while my colouring and style of dress could, just possibly, allow me to pass in some circumstances, few Bengali women of my age would be seen without at least some slim token of their Muslim religion, a scarf for example. I never made any attempts to dress in Bengali style, although some friends said that they could never really *see* who I was since I did not wear a *sari*.

Within shops, Bengali assistants, or perfect strangers to Jahanara would look with intense interest and more often than not, come up and ask who I was, especially if they overheard our conversation about vegetables or fish in Sylheti. Following Jahanara's lead, we would be rather vague and aloof with some, such as eager, threatening-to-be-vulgarly-immodest women, and actively avoid eye contact and the physical space surrounding most men. If a delivery of stock was in progress this made moving round a small shop something of a dressage exercise in controlled body movement as burly young men came in and out with baskets of fresh produce. It was possible to be more indulgent with others, especially the elderly, but I could not always guess in advance who would be favoured and who despised. "Who were they?" I would ask afterwards, "*Kheeou nai*", ("Nobody I know") was often the reply, or she gave the slightest classification, "*Mouk firrisoi*" ("I know them by sight" - literally, "I know her face"). As often as not, however, a pleasant social chat among a group of us might be set up in the shop which would be punctuated from time to time by English people who popped in, navigated the cigarettes and milk end of things and seemed blind to the inner recess of the shop stocked with fish, meat and vegetables and its now immobile group of talkers. The chat would stop but the English customer would not notice the hiatus and after they left, the conversation picked up again, only the shopkeeper continuing to act in both spheres.

New friendships appeared to be struck up with ease and someone met in the street a few times could be invited back to Jahanara's flat for tea and small talk about their family life. Those who stopped to chat in the street or in shops were not just *mouk firrisoi* but also *neshdoor* (neighbour), a term that covers those people in the area who know or have visited each others' houses. Frequent visitors could unburden themselves of their household anxieties and frustrations. Everyone found it interesting, but not awkward, that I had somehow stepped into Jahanara's social world. It is a little different in households where I am primarily the friend of the father of the house and my professional (masculinised) role of a doctor is more clearly emphasised. Male friends of friends usually treat me initially to a disquisition on moral or religious matters or ask for specific medical advice whereas in the female company of Jahanara's house the latter strategy is noticeably absent and the immediate theme of conversation is nearly always one that seeks to place me more accurately in important social terms. "How many children do you have? Do you live with your husband? What is his job?" and other similar questions allow them to 'read' me through my domestic particularities. Once past the small talk, however, divulging personal troubles is common in both contexts and although again this might be because I am doctor, other authors note that sorrow and pleasure are commonly combined themes in Indian women's domestic colloquies (Raheja & Gold 1994)

Over time, in the districts adjacent to the practice, I was the one who knew no-one whereas my Bengali friends frequently met people they knew on our way to school or the shops. Some of these walks were near to my own home: social geography calculations show that even in the areas most densely populated by Bengali people they will meet on average three non-Bengali people for every one Bengali person (Peach & Rossiter 1996: 126). Combined with my observations, some (unsurprising) judgement can be made about the relative inclusiveness of Bengali social networks compared with those of middle-class white urban residents such as myself. Again the simultaneous thickness and thinness of the Bengali social world suggested itself. Not only were informants well supplied with social contacts whom I would think of as significant, more than just a person seen in the street, there was evidence that there could be too much of this sort of thing and some could afford to pick and choose among acquaintances. One friend said that if they went to every wedding for which they had an invitation, they would spend most of their weekends at weddings. On another occasion, driving with a friend through Whitechapel he said, "Oh look, my uncle-brother (son of maternal aunt and uncle, MZHS - *khalu-goro-bhai*)". Alerted to field-notes mode, I duly started asking about their relationship and he said that the old man was tiresome and if they met by chance would always complain that they hardly ever saw each other. My friend chuckled, "I just say - you know this is London, your house is too far."

Acquaintances, particularly adult migrants, explore the potential for friendship or mutual connections by asking first about their respective originating villages in Bangladesh before asking where they live in Bethnal Green, or their names, jobs or family. People do not say early on in a friendship that they are from this or that *foribar* (family), *gushti* (patrilineage) or *bongsho* (clan, wider patrilineage). Their name may denote a certain status but that might be falsified by an act of deed poll that inserts the nobility of Sheikh or Soyod/Saiyed into a title. Asking about village origins modestly veils the far ruder question, if put directly, as to which *'jat'* (strata or caste) the other person might be. Using villages as a primary referent also allows contiguous social networks to be examined. Aziz only gained informants' confidence as a fieldworker in rural Bangladesh once they knew his village origins. His provenance as a scientist from a research centre counted for little without this vital information (Aziz 1979: 12). The only verifiable knowledge about others comes from eye-witnesses of their village *bari* and kin relations. Even younger informants, educated, if not born in Britain, say that you can place anybody given a minimum of the right information. Women hiding from violent husbands point out the hopelessness of relocation in temporary 'safe houses' in London since someone on the block is bound to be connected somehow to the husband's social circle and he will hear of her whereabouts.

The basic introductory question, *"Kun gram-o takhoyinne?"* ("Which village do you come from?") is asked, not because each village has a special regional character (which they do), but because once this fact is fixed, nitty-gritty social knowledge becomes accessible through connections. Relationships here are accelerated or broken off early by the tracery of connections at home; recognising someone's co-ordinates in Bangladeshi village terms can be a felicitous starting point for friendships that begin with a chance meeting in shops, the street or neighbours' houses. The connectedness allows not just for shared conversational subject matter but also for accurate social placement and a potential increase in the kind of knowledge which might be used for all sorts of purposes, for example for children's marriage prospects (see before, p 92, for the search for spouses).

The layers of knowledge about other people in Bengali social circles can be ordered from the outside in as comprising firstly, known by sight (*mouk firrisoi*), then neighbours (*neshdoor*) and finally those who come within genealogical kin categories. These Bengali kin categories are broadly inclusive, stretching to almost anyone with whom one has a social relationship of any importance. In Bethnal Green this potential world of kin is not conceptualised as consisting only of other Bengali people, nor is it always found in practice to be coterminous with shared ethnicity. The concept of relative (*shomporkor*) extends far beyond known genealogical connections. The inclusive term *kutum* describes this extended, or theoretically unbounded world of social relations. There are no essential qualifying shared attributes such as genealogy, ethnicity, property or religion that must pertain before one can become *kutum* except that of forming a significant relationship one with another. *Attio* describes closer relationships within the *kutum*; *gushti* refers to the patrilineage; *bongsho* means the clan or lineage origins of any family rather than denoting a particular relationship between living persons, and *jat* is the caste-like status of any family. The most exclusive group term is *foribar* or immediate family. Moving outwards again from the family, the grouped terms, shared house, shared household and shared village (*ekkee ghor, ekkee bari, ekkee gram*) delivers an alternative, spatially graded perspective on relatedness within the *kutum*.

In common with other populations from the Indian subcontinent, non-genealogical social relationships of any significance are given classificatory kinship terms of reference and address extrapolated from genealogical kin both in Bangladesh and in Bethnal Green (classificatory is used here to denote non-genealogical kin connections; I am aware that such a distinction is one that is imposed rather than emic). The range of Sylheti kinship terms is extensive and most remain in common usage even among fluent English speakers but familiarity, obviously enough, depends on maturity: young children may be quite ignorant of sibling's affines terms if none of their siblings is married. The 'reason', if any can be adduced for such an extensive elaboration and usage of kin nomenclature, is given by some as a kind of institutionalised avoidance of corporations in favour of expanded kin networks (Asghar 1996: 306, Aziz 1979 passim, Maloney 1979: xiii). Whilst I am not in a position to contest these author's ethnography (Aziz' study is based in Bangladesh and Asghar studied community organisations exclusively) my experience leads to a different formulation.

The functionalist inferences of Aziz and Asghar can be rejected and the analytical problem recast. The conundrum is that Bengali kinship is reckoned both extensively and cognatically, yet patrilineal, corporate and caste-like ideologies and groups are also discernible. The processes that lead simultaneously to apparently boundless centrifugal networks and bounded centripetal institutions are not, I argue, separate or at cross-purposes, nor is one 'weak' and the other 'strong'. Bengali relatedness is rather a form of productive dynamic tension whereby the maximum extent and shape of any individual's network is built concurrently with a strong sense of *gushti*, *bongsho* and *jat*. The advantages of networks and corporation are recruited together in counterpoint and not despite each other. It follows that any person's social provenance and status cannot be given simply by virtue of their membership of a group. Groups do have their own importance, for to be of *Talugdur bongsho* (landlord lineage) or of *Soyyod bongsho* (the Prophet's family lineage) is to be far superior to those from the fisherman's *jat*, but until all social connections are revealed, a complete social placement of any individual cannot be made. In summary, who people are by virtue of membership of any particular group in Bengali society does not suffice without specific information as to where their social connections lie. For this reason, *"Kun gram-o takhoyinne?"*, is the most potent introductory question since it will reveal the crucial dimensions of the social network.

The technique of using village co-ordinates is, however, only a start in getting to know people well and behaving as social intimates. The generational position of persons with non-genealogical connections to any ego are guessed at, and rounded upwards if there is doubt. Kin terms of address are always used if Bengali people of the older generation are present. Thus, as in other Indian kinship systems, hierarchical norms of social behaviour are codified by the lexicon of the kinship vocabulary. Use of first name terms by senior to junior persons demonstrates the hierarchical order but knowledge of first names and nicknames among *equals* is only acquired through intimacy that is normally afforded only to very close kin. Several layers mask the names of people from non-intimates which means that conversation can only include the more distant modes of address. This can make small talk about absent third parties rather awkward to an English person who is not familiar with the extended social network. Instead of names, social co-ordinates are given, usually by the use of junior kin's first names, for example *'Forida-err amma'*, Forida's mother, *'Aleha-err borrobhai'*, Aleha's eldest brother. If the junior kin's names are unknown then it will be "The woman at number 11" and "The Manor Road shop-owning man's wife" and so on, but the actual name cannot be used since no-one may know what it is. There are also nicknames used only within close family, so that a friend may say *"Forida-err amma"*, but an aunt could say *"Kushi-err amma"*, where Kushi is Forida's family nickname. For all Bengali people, then, their most personal, family identification resides under several covering layers that may or may not be revealed to others, and circumlocution allows the layers to remain undisturbed. Even children, whose names are enunciated in public, will retain a private layer of identification by masking of their nicknames. In other words, anyone can be placed more or less easily through the network, but exactly who they are remains obscured except to close relatives, family friends, or others who are knowledgeable about their connections. Given the extensive range of Bengali social connections, it may not be very difficult to find someone who does know.

These coverings disappear in mixed society: workers in supermarkets, hospitals and the surgery use first names in that setting as address and reference (cf. use of kin terms in work-places in Bangladesh, Kabeer 1994: 176). In the surgery, first and second names without any titles are used to call patients from the waiting room since spouses and siblings of all backgrounds no longer share second family names consistently. This crudely removes the customary layers for Bengali patients who sometimes register their formal names but sometimes their middle names or even their nicknames since the first name for a great number of men and boys is Mohammed (some parents say this is a title, not a name) and they may not be used to hearing their middle names used. Teachers report difficulty with young primary school children who are not clear about their own names outside the home. Merely to overhear someone's name in a waiting room does not of course entitle you to use it in another context.

To recapitulate the points made so far, the first impression gained of Bethnal Green Bengali social connections is that of a group of people who feel bereft of their habitual comfortable social milieu yet sustain a thickly populated world of relationships. Who people know and how many people they know in some sort of a network is an inadequate description of any person's social circle. Good connections are not limited to Bengali people and not all Bengali people are good to know. Knowledge of other people's social connections, especially those of the originating village *bari* allows for the exact placement of almost any acquaintance. Kinship terminology is important as a part of social etiquette but so far this has not been found to have any uniform correlation with closeness, social behaviour or personal feelings. Finally, detailed personal information can be masked from outsiders.

5.5 Migration distorts kinship

I will now move from the exploration of the ways in which Bengali people build social networks in Bethnal Green to the effects of migration and settlement on the shape of these aggregated social relationships. Bengali households superficially appear to be much like other households in the area. Household composition is not so dissimilar from the rest of the local population and missing pieces in the kinship picture are not immediately obvious. Inter-household relationships appear to develop with ease but not without discrimination. Those with no local connections are by no means marked out as especially unhappy or odd, for residents of three-generational households complain of social dilution and loneliness just as frequently as those in isolated nuclear households. For the most part, Bengali parents are proceeding in just as rational a fashion as anybody else in Bethnal Green to shape their children's future. In general parents provide for their children's welfare, send them to school, teach them about Islam, tell them how they should dress and behave and at the end of childhood all reasonable offers are considered for their future jobs and marriages.

While all this ordinary business is going on, however, there are social facts unfolding consequent on migration to Bethnal Green that, if not exactly beyond the control of the actors, nevertheless they cannot be readily grasped and dealt with in the same way that people cope with the more immediate tasks of running a household. The rational enterprise of continuing a good Islamic Bengali life with the added value of education and employment in Bethnal Green is vulnerable to alterations in kinship ideologies and practices occasioned by migration. These changes may not be felt to matter very much until an immediate personal problem precipitates sharp feelings of anguish because the 'right' person who would usually be expected to help is not there.

We cannot extrapolate from what is known about Bangladesh to predict what might be found in Bethnal Green, nor can we assume that families are only trying to reproduce here, give or take a few practical adjustments, an idealised reflection of family life in a Bangladeshi village or town. It is not just a matter of mapping the kinship system onto a larger geographical grid, especially given that Bengali families have settled only recently in Bethnal Green. We cannot draw a diagram of typical social networks in Sylhet and then expect to find it writ large on another diagram that includes Bethnal Green, Britain and the rest of the world. It is not just a matter of managing to overcome the physical distances between different persons or families in any one kin network, although this is part of the problem. We may be able to discern attempts to bridge gaps as if they were merely practical logistic problems, notably the proliferation of phone shops offering discounts on overseas calls and so on. That there needs to be some adjustment is obvious, but not all of the alterations wrought by migration or by living as part of a minority ethnic group in London can be anticipated in advance of migration or at the point of embarking on life as parents. The idea that kinship and other social relationships here are not simple refractions or extrapolations of those in Bangladesh may seem to be an overly obvious point to make except that the contrary view is, as has already been said, a prevalent local opinion.

I argue that very few families want only to reproduce the traditions of Bengali family life here without any regard for British social values, and likewise very few want to become entirely like their British neighbours. The process of development is continuous throughout the life of the household, since any individual family's particular aspirations are likely to need frequent adjustment in the face of anticipated and unexpected outcomes of their own and others' actions. Bengali people here reflect on what they can observe of their British neighbours and consider their own traditional preferences in the light of such observations.

To begin with, the change is not just sudden dislocation, a once and for all transposition but it has a history for the population as a whole and for many individuals, particularly among the men, it is a slower trajectory away from, and a retention of an important relationship with Bangladesh. On a smaller scale similar changes occur within Bangladesh when people move from villages to Sylhet town or Dhaka, and Bengali people do draw a parallel with London and Sylhet town in this respect (cf. Chandavarkar 1994: 150ff., Vatuk 1972). The period of time when working men were living in London without their wives and children allowed enduring friendships with other Sylheti men and non-Sylheti men to develop over many years (Adams 1987). They may arrive here from very different areas of Sylhet district but become *bhai* (brother) to each other, and their children call them *sassa*, (father's brother), and some may develop a close feeling for their brother's children: "I know that woman, her father is not my real brother but we were close when we worked together and she and her little brother call me uncle. In our country we say, by my hand I made them, *ath-or failchee*". Female migrants do not have the equivalent experience since their travel is initiated by marriage or family relationships and not usually because of employment. In some respects the movement of women from Bangladesh to Bethnal Green is homologous with the expected life patterns of women remaining in Bangladesh where virilocality and exogamy is the desired norm. British Bengali children born here have not migrated from anywhere but have an important relationship to the (also changing) state of Bangladesh through their families and marriages.

Once families are settled in Bethnal Green, even the larger households are felt to be very different from those in rural Bangladesh (cf. Jeffery 1976: 122ff.). The traditional village *bari* in Bangladesh comprises related families from several generations living in adjoining apartments so that a certain level of kinship density obtains. Nuclear households have significant relationships with the larger *baris* although it is possible for branches of an original patrilineage to move away and over a period of time effectively break off (Gardner 1995: 102ff.). In any case there is likely to be a fair mix or scatter of all the representatives of the kin system living in proximity to each other, or, where there are gaps, classificatory relatives living nearby in the village who can be 'recruited' to fill vacancies. This is, of course, a representation of an ideal type but one that conveys the notions of idealised kinship and residential patterns described by Bethnal Green Bengali people. London families visiting Bangladesh continue to contrast populous *bari* life with the less dense patterns of co-residence in Britain. Ethnography from Bangladesh, on the other hand, points to depletion of the density of *bari* life. Demography and emigration means that ideal sets of kin relations cannot always be found in Bangladeshi villages. Households containing three, let alone four or five generations are few in Matlab district of Sylhet (Aziz 1979: 49) and Talukpur (Gardner 1995: 30). As discussed in Chapter 4, emigration from Bangladesh has a parallel effect on the patterns of co-residence in villages to that of residential patterns in Bethnal Green. Women stay at home while the men follow routes created by chains of men, leaving spatial 'gaps' in the ideal residence pattern. *Baris* may empty, leaving one lone caretaker (Gardner 1995: 227). Kin diagrams from Sylhet and Bethnal Green are likely to be different in many respects, but absent menfolk and home-based women will figure in both. If the demographic differences are not supported by statistical data, the comparative social experience is not necessarily gainsaid. More to the point, the contrastive social experience is, in all probability, not dependent on the objective statistics of social demographics, but on the subjective experience of a different social atmosphere.

Firstly, to give an overall picture of the extent and density of inter-household kin relationships of Bengali households in Bethnal Green, some preliminary general observations can be given where I have sufficient data. There are sixty households among the study population whom I have known for sufficient time to be confident in my knowledge of their most important social connections. Among these, only a minority (ten) have no local kin: local in this context means having relatives living in adjoining areas of the borough such as Spitalfields, Aldgate, Globe Town, Stepney, Bow and Whitechapel. Most of these have some relatives living outside London but within Britain, and a very few are truly isolated with no social connections at all within Britain. Some may have up to four or five same-village (*ekkee gram*) relations within the borough but the activity of these relationships is contingent on context. Of the fifty or so families with local consanguinal or affinal relatives, the majority have mutually supportive kin relationships. A small minority have predominantly difficult relationships with local kin, serious enough to come to my notice without specific enquiry. These include not only those that are so by definition (i.e. broken homes through divorce), but also some married-couple nuclear households. The remaining households have mixed relationships: they get on with some but not others and on the whole it is the husband's family who are seen as problematic rather than the wife's family. In other words, difficulties with mother's family are not as socially significant, can perhaps be take-it-or-leave-it in comparison with quarrels within a patrilineage. Contrary to my initial impressions of isolation, the majority of Bengali households are meshed with local related households, but a significant minority are voluntarily or otherwise isolated from such relationships.

124

Paternal grandparents, *dada* and *dadi* are still commonly missing from Bethnal Green Bengali families, but sometimes maternal grandparents, *nana* and *nani* and other maternal kin may be 'unnaturally ' close. Where it is the husband who has come from Bangladesh and lives either with his parents-in-law or in a nuclear household with his wife and children nearby, the *nana/nani: nati/nateen* (maternal grandparent: grandchild) relationship can flourish. Some will even foster the child of a working daughter, or at least help with daytime child care. This receives no opprobrium from either British or Bengali society and is popular with those women who would like to work but worry about child care outside the family. The maternal grandparent's care and attention to their daughter and her children has a natural feel to it and is never the occasion for a funny or awkward remark. *Dada* and *dadi* may be too far away in Bangladesh to be able to do much about this but there is no evidence that they mind, given that their son is now in Britain.

Likewise, the proximity of married sisters, who would otherwise be dispersed in Bangladesh, is almost always enjoyed. A man's affines, for example his wife's older brother, *shomondik*, (*mama* to the children), can be very close both to his sister's husband and their children. This would sometimes be difficult to achieve geographically in Bangladesh except on an intermittent basis. The rationalisations 'distance' and 'this country' can be used to maintain distance if desired or are seen as an obstacle. Relationships that are now geographically closer than is usual can be favoured, or alternatively cannot always be gainsaid. Although it is not difficult to find husbands who grumble about their wife's family if they live close by in Bethnal Green, the more usual finding is ease and pleasure at least with same-generation affines such as their wives' siblings and cousins.

Specific gaps come to light when families are in difficulties. The negative consequences occasioned by a lack of generational breadth as well as depth is revealed by the troubles facing parents of teenagers and unmarried young adults. The problem of finding the right person to advise such young people is a perennial problem. Good Bengali parents should maintain the respect of their children by dignified behaviour. To this purpose certain subjects are *shorrom* (improper, requiring modest conduct) for mutual discussion between parents and their children. These include not just the obvious one of sex, but also any mention of marriage. Older daughters eavesdrop and cross-examine younger siblings who may have been present when the older generation sit in convocation (*allossonna*) in order to find out if she is to be married. In some families, nothing direct will have been said until just before the appointed day when she is to meet the prospective groom. A daughter may refuse a particular choice and so the search begins again, but still without any open discussion. On the other hand, many Bengali parents do incorporate their daughters' wishes and choices in marriage negotiations (Gavron 1998). In general, a completely open family discussion, well in advance of any specific negotiation, would still go against the grain of *shorrom* norms for most Bengali parents except in unusual circumstances.

The norms of *shorrom* behaviour work in both directions: if daughters should ideally be silent during the period of marriage negotiations, parents should ideally have no need to discuss romantic relationships with their children. Recalling the predicaments of Rahmat Khan and Fazlul Ahmed in Chapter 2 (p. 55ff.), however, it is extremely difficult for some parents to remain silent if they become aware that their daughters are risking scandal by their behaviour. Tidbits of gossip, abruptly ended phone calls, mood changes and packets of pills from the doctor suggest that something is afoot. Some, such as Rahmat Khan confront and browbeat the girl and my role in the situation, according to his daughter, was intended to be purely instrumental. Fazlul Ahmed, on the other hand, asked me to intervene as a trustworthy family advisor. While he is not so different from anyone nowadays who thinks that a doctor's role includes solving any personal problem rather than being restricted to diagnosing and treating illness, Rahmat Khan is more typical of Bengali patriarchs who are often hostile to outsiders' interventions in family matters. I am labouring this point to ensure that I am not considered to be a peculiarly energetic doctor who interferes in family matters whether requested to do so or not. I was aware that Fazlul Ahmed's request for help was unusual and so I looked for opportunities to observe and enquire as to whose job it should be in Bengali families, if it was not that of the parents, to deal with personal and potentially embarrassing or shameful matters, and this enquiry yielded the idea of the actual and idealised roles of women who are *bhabi*.

A *bhabi* is an older brother's wife or someone in a classificatory older brother's wife's position, such as a cousin's wife, or, for a married woman, her husband's older brother's wife. One realisation of the *bhabi's* role is quite formal and is not necessarily personal: it is she who gives the prenuptial advice session to grooms as well as brides, and she can be trusted to advise wisely without any embarrassment. She must be at wedding ceremonies and check that protocol is followed. There are others with similar formal roles, such as *ukkil mabaf*, parent substitutes, who protect a bride in her husband's village. In another manifestation, a *bhabi* can be a confidante to her husband's younger brothers and sisters. For the former it is an informal joking relationship, although the limits of such informality are narrow in Bengali households.

In a large *hari* there may be several women of different ages who have this relationship with young adults although the young men by this stage will be spatially separated from adult women. In London, a *bhabi* could provide much needed support and intimate advice on personal and domestic matters, even if she lives some way from her relative's home, since transport in Bethnal Green compensates for distance. There are, however, more significant difficulties than the matter of local geography. For young Bengali women growing up here, an older brother's wife is more likely to come from Bangladesh than London. If so, then the difference in backgrounds between the two women undermines the *bhabi's* potential usefulness as a social advisor in London. There may even be a significant language barrier between a *bhabi* and her husband's younger siblings. Those *bhabis* who are UK-born will have more in common with their *nonons* (husband's younger sister) but their schedule may be busy, taking them to college or work. The actual older brother's wife, being so close to the older men and women of the patrilineage, is likely to have split loyalties, at least while she is living with her in-laws. It can be too tempting for her to pass on information to her husband; if she maintains strict confidentiality about her husband's younger siblings behaviour, she may be severely criticised for not informing the rest of the family about what was going on. Married female friends living close by who are not kin can certainly fulfil the role of *bhabi*, and if they have small children, they are conveniently grounded in domesticity and therefore relatively available to their unmarried contemporaries who can visit them on the way home from college without the disapproval or (for strict families) the knowledge of their parents. Not all married women are deemed suitable by Bengali parents as advisors to their children.

Bhabis who are beyond the immediate family can be more easy going than married-in patrilineal women. In this way, non-Bengali adults with pastoral roles for youth can, on occasion, be more trustworthy confidantes for major issues, but they are usually unfamiliar with the everyday details of Bengali family life, and parents like Rahmat Khan may not read their intervention as one that is sympathetic. Some Bengali girls have found that after confiding in their teachers or social workers, these concerned adults have volunteered themselves to act as negotiators with the girl's parents. The parents, however, may choose the paradigm of institutionalised racism to cast the behaviour of the negotiator in a negative light, and I have never heard of an instance where the parents were persuaded by such negotiators to follow a course of action other than one formulated by the extended family. In so far as those with pastoral duties may limit the parameters of such discussions, without due reflection, to the opposition between so-called 'Asian family values' and idealised Western liberalism, these Bengali elders may be right to mistrust the intentions of such negotiators. It is not impossible to find practical rapprochement between these two discourses (Sen 1997) but the moment of a particular predicament is likely to be too fraught with anxiety on all sides to allow dispassionate and free-ranging discussion of several alternative strategies.

My pastoral role is variously interpreted by Bengali patients as that of older sister, aunt or *bhabi*. There are no perceptible taboo subjects for discussion on the grounds that I am female or a non-Muslim or non-Bengali. On the whole, parents are comfortable and happy with the notion that I am a married woman (not divorced) and a mother in the same generation as themselves. In this mode they can be trusting of my advice. Although some monolingual Bengali people call me 'afa' as a routine form of address, English-speaking Bengali women who call me 'Doctor', if they have been able to unburden themselves of an emotional problem will often say, "You are like a sister" or "It is like talking to a sister". To their small children they explain that I am khala (mother's sister or any non-patrilineal woman in the parents generation). Teenagers may be trustful and confiding but their respect shades into cautious reserve. If they do divulge intimacies, they frequently comment that they cannot discuss these sorts of things with their parents. Most commonly I am a maternal aunt for little children and a quasi-bhabi for older teenagers and young adults (especially during first pregnancy). Older men are also confiding and intimate with me on certain matters, as with a bhabi.

Bengali families in Bethnal Green perceive an absence or thinning out of the women who are both able and willing to act as social advisors to young adults and married women. Some people, children as well as parents, are relieved if they can find a substitute for such a person. If they cannot, then the strategy of enforcing hierarchical norms with more than usual emphasis and even violence may be used. Without the middle role of the bhabi, differences of opinion between Bengali parents and their children evince a particular configuration of what might generally and vaguely be called the 'generation gap'. Firstly, as already described, the gap may be filled by the rhetoric of 'cultural difference' whether spoken of by the children or by non-Bengali supporters and negotiators. Secondly, the absence of a bhabi, in combination with the maintenance of the strictly dignified behaviour of parents, leaves a social space for deviant behaviour, and if children are artful enough, they may exploit this freely. If Bengali parents are not allowed to raise certain subjects with their children then it is relatively easy for the affairs of children to remain hidden from view. As described in Rahmat Khan and Fazlul Ahmed's stories, quite astonishing long-term secret liaisons and relationships are managed by teenagers. This is understandable in the case of boys for whom association with friends in public is not so vulnerable to gossip. The scope of the risk-behaviour of Bengali girls is startling given the sanctions which may be employed against them. Periodically, parents make long visits to Bangladesh, and rather than disrupt their older children's education, they leave them alone or under nominal supervision of the eldest child or other relatives for several weeks. Through this and other means, young Bengali men are able to control spaces sequestered from parental view, where they can entertain girlfriends. Young women are then beholden to the friends of their boyfriends who have the power to talk about them on the gossip network, so this can hardly be seen as a major gain in young Bengali women's freedom. What is seen as delinquency in the younger generation is a common theme when a Bengali parent or grandparent is in the mood to complain about their problems, but the reason often given for the children's deviance is the difference in atmosphere between Bangladesh and Britain rather than any specific gap in the kinship system as it is found here.

5.6 Batash

In Bangladesh, as envisaged or recollected by parents in Bethnal Green, the rules for bringing up children make up a set usually contextualised by village life where social knowledge is prolific, pervasive and dense. Again, the disparity between such recollections and the facts of contemporary Bangladeshi village life does not gainsay the experience of difference through change of place. The particularities of these roles and rules of behaviour are generally well understood by Bengali people in Bethnal Green but what marks the difference between Bangladesh and Bethnal Green family life, apart from demographic change, is not so easily specified by the actors themselves. Social morality and custom or habit (*obyash*) is, I am told, imbibed with the air you breathe, but here in Bethnal Green the children do not grow up in the same *batash* (atmosphere). Some describe this by saying that here is no 'fresh air' unlike Bangladesh[14]. Simple explanations and logical instruction cannot take hold in Bethnal Green because of the altered atmosphere. For this reason, some parents explain, children cannot be expected to stay on the rails without immense effort because the correct *batash* is not all around them as it is in Bangladesh, and moreover the wrong sort of knowledge can go around in the atmosphere here. The custom and culture of the old country cannot be boxed up, transported intact and unpacked anywhere: it only works within a particular density and configuration of actual social relationships, without the interference caused by certain interpositions of non-Bengali people and the insensitive long arm of British law.

The *batash* in London is felt in social terms to be thin and distorted by juxtaposition with a non-Bengali social discourse. This destabilises the security that parents feel about their individual family's social strategies. Habituation to a particular density and configuration of social knowledge maintains their practical consciousness making the conduct of daily life routine and unproblematic (Giddens 1991: 35ff.). Removal to British inner-city life can thus engender a feeling of stepping backwards into thin air where unpleasantly conscious efforts are needed to stay on the right track. This constellation of not entirely anticipated effects (the dispersal and distortion of an ideal kinship pattern, the dilution of social information and the interfaces with different aspects of British society) causes practical consciousness to founder. The ideal pattern of social life can still be discerned within the residual partial or altered picture by the older generation who spent most of their formative years in

---

[14] This correlates with a general preference for the fresh food of Bangladesh compared to frozen imports flown into London. British born people comment after their first visit to Bangladesh, "The food is really good there, so fresh".

Bangladesh, and some adjustment in the light of that experience can at least be entertained. Younger married adults, in particular, may express regret that the large extended Bengali family, which they applaud in principle and in preference to their idea of standard British family values, can so often founder in a welter of dispute and discord. For the younger generation brought up in Bethnal Green, the cultural norms of Bengali family life are likely to make only partial sense and may be meshed together with other kinds of local discourse to make a new scheme of social logic.

Gaps in knowledge for younger children about matters such as *jat* and *izzat* (honour) may pertain to Bangladesh as much as Bethnal Green, depending on the composition of their family home, but they will inevitably pick up such knowledge as they mature in Bangladesh. The social maturation of Bengali children in Bethnal Green is much less predictable: where parents and children diverge this cannot be glossed vaguely as a falling away of traditional knowledge through diasporic effects, nor only as teenage rebellion against Bengali traditions. The integrity of such traditions, in the sense of making some kind of readable or patterned continuity of meanings (that were always, of course, mutable and open to question) has not simply altered but, for some, has been traduced.

It should not be thought that all families or individuals are trying to darn the holes in a ragged system or that change is necessarily and always interpreted as damage to something that was once whole. This is a view of some, particularly of parents who are considering the personal difficulties they may be experiencing with their children. In other contexts, they, and others, find advantages in the altered social environment which can serve as a useful rationalisation for novel relationships, or they manage to maintain a reasonable sense of social stability. When I raised the question of *batash* with an upwardly mobile acquaintance who regretted the loss of 'culture' among her peer group, she rejected my interpretation entirely. "*Batash* is not a good word to use" she said, "That is something that goes round, you know something that touches people." She made a moue of distaste, so I asked her to explain further. Just as in English the word atmosphere can be used metereologically or socially, if *batash* is used without positive or negative qualification the social meaning implied is that of a bad or at least a problematic social atmosphere as in the English phrase, "There was a bit of an atmosphere". The recruitment of *batash* to a discussion about Bengali culture was not at all in keeping with this woman's 'heritage' model. For her, Bengali culture is contained in certain traditions and customs of language, dress, aesthetic and religious practices. These customs may be inherited and passed down through generations regardless of the prevalent tenor of social relationships or *batash*. She implies that the tenor of social relationships would be morally improved if people adhered more closely to virtuous traditions. This subtle detachment of 'culture' from the social relationships that subtend cultural discourse, from lived praxis to routine practice, makes it easy for her, and others, to classify problems within families as being 'social problems' while preserving intact a mental model of inviolable 'culture'.

For those with troubled lives, whose sons are a problem at school because of violence, or who pawn their sister's wedding gold to buy drugs, or whose daughters are pregnant before marriage, or who drink alcohol and smoke in the street with boys, *batash* sums it all up. The non-Bengali working-class counterparts of these families likewise blame the area, Bethnal Green, as a total social fact which engenders harm, rather than any particular sub-text of the local social environment, "What can you do when they're taking drugs? Its the *area*. If we could, we'd move out." The experience of these informants enables them to put their finger on the sum total of the effects of the atmosphere, or culture in Bethnal Green even though they are not at leisure to disaggregate and analyse the components of this wholeness. The contained and essential formulation of culture, detached from social practice can be seen to be favoured by some (those who need not or do not wish to dwell on the problem of contingency), while the contingent experience of culture falls largely on those who are forced to face up to the difficulties of life in a mixed social environment.

5.7 Summary

Observation of expectations about Bengali social conduct reveals a normative discourse of ideals that is grounded in kinship. The ideology of kinship encompasses friends as well as genealogical connections and may be used to enhance or diminish the content of relationships. Kinship ideology can be invoked rhetorically to illustrate the morality of any one person's behaviour and it can be recruited to enhance the strength of feeling in a non-genealogical relationship. It can be understated and neutral, but it is a readily available, ready-made schema of the moral and emotional possibilities of any social relationship. A death in the family automatically recruits people with structural places in the system to fulfil certain roles and marriages call up the entire *attio*, but daily life is shaped as much by personal preference as anything else, albeit contextualised by kinship normative behaviour.

Who people are is finally unmasked by another person placing them correctly in a kin network and filling in as many connections as necessary to fix their social status. Other traits like job, appearance, name, education level and income are important but can be undermined by the complete picture which is only given by intimate social relationships which must include (for those who really know about such matters) village connections. This social order is perceived by actors to be altered or distorted by migration. Specific gaps in the supportive social relationships are discerned but also a more overwhelming sense of a difference in atmosphere between Bethnal Green and Bangladesh. The

131

alteration in atmosphere arises not just from missing pieces in kin connections but also from a general alteration in sociability through migration to Britain and the juxtaposition of Bengali and non-Bengali systems of social knowledge.

Prevalent social difficulty is not always felt sharply until something goes wrong in personal terms which disturbs the routine flow of practical consciousness. It is in these moments of disturbance that the explanation given throws into relief the contours of a desired pattern of social relationships. When someone says "We are orphans," or "The *batash* here is different" they are trying to finger the guilty party in Bethnal Green rather than describing in accurate terms an actual social system elsewhere that is not in such disarray. The point is not that people lack or deny insight into their personal relationships and fail to see what is the same or different between Bethnal Green and Bangladesh but they are entirely right that the whole is not simply the sum of its parts. During the time that Bengali families have settled here, all the component parts have become available and yet they do not always make up a complete picture of social comfort.

A particular manifestation of the wrong *batash*, the atmosphere that inappropriately touches people, is the pervasive and discomfiting schema of disembodied social harm: gossip, evil eye and black magic. This is the subject of the next chapter.

CHAPTER 6: NEGATIVITY

6.1 Introduction

This chapter examines negative social and spiritual relationships. This allows for further elaboration of diversity within the Bengali population of Bethnal Green, and in this case, the distributions of beliefs and practices of gossip, evil eye and black magic. I describe how the destabilising effects of an attenuated and distorted social atmosphere are amplified for those who feel that the area is 'thick with spies' and who worry that everybody is watching them. With regard to living in a mixed society, although non-Bengali people do not figure prominently in this chapter, their imputed role of blocking information channels is found to continue in the way that spirit technology does not always work reliably when transposed to the mixed society of Bethnal Green. At this point it should be said that traditional Cockney people, and probably a wide spectrum of Bethnal Green residents, are more alike than different from their Bengali neighbours in their inclusion of spiritual beliefs among the causes of misfortune. The East End colloquialism, 'putting the mockers' on someone is similar to, if less dramatic and less widespread than the Bengali belief in the evil eye (*nozzor*). Bengali and non-Bengali people alike think that you worry yourself to death or develop cancer from shock. Non-Bengali East End people may also visit spiritualists and mediums from time to time.

A preliminary sketch of Bengali ideas about gossip, evil eye, and spiritual harm is again shaped by my fieldwork trajectory of uncovering these matters. This is followed by sections devoted to each of the three categories of harm and an account of the means of redress.

6.2 Fieldwork discovery

Before starting fieldwork, the *tabiz* (charms) that Bengali people wear and visits to faith-healers that occasionally came to light were construed by myself and colleagues roughly as a system of folk-spiritual healing that seemed to be generally 'a good thing': a different, complementary system like Homeopathy, Acupuncture and other alternative therapies. The lack of curiosity to find out more can be explained partly because at that time I did not understand Sylheti. Conventional medical attitudes to minority groups and their 'cultures' are also relevant: Bethnal Green offers an increasing number of alternative therapies, perhaps because it is an area with high morbidity. Few allopathic practitioners would argue with patients who shop around a little among the fringes, nor do they regularly dispute the scientific basis of different therapies with patients, being aware that the evidence-base for allopathic treatment is also open to criticism (see for example the journal, *Bandolier*). This *modus operandi* of tolerant practitioners tends to overlook the specific meanings of cultural practices in favour of a generally sympathetic stance towards alternative therapy as long as the doctor-patient relationship is not injured and the patient does not appear to be the victim of exploitation, financial or otherwise.

One corollary of the practice of Bengali faith-healing, that is, the possibility that these practices could also be used to harm others, as well as Bengali notions of illness and disablement through the agency of spirits and social spite were likewise overlooked. This was partly because of the tolerant oversight already discussed, but also because Bengali patients are unsurprisingly reticent about spiritual matters with doctors. In retrospect there were, however, tell-tale traces of the fear of exposure to evil by Bengali patients, but these clues were misinterpreted in our clinical practice. For example, the home-knitted covers for babies' bottles were thought to be simply for warmth, or decoration, rather than a protective veil hiding a child's healthy appetite from sour onlookers, because the covers look homely rather than religious. Ethics of confidentiality were also a distraction from what were sometimes quite different concerns of our patients. The example I now give of disputes about third-party interpreters is also cogent to the issue of relations of cultural difference.

If a married couple asked not to have a Bengali interpreter, although the nurse, midwife or doctor felt that the husband's English was insufficient, the clinician often assumed that the husband wished to maintain propriety with excessive zeal, or thought his English was better than it was, or he wished to control the information that his wife could receive. A feminist or a race-relations paradigm often came to the fore. At times, a stressful dispute could arise between husband and clinician (apparently so, for the wife, it was assumed, would agree with the feminist) about whether an interpreter was needed or not. The practitioner would press the point if they felt that the woman would be neglected without such a service. Anonymous telephone interpreters were not convincingly more acceptable. The usual excuse given for declining the translation service, as far it was understood, seemed to be shyness and embarrassment in making disclosures to third parties, especially if it was about something like pregnancy. This was usually accepted by us at face value although there is plenty of evidence that various Islamic authorities are flexible on such matters (Sheikh & Gatrad 2000: 68) and many Muslim patients say that they do not see contraception as sinful if it is in the best interests of their (Muslim) family life. What was not realised was that if the couple's *specific* identity was recognised by a third party, this might expose them to the uncontrollable effects of gossip and spiritual affliction.

My attention was drawn to gossip when informants recurrently used their hands in mimicry of a mouth talking while they said, "Oh, you know Bengali people - they like to talk, they talk too much" (*matta beshi*). Enunciating the verbs that specifically mean 'to gossip' or 'back-bite' (*bodnam koraowar, fisedi matta koraowar*) is avoided, and 'talk' (*matta*) is often substituted. I found out about spiritual modes of harm (which at this stage I conceptualised quite separately from gossip) by discovering that some informants were *khobiraj*, Bengali herbalists who have a variable amount of knowledge about *tabiz* and spirits (Gardner 1995: 251). I learned something of their methods and casework from *khobiraj* who were not patients. I did not, however, once armed with 'expert' knowledge, cross-examine likely candidates among patients about the possibility of a spiritual dimension to their symptomatology. Instead, I found that one of the simple questions that is a routine part of any doctor's repertoire, asked in Sylheti, was enough to allow patients to mention spiritual affliction if they wished to discuss such a matter. The suggestive line of questioning, 'What do you think about the problem? - what *sort* of illness [might it be]?, (*"Afnar oshibida lagi, kita monay koroinne? - ki jat bemar?"*) suggests the taxonomy of Bengali epidemiology which includes causes that are physical (*shordi-bemar, kencher-bemar*), psychological (*sintha-bemar, fagoll-bemar*) and spiritual (*Allah-bemar, jinn-bemar*), on occasion evoked an unhesitating direct answer, *"Uffri-bemar"* (generic spirit or immaterial illness). As will be discussed later on, a diagnosis of *uffri-bemar* does not preclude an allopathic remedy, so the ability to understand this dimension of Bengali patients' morbidity has enhanced rather than exoticised my medical practice.

Over time I heard similar stories about gossip and *uffri-bemar* from many patients as well as from informants outside the practice. As will be discussed in greater detail below, in a field-setting where social change is marked, the nature of the relationship between victim and perpetrator is found to be more illuminating than the social-structural position, of one or other participant.

6.3 Gossip

6.3.1 INTRODUCTION

Bengali normative codes are taught from a young age: prescriptive rules of conduct enjoin dignity and respect (*shomman*) towards your elders and betters. Parental guidance is reinforced by moral and religious instructions from *mullahs* (people with specialised knowledge of Islam). Many children attend after-school classes at *madrasahs* (Islamic schools). The number of *madrasahs* has increased in the area, in line with the expanding Bengali population. Children attend *madrasahs* from the age of about seven, learning recitation of the Koran as well as receiving moral instruction and Bengali language tuition. Some families engage home tutors for such purposes and others pay for their children to attend *madrasahs* for their entire secondary school education. The religious and moral education of Bengali children inculcates a 'natural' feeling of shame (*shorrom*) when deviant behaviour is exposed (Gardner 1995: 207). These norms are given further emphasis when it is learned that not only will misbehaviour result in guilty feelings but that such conduct or circumstances may occasion gossip.

Bengali people who do not explicitly believe in spiritual harm recognise the similarities between gossip and what they see as superstitious beliefs. Many authors make this connection and bracket gossip and witchcraft together as both are regarded as products of jealous or soured close social relationships (Bleek 1976). This is satisfactory in so far as the argumentative links between technically diverse social and spiritual practices are justified by their shared context. There is a danger, however that the regularity with which gossip and witchcraft are found to coincide with certain societal types could be mistaken for a complete account of cause and effect. Whilst my data show a similar connection between relationships that have gone wrong and the practices of gossip and spiritual harm, I wish to extend the explanation beyond a correlation of social facts.

When patients tell me of trouble in their lives I may ask if they know anyone with whom they might confide about their worries. This often causes an embarrassing hiatus in the conversation. They may say no at first, but with equivocation as this implies that they have no friends when this is patently untrue, and if pushed, the recurrent answer is, "I can't really talk to anyone, - you know Bengali people, they like to gossip" to which is added the characteristic gesture with their hand opening and shutting. Sociable chatting (*goff koraowar*) is distinguished from gossip which literally means giving a bad name (*bodnam koraowar*) or talking behind someone's back (*fisedi matta koraowar*). Gossip and talk in the context of personal trouble is, I am told ruefully, a characteristic weakness of Bengali people. In parallel with this rather shameful practice is, of course, widespread neighbourly and kin support which is enabled through the same informal social networks (Bott 1971, Yanagisako 1977).

If, for some people, the social milieu in Bethnal Green feels thin in comparison to their experience, recollection or imagined notions of a richer social life Bangladesh, the atmosphere may still be too thick when it comes to misfortune and trouble. If common talk or chance observations about a person's behaviour is worthy of note, then a narrative of gossip may develop (cf. Gilsenan 1989). The occurrence of gossip as 'common knowledge', is frequent and effective enough for some to avoid public gaze wherever possible because of the *shorrom* they anticipate if they thought they had been even potentially gossip-worthy in behaviour. A young woman who thought she was strong enough to resist such pressure capitulated when somebody reported her standards of dress to her uncle, "I used to walk about in shirt and skirt - but now I wear *shalwar kammeez*; I don't care really, it's easier but I get fed up". Since she is otherwise an assertive personality, and since many of her fellow students do not wear *shalwar kammeez*, it was not immediately clear to me why she should be talked about and brought into line while others continued to dress as they pleased without criticism. There was obviously more to this story but at the time I was unable to resolve the loose ends.

It appears to be the case that a bad name is earned through unelaborated reports of shamelessness or personal tribulation being sent back to those whose may take pleasure in that person's social downfall or to those whose status is vulnerable to their misdeeds by association. Slander or distortions of the truth for the sake of getting someone into trouble is not the common event. The medium is the message, and the fact that gossips find other people's behaviour of enough *interest* to shape into a little narrative is sufficient to cause embarrassment, however minor or even non-existent the reported peccadillo. In fact, infraction of norms *per se* is not sufficient (nor in some cases even necessary) to qualify a person as a subject for gossip.

6.3.2 GOSSIPS

Few people admit to gossiping maliciously, but the boundaries of innocent chat blur with those of more harmful gossip. Some housewives have told me with guilty pleasure that daily gossiping sessions in their neighbourhood can be an addictive habit. Everything under the sun is talked about, particularly other peoples' bad habits in standards of behaviour and dress, non-Bengali and Bengali alike. Snippets of social observation can be chewed over repetitively to extract every detail of possible interest (Gluckman 1963: 315), even something as slight as why a person was seen in the street with her older brother. When I sit in the kitchens of Bengali friends' houses the talk is mostly confined to the social troubles and daily events in the lives of the people present with a lively mixture of bemoaning the sad things in life and entertaining funny stories of misunderstandings or foolishness. Others might be referred to, but it is quite possible to do so with respect and sympathy. It is obvious that my status as an outsider might constrain the agenda but there is never any noticeable struggle to keep the conversation 'clean' nor any signs of particular subjects being suppressed or of any frustration because of my presence.

There are plenty of conversational subjects that should be covered up such as pregnancy, marriage and so on from the ears of men. General social chatting is relaxed in both same-sex and mixed company. In fact, gossip that shades into *bodnam*-slander is something I witness more often when men are talking together. Once, while waiting for lunch to be ready, I sat in the front room of a friend's house listening to two men hunched close over the coffee table discussing the story of a neighbours' wedding where the groom refused to show up. The tale was relayed in enormous detail and excited tones even though it turned out that the parties involved were only slightly known to one of the men present. They seemed to find it easier to forget about my presence, or to consider it neutral, vaguely masculine since I was a doctor and the guest of a male friend, sitting in the front room rather than the kitchen. It was also true that my Sylheti could not always keep up with their conversation so inhibitions were easily dropped. In female company, as the guest of a woman friend I readily become another woman in the group for a little while rather than an outsider-English doctor.

Bengali women may be thought of as typical gossips (Gardner 1995: 202) but the channelling of social information through men is more powerful in its effects. It is virtually a duty for men to pass on interesting social information and commentary and they are likely to do so to other men. Women on the other hand, although they will certainly gossip, will only do so to other women outside the family. Gossip can build up in female circles but may remain sequestered there. Public airings of a family's misfortune in male society, on the other hand delivers a more immediate and sharper feeling of shame to the victims even in an unvarnished version of the truth.

A man who had suffered at the hands of his brothers when the joint family account was broken up told me that he could talk to no one about this because it would bring his family's reputation into disrepute. He and his wife cut off relations with neighbours because they looked like people who might gossip maliciously. Their demeanour was often constrained and awkward since they could not help meeting these neighbours on a daily basis. It was noticeable that his wife bridled if any reference was made in passing that might emphasise her familiarity with Bengali customs, "Don't ask me about those sort of things, I don't know what *they* do or think - I went to school here, I've lived all my life here really".

Men are open channels, unable to constrain the flow of essential social information whereas women, although processors and creators of gossip narratives, are more like containers in this metaphor. A wise woman is thus a better confidante and if well-disposed, will refrain from publicising the heartaches of others. There is, of course, room for compassion and the depth of compassionate behaviour is the converse of the cruelty of loose talk and gossip that takes place through informal social networks (Bott 1971: 133). In like fashion, the open channels of masculine information systems, when in positive mode, has its counterpart in the usefulness of such connections. It is women's relative political powerlessness that makes them low risk, low gain confidantes (unless counselling is valorised for itself) and conversely it is men's social power that makes them high risk, high gain recipients of personal disclosures (if practical stratagems are valued). The fact that it is men who guard the reputation and honour (*izzat*) of the family means that they are strict in matters of controlling the behaviour of women, but they also look to the female presence in the family for confessional guidance and support (cf. Abu-Lughod 1986, Raheja & Gold 1994, Yanagisako 1977, for similarly gendered divisions of social labour).

6.3.3 BODNAMI

Women feature more prominently but not exclusively as gossip subjects (*bodnami*). Variations on the story of the young woman who was made to wear *shalwar kameez* because of 'talk' are heard so frequently that it is almost a 'natural' fact of life for young Bengali women. Junior male kin are also found to be vulnerable to negativity of all kinds. Gossip is not confined to the less educated although it is commonly described as a 'low' activity. Likewise there is no direct relationship between increasing educational and career opportunities and a decline in self-consciousness about one's public persona. It should be emphasised, however, that the rapid social changes within the Bengali population in Bethnal Green means that categories of class and socio-economic status, and the vulnerability to gossip and affliction which may correlate with these categories, are not uniform across or within households, nor stable for any individual. In fact, those who are in the process of changing social position are those most likely to attract the attention of gossips. The professional classes may be less anxious, generally speaking, about gossip from idle onlookers, but within the privacy of the middle-class enclave, the family can behave in a similarly dramaturgic fashion:

A young teacher arrived in London to join his wife but found that she had been having an affair. He protested to his in-laws but not only did they make no attempt to deny the facts of the matter, they took her side and began instead to spread rumours about him within the family circle. He saw a counsellor who found him 'rather paranoid', seeing himself as a 'victim of conspiracy by his in-laws'. Given that his visa and career were both threatened by this turn of events, his paranoia (as judged by the counsellor) would appear to be justified. The observation of a paranoid flavour to his presentation, however, indicates the dramatic qualities that he relayed to the counsellor about the family relationships. His problems resolved through the counselling and subsequently remarriage.

Women of all backgrounds are often the focus of more salacious stories but their male relatives suffer equally as a consequence of gossip and are spurred on to take action to abbreviate its scope. Surprisingly, in such situations the anxiety of a kinsman about controlling *his own* behaviour may be as important as the necessity of controlling that of his *bodnami* kinswoman:

A young man, Kamal, has reached the end of his tether with his sister because she had been seen by his brother talking to a young man in the street and refused to confess to being guilty of any offence. Kamal worries that neighbours will gossip about her. She did not deny that she had been talking to the man in question but protested her innocence as to their relationship. Kamal feels, but does not know, that this was probably only one of several improper trysts between his sister and her friend. He is furious that she will not state categorically that she will never see him again. She is otherwise a quiet compliant daughter in an upwardly mobile family and is the only unmarried child in a household where one brother has married and left home and the other is married with a baby and living with his parents. All the children have established careers, father is well respected and mother has an unimpeachable reputation. I had thought that the reputation of this family would be robust enough to weather an unsubstantiated rumour. In any case Kamal had no evidence that anyone was actually talking about her. When pressed, he is unable to specify any particular person or group of people who might have noticed her behaviour, or who might have a grudge against them and make something out of nothing. "But you see, *I* might let something drop" he says enigmatically. He goes on to describe how it is only neighbourly to visit people living in the same street but he if he stays and chats for any length of time in their houses, he might, in an unguarded moment, drop something incriminating about his family into the conversation. He is not so inexperienced as to imagine that he would blurt out specific facts, but thinks it is almost inevitable that he will say something, quite unrelated to his sister perhaps, but he will let words 'drop', and like the proverbial penny, the hearers will divine the hidden meaning. He is quite certain that the neighbours would not intentionally look for tidbits to elaborate into gossip but that he, through 'natural' weakness will say something to inspire them, almost force them to talk about him after he leaves. The problem is that he cannot anticipate what he might say that would be incriminating, and afterwards he will never know what it was he said to trigger the gossip.

Aware of his own weakness, controlling his sister remains the only (secondary) strategy for maintaining propriety without which gossip will ensue. Other informants have concurred with this counter-intuitive idea that they are, at least in part, the architects of their own misfortune and so other people are almost helpless to do otherwise than fashion a gossip narrative. A further example of anxiety about self-betrayal illustrates this:

A married woman is ambivalent about her pregnancy because her first child is only a year old. She is English-speaking and had a job as a nursery nurse before marriage. Near to the birth she asks if she can transfer to a hospital in another borough, "You see, if I go to the local hospital, Bengali people will say things". "What will they say?" I ask, expecting a disclosure, "Oh, you know, they'll say something about me having another baby so soon". Given that she is married and that Bengali women have a high fertility rate I wonder how they will notice her as being especially gossip-worthy. In any case the evidence of her poorly controlled fertility (for an educated woman) or hidden adultery will be plain to anyone who bothers to take an interest once she returns home from hospital. Neither her demeanour nor what I knew of her family life suggests that she is covering up a more shameful problem such as adultery, but her anxiety is palpable. She cannot say exactly who will talk about her and is not willing to think about the problem from this angle. She returns to her original request, emphasising that she feels that it will be extremely awkward to deliver this baby in surroundings where she might be observed by those who can see what was going on.

Her fear is that she will be unable to hide her *feelings* about this birth (even though others might not particularly care nor be censorious about fertility intervals) and so others will *unintentionally* detect her distress and then a gossip narrative will be born with the baby, one that might perhaps include a story of adultery. Visible anxiousness about other people's talk alerts the gossips and such feelings cannot be masked effectively by feigning cheerfulness and insouciance but only by concealment from their line of vision. The young woman who felt she had to wear *shalwar kameez* knew that when she wore Western fashions others would find her *demeanour* more interesting than the clothes themselves and this would betray the fact that there was more to her adopting one style of dress than simple preference.

It appears to be the case that gossip narratives are only successfully created where the potential victim signals to gossips, self-consciously or unconsciously, that they recognise the potential for dramatic interpretation of their current predicament. In this way, gossips can hardly be blamed for the stories. Presumably gossips may try in the general course of conversation to realise stories where this does not pertain, but the impression gained is that there is something particularly contagious and juicy about gossip stories where the subject's awareness of vulnerability is apparent or lies very close to the surface. People may say spiteful things about anyone but it will not 'take off' if the target is dully phlegmatic. The vulnerability to shame does not, then, depend on any fixed scale of acceptable or unacceptable social standards. If that were the case it would be relatively easy to stay within the bounds of propriety. For Bengali people, to be at fault (*dooshi*), or to commit a sin (*goona*) is not the primary concern in relation to gossip. No-one is perfect and only Allah can know true intentions in a believer's heart of hearts when making difficult choices so no one can be condemned out of hand merely on the grounds of sin. A temporary straying from Islamic precepts is forgivable for Islam is a redemptive religion and such faults, even if publicly known, do not inevitably precipitate gossip. It is rather when behaviour, good or bad, can be realised as a narrative worthy of discussion and shaped into a social drama that danger ensues. Like media spin, the stories develop without regard for the feelings of the actors who protest in vain their innocence or their version of events. Each person, then, carries with them the ability to affect other's lives profoundly if information passed on innocently becomes a narrative of gossip and by the same token they themselves are vulnerable to the narrative power of others. The robustness or weakness of self-esteem is thus the primary factor in considering the vulnerability of any individual to Bengali gossip.

There is evidence of relaxing standards for public behaviour: young women work in supermarkets alongside men and wear a variety of Western clothing. At the same time increasing numbers of Bengali women take up the veil in its various manifestations as already described. Some wear the plain *hijab* typical of 'international' Muslims, others wear complete face coverings, described by some wearers colloquially as 'ninja style' because of the apron of cloth tied round the face leaving only small slits for the eyes. Others wear expensive and fashionably styled scarves and *burqas* denoting wealth and status as much as piety (Gardner 1995: 208). The most complete covering of all is afforded by residing entirely within the home. The degrees of seclusion are variable: the extreme situation of a Bengali woman who only goes out of her house to travel to the houses of relatives in a car is not unusual, but nor is the behaviour of those women of a similar age who perambulate in mixed shopping streets wearing only a cardigan for warmth. Exemplary *purdah* is primarily a religious practice, but variations in its form speaks of other influences including an awareness of gossip. Ultimately, just as Allah knows someone's true intentions whatever the outward appearances, so do gossips, and the searching eye can easily discern those who are, despite their coverings or apparent confidence, vulnerable.

Bengali men also pay attention to the proprieties of appearance as a form of insurance against gossip. Gravitas of demeanour increases with age, and the growth of a well-trimmed beard by mature men is usually matched by an Islamic style of dressing so that 'ordinary' clothes are left behind at this stage in life. Their lips are sealed by a prevalent anxiousness about the flow of social information along masculine channels which pushes public male discourse into an impersonal mode.

Despite the strength of the negative sanctions on bad behaviour, plenty of people provide blatantly obvious case material that excites comment. A few are apparently proof to anxiety about gossip and some even appear to court such attention by flaunting their misdeeds. Those who sail close to the wind allow a dialectic between gossip and *bodnami* to grow. They risk such notoriety not only because of the (slim) chance of getting away with excitement and flamboyance without punishment, but also because they are controlling the drama as much as the gossips themselves.

A young mother, Rahela, found married life difficult. Brought up in a strict household, she was keenly aware that her mother had been unfairly oppressed by the systematic deployment of Bengali patriarchal power. Rahela neglected even minimal standards of housework and her two daughters were noticeably unkempt as well as being badly behaved at school. There were frequent rows between Rahela and her husband and she did not hesitate to raise her voice or even have a shouting match with him in the public spaces in and around the tower block where they lived. She cursed loudly the neighbours whom she knew were talking about her and dismissed as 'scum' the white neighbours who studiously avoided taking any notice of what was going on. Such behaviour attracted the attention not only of her male kin who sat in convocation to discipline her but also that of numerous official family support workers. Nevertheless she consistently failed to commit herself to any planned strategy to ameliorate the situation. She manoeuvred to shift the blame on to her husband and accused him of long-standing aggression. The facts of the matter were never clear and he remained a disconsolate and usually silent participant in the affair. She frequently complained to me of bodily pain and mental anguish. During difficult and, at times, disturbing consultations, she referred to her *bodnami* status with relish. In fact one neighbour was her '*bodnami*-mate', and she described with pleasure how they could manipulate credulous gossips by flaunting their disreputable behaviour.

Without resorting to a psychiatric paradigm, Rahela's story can be analysed as the development of a social drama in which both gossips and *bodnami* were equally strong characters. In the reciprocal relations between gossip and *bodnami* the balance of power may predominantly reside in one or the other but rarely, I argue, in one wholly to the exclusion of the other. Whereas robust characters carry on without too much regard for the opinions of those who while away the time elaborating tales, others falter on the least provocation. Once the dramatic dialectic gets underway, the process enmeshes both gossips and *bodnami*. The reaction of the victim only fuels the certitude with which others predict their downward slide. The key distinction between gossip and other forms of talk is that the former is emotional and dramatic in quality (Goodman 1994: 6), violating the codes of practice of more prosaic conversations (Morreall 1994: 61). Drama is, in fact, a critical feature of all the forms of negativity discussed here: during performances of gossip, discussion of evil eye or during séances, voices thicken with emotion, female heads are covered suddenly, doors closed to obstruct eavesdroppers and the atmosphere (*batash*) intensifies. The structuring narratives of well-developed gossip dramas are vivid and steamy; the endings are as predictably constrained as folk-myths despite attempts by *bodnami* to manoeuvre out of their predicament. The final choice is that between surrendering in shame to the gossips version or continuing to deny it, risking escalation of the drama.

Unlike exorcisms, or public meetings found elsewhere in gossiping societies (Brison 1992, Knauft 1985) the fall-out from Bengali gossip is not resolved by specific community action. The dramaturgy does not include closing speeches by people of wisdom and judgement, nor any system of expelling well-known gossips from polite society. *Bodnami* undoubtedly suffer on the whole but some, such as Rahela, can enjoy in an apparently perverse way the notoriety given by their gossip status. Fellow sufferers can band together, facing down the wagging tongues with dramatic displays of emotion in public spaces, revelling in the consternation and fuss that they cause in the neighbourhood.

The behaviour of *bodnami* women is likely to attract the attention of social workers and health visitors where young children are involved. The behaviour is commonly regarded as neurotic, hysterical and manipulative, but management is based on an understanding of the social context of the whole family. The contrast between the two readings of the situation, that of the social worker and *bodnami*, can be caricatured as plodding dull rationality taking on volatile dramaturgy. This contrast is not lost on the actors involved who often have remarkable capacity for insight and ironic reflection on the absurdity of their predicament. Some may indeed appear to be manipulative, playing one set of characters off against the other with ease; others make use of interventions from outsiders such that non-Bengali social mores (as read by the actors), and their representatives (the public servants) can be recruited as sources of counter-argument and direct assistance.

6.3.4 DISCUSSION

Gossip in social science literature is divided between analyses of why gossip exists (the functionalist view - see Gluckman 1963 and the ensuing debate), gossip as a narrative verbal practice (a linguistics or praxis analysis of gossip, Abrahams 1970), philosophical analysis (Goodman 1994, Holland 1996) and the settings in which gossip is likely to be found (Bleek 1976, Gilsenan 1989, Murphy 1985). The consequences of gossip in any particular society are also given due attention which in some cases, usually where gossip leads to witchcraft accusation, can be fatal (Knauft 1985). Each of these approaches has its merits and drawbacks. I argue that gossip, as dramatic speech practice, is not essentially and uniformly moral or immoral, but has a greater propensity than other speech practices to be used either for harm or for increasing social cohesiveness. Most of the Bengali informants for this study would say that gossip was a vice rather than a virtue. In this ethnography I have emphasised the agency of potential or actual victims of gossip in creating scenarios that they hoped to avoid as this is a theme that continues through the other forms of negativity that will be described.

The comparison of the all-seeing eyes of gossips with Foucauldian panopticism seems at first blush appropriate. In *Discipline and Punish*, panopticism is used as a sweeping metaphor for every modality of social discipline, from specialised institutions to intra-familial relations (Foucault 1979 [1975]). Later, Foucault finds it important to draw a distinction between panoptic disciplinary *institutions* and the reciprocal relations of power in *non-institutional* social settings. He argues against *a priori* reification of 'power' in favour of the observation that reciprocal *relations* of power at ground level may not always become social *formations* that are disciplinary institutions (Foucault

1982: 218ff.). Foucault's emphasis on reciprocity (he notes the dual meaning of 'conduct') has a bearing on my observations of the processes of Bengali gossip. The Bengali 'system' of gossip is not a normative disciplinary institution but an observable regularity of relationships between people who share a sensitivity to the representation of social behaviour as dramatic narrative. Bengali society has disciplinary institutions, ranging from the patriarchal family convocations, which sit in judgement and persuade or punish the wayward into conformity, to the authority of the Muslim elite, the *ulema*. It could be suggested that the formality of such institutions will ensure that gossip remains a contrasting informal social formation. I argue that it is important to make explicit the distinction between different locations of social discipline in the analysis of Bengali gossip to avoid the generalisation that Bengali society is 'gossip-ridden'. While some informants feel it is so, others neither find the need to gossip nor fear its effects. The immunity to gossip is not given simply by social position in Bethnal Green, but depends, as already stated, on robust self-esteem or sense of ontological security in a changing world (Giddens 1991).

It is apparent that it requires less social density to knit up a skein of gossip than to build a strong network of supportive social relationships. Ontological security may therefore be relatively more difficult to attain in a transnational population. Because gossip can be sustained across long distances adequately through communication technology, it is not halted, inhibited and distorted to the same extent as positive, supportive relationships. Bengali gossip as a systematic social fact (as distinct from a particular gossip narrative) thus moves from Bangladesh to Bethnal Green with fewer distortions than kinship relations. A quantitative measure of attenuation is difficult to arrive at: some people talk of the lessening of gossip in Bethnal Green, and of how Bangladeshi villages are hotbeds of gossip and jealousy. Residence in Bethnal Green affords some relief for such as these. Rather than trying to measure thickness or thinness we can say that for those who had a particular problem in Bangladesh, migration to Bethnal Green possibly puts some distance between *bodnami* and potential gossips. Despite living in Bethnal Green the same situation may arise in which case it is not so easy to hide from gossips within London or outside the city. The restaurant network and even Bangladeshi villages are sometimes used as bolt-holes where change of place is thought to be of use but it is unlikely that anyone will thus remain reliably hidden. This combination of immateriality and a lack of resolution through any mechanism to punish perpetrators of malicious gossip is found also in the practices and experiences of spiritual harm.

6.4 Nozzor

6.4.1 DESCRIPTION

Nozzor (evil eye, known in India as *najar*) describes the ill-effects of one person's envious or baleful glance on another. To give the evil-eye (*nozzor deowar*) involves no ritual practice and may even be unconscious (Pocock 1973: 30). Jealousy (*ingshyia*) on account of another person's good fortune is the harmful emotion and can be prevented by material coverings as well as by censorship of personal information in order to block the view of potential victims from harmful people. Its effects can be deflected and countered with the wearing of *tabiz* or other magico-religious practices. No-one is immune to *nozzor*, but the likeliest victims are those who are physically or socially vulnerable: babies, young wives and younger brothers. The typical finding that well-educated people do not believe in *nozzor*, and that the superstitious are also lowly in social standing is generally true in Bethnal Green (cf. Fuller 1992: 239, Pocock 1973: 39). Nascent belief can be realised, however, by the occasion of misfortune in almost any person, and this is more likely to take hold, as with gossip, if they are socially mobile. In other words, those in stable social positions may also have stable beliefs that correspond with their level and type of education, but those who are socially mobile in Bethnal Green are susceptible to belief contingent on personal circumstances.

Babies must be brought to our clinic for regular checks from birth onwards. During the first examination by the doctor, black dots of ink can be seen on their heads that have been shaved to ritually cleanse the child of the mother's polluting *naffar* (female genital tract fluids). If asked, parents explain that this spot protects the child from evil eye; it is more or less a routine procedure for new babies and does not indicate that the parents are particularly anxious. A *tabiz* may also be pinned to the infant's clothes particularly if there has been any neonatal illness. Likewise healthy babies' bottles are covered and mothers are uncomfortable if the Health Visitor makes pleasantries in public about the visible health of an infant, "*Marshah Allah*" mothers mutter under their breath to avert the *nozzor* that might be attracted by such a pronouncement.

Sickness caused by *nozzor* in older children and adults may be understood by the family as socio-spiritual misfortune but this does not preclude using orthodox medical treatment as part of the overall management of the problem. The doctor may be alerted to the possibility of spiritual misfortune when anxiety about illnesses persists despite what would seem to be an adequate explanation of the cause and reasonable prescriptions of orthodox medicines.

A child with intractable and disfiguring eczema is brought by her mother over and over again to see me as well as visiting a hospital specialist. The family typically presents *en masse* and has a habit of crowding in on me, engaging me closely, physically as well as emotionally. They lean over my desk in a cluster, interrupting each other before one has finished speaking and do little to restrain younger siblings who explore my computer and cupboards distractingly. I explain once more what it is that I advise them to do for the child's skin with a somewhat repetitive tedium. They reply hesitantly, equivocating, the child swings around on one foot looking embarrassed and her mother fixes my gaze with piercing intensity. I ask her outright what *she* thinks is the cause of this problem, '*Ki jat bemar?*' She says it is *nozzor*. Pressed to be specific it turns out that the child's 'cousin brother' (*mama ghoro bhai*) had wanted to marry her but the family would not countenance the match so he gave the evil eye *'nozzor disse'*. They had got *tabiz* from a *mullah* and performed prayers but without any help, ("And he charged £50"). It seems that nothing more can be done at present and while they continue to press me for new kinds of treatment they are resigned to the chronicity of the child's illness.

The disclosure of the spiritual dimension did not, in this case, afford any relief nor did it alter the way that the family persisted with trying anything on offer that might help their daughter. Spiritual remedies do not always work and the healers, as far as I can gather, have a similar case-mix of acute and chronic patients as orthodox practitioners (cf. Parkin 1995: 154). At times, however, the explicit discussion of *nozzor* with a medical doctor can enable the patient to make efforts to improve their health.

A young Bengali man telephoned the emergency service late at night. His symptoms of headache and difficulties with vision and use of his arms could possibly have been due to serious neurological disease such as a tumour. However, further questioning revealed that the problem was chronic and the precise diagnosis had proved elusive despite examinations by several other doctors. It was hardly appropriate for him to call urgently after hours just because his symptoms had worsened slightly. He skilfully directed the conversation in accentless English so that it proved impossible to persuade him to wait until he could see his own doctor the following morning. He arrived at the hospital with his wife, anxious young children and his parents together with two brothers forming a silent, self-conscious and unusually numerous group for a late-night consultation. Only the patient spoke and my assessment, after due process, that this was a troublesome but not serious musculoskeletal problem, was easily understood by the patient. It seemed that he had heard similar diagnoses from other doctors. He was slight in build, calm and careful in his demeanour; face to face he was a little more superior and less ingratiating and familiar in his tone and manner in comparison to our telephone conversation. I concluded that his pain was caused by his admitted excessive use of body-building weights, betraying an anxiety, as it seemed to me, about both his physical and social stature. During the course of the examination a large cluster of *tabiz* were impossible to ignore as they were tied round his waist and both arms on fresh violet coloured threads. Many, if not most, Bengali patients will have one or two *tabiz* on a black thread around the neck together with jewellery, safety pins and other oddments, so this man's threads stood out in their freshness and bright colouring.

"You've obviously been to someone else as well", I said. "Yes, a spiritual healer" he responded with a little self-deprecation, "Sometimes they can help, you've got to try everything". He trailed off with an air of despondency, prompting me to offer polite and sympathetic general agreement to his remarks. I asked what the healer's diagnosis had been. At this the older brother woke up a bit from his passivity and said, "It was *'nozzor'* - that means, if someone is doing very well, someone else may be jealous and curse you". The healer, by their report, had thought something 'inside' was wrong. The story unfolded that the patient was accelerating through his career in the local civil service but this had been suddenly halted three months previously when his illness caused him to take time off work. He showed emotion for the first time by saying that on account of this pain he was behind with his work although he was confident of his eventual achievements. A cousin who was less fortunate was thought to be to blame for harming him. I accepted this explanation but suggested that practical measures to improve his problem might also help in conjunction with the spiritual methods that they were using and this in combination with acceptance rather than rejection of the co-existent *nozzor* afforded visible relief.

This young man shows that the spiritual and physical dimensions of *nozzor* are joined. Since they had only recently seen the *mullah* it might be thought that they should have given his remedy a little longer to work before asking to see a medical doctor. This is faulty logic, however, because if the *nozzor* effect is serious the subsequent illness might be imminently fatal, hence the urgency in seeking orthodox medical help while the *tabiz* would disperse the underlying cause in due course.

6.4.2 DISCUSSION

Nozzor is pervasive because the perpetrators can be provoked to harmful looks by a pang of jealousy sparked off quite unconsciously by a chance encounter in public places. On the whole it is not imagined that people behave in a deliberate instrumental manner to engender *nozzor*. The inability to suppress jealousy may be disliked, or considered a character fault, but it is not in itself sinful (*goona*). If a baby does not thrive, then *nozzor* may be adduced as the cause, even though no occasion of harm can be recalled, nor any likely perpetrator identified. Where the likely person can be guessed at, as in the examples given, they are usually socially close kin or acquaintances. It is, however, useless to confront them for their envy cannot be neutralised nor their emotions denied once a certain level of animosity has been aroused. There is no system of exposing those who give *nozzor* and resolution cannot be achieved through a process of naming and shaming. Apart from the black spots, *tabiz* and coverings, only a firm confidence in personal invulnerability can render someone proof to the free-floating negativity of others' jealousy (cf. Pocock 1973: 36).

In India and Bethnal Green, powerful and rich men are largely proof to *nozzor* and poor women are very likely to be both targets and suspects (Fuller 1992: 239). Structural inequalities do not, however, inevitably give rise to *nozzor*: the envious do not always give *nozzor*, nor do the paranoid always suffer. As with gossip, it is occasioned by the *conjunction* of one person's awareness of their vulnerability in the vicinity of someone who is alert to this self-consciousness. Pocock's account of *najar* in a Gujerati village illustrates pungently the reciprocal relations between those who are recurrent victims and those who are recurrently accused of *najar*. The 'chorus' in his evocative description are the ordinary villagers who discount the importance of structural positions in favour of remaining proof to fearfulness thus avoiding any embroilment with evil eye (Pocock 1973: 30). Fuller's review of *najar* in India accords with the recurrent finding of an emphasis on the victim's vulnerability through their own 'internal disposition' as a partial explanation of the selection of victims. Fuller also notes that awareness of evil eye is sometimes seen as a device which acts as a 'brake on the ostentatious flaunting of success' (Fuller 1992: 238-9). In Bethnal Green, it is certainly commonly understood that it is the reciprocal relationship between someone with a weak and anxious personality, or who is temporarily so disposed, and another who is troubled enough (again by permanent disposition or temporary circumstances), to feel easily jealous that realises the process of *nozzor*. Moreover in Bethnal Green the correlation of fixed social position and *nozzor* does not apply as closely as in the relative stability of an Indian village. Those who are noticeably changing their social status are more likely to move into the line of fire than those who are settled.

If it is, in the end, all about envy, does it matter whether the envy is apportioned to the perpetrator or is seen as a projection of the victim's paranoia? (see Freud quoted in Dundes 1981: 195). Is the attempt to place the moment in which *nozzor* is realised in the inter-subjectivity of victim and perpetrator a more accurate and illuminating analysis, or just a prim avoidance of apportioning blame? I argue that a shift away from the question as to whether envy or fear in one or other party causes *nozzor* towards an examination of the inter-subjectivity of *nozzor* practice is helpful for three reasons. Firstly, it ends the unresolved oscillation between whether fear or envy has the upper hand in this society (and therefore why the society is unusually, in the scale of things, paranoid or envious). Secondly, this move returns us to the question of why the eye is the significant body part in *nozzor*.

Eye contact is the most mutual non-physical body-practice in public spaces. The giving of *nozzor* does not depend on mutual eye contact but I am here talking about what the entire script enjoins or proscribes. The substitute eyes (such as painted black spots) which attract and deflect *nozzor*, unlike the hidden armour of *tabiz*, do speak of potential mutual eye contact which is side-stepped. From the point of view of the fearful potential victim, direct eye contact with someone who is socially unequal engenders a moment of uncomfortable self-awareness:

> "[M]utual looking is a basic mechanism for intersubjectivity because to look into another's eyes is not just to see the other, but to see the other seeing you." (Gell 1998: 120).

This mutual awareness effaces the safety of customary boundaries and, in the case of *nozzor*, dangerously.

Thirdly, the move away from the dualism of envy and fear allows consideration of alternative inter-subjective modes of managing unequal relationships. *Nozzor*, considered as an available practice in the social environment, perhaps kinaesthetically learned (Jackson 1983), is a way of acting in certain types of relationships for some, but not all Bengali people. The *nozzor* 'script' does not primarily encourage people to find targets and 'take them out'. In the first instance, preventative care is enjoined for both parties in order to avert the occurrence of harm. For believers, the *nozzor* script is a practice that allows distance to be maintained from those with whom it is difficult to stay on good terms because of status asymmetry. Sceptics must manage without this practice and can take pride in their ability to do so; even *nozzor*-believers state that it is admirable to be fearless and self-confident about such matters. People who are aware that they are likely to be uncovered as a little smug and self satisfied may then fall in with a way of acting in public that prevents discovery by using the *nozzor* script for action, and the same holds for people who are easily made self-aware of their enviousness. The script, of course, may not always play out according to the wishes and desires of one or other party, in which case the *nozzor* moment of harm is realised and its consequences rationalised *post hoc*.

The evil-eye does not, then, denote a paranoid or envious society but one in which ways of avoiding social difficulty include a scripted, ritual avoidance (which may sometimes fail and therefore reinforces the need for close observance of the practice) as well as a more ideal, unscripted (or less ritually prescribed) mode of addressing awkward social encounters. If *nozzor* comes out into the open, avoidance strategies are lost, the gloves are off so to speak and the damaging effects of envy debilitate the fearful victim. There is time and scope, however, for the negative cycle to be turned around by personal or assisted efforts to weaken or eliminate the effects of *nozzor*. Less easy to countermand are the purposeful harmful actions of *jinn*, or of those who engage *jinn* (*jadhu-kor*) to prosecute their evil ambitions.

6.5 Jinn

6.5.1 DESCRIPTION

Allah created mankind, the angels and then *jinn* (in Sylheti, *assib*). In this era they cannot die and are invisible except to adepts, unless they inhabit by possession a human body. When this world ends, however, they will be mortal while humans will enjoy eternal life. Some *jinn* are good, (*momin* or *muslim*) and may be *pirs*, *mullahs* or *ilim*, and some are wicked (*kharaf*). There are innumerable sub-groups of *jinn*. This sort of information, and the extent to which it is shared by the general Bengali population, is only gained in question and answer sessions with specialists from which it is difficult to contextualise the catalogue of knowledge.

For most sufferers, '*jinn-bemar*' (*jinn*-illness) without qualification is sufficient explanation and the exact sub-category of the noxious *jinn* is superfluous information. Of greater importance is the social context and immediate circumstance that precipitates *jinn* activity. The majority of Bengali people will accept the notion of *jinn* but the immediacy of the belief, the palpable fear of *jinn* possibilities and the effects of their actions varies from individual to individual. As with gossip and *nozzor* we cannot read off the likelihood of belief in *jinn* from social class and educational achievement but there is a general alignment, as with gossip and *nozzor*, such that middle-class professionals know about *jinn* as part of their religious knowledge and those with less education are more likely to see *jinn* at work in their everyday lives (cf. Parry 1994: 246). Again, latent belief turns into palpable experience more commonly among those who are making changes: social mobility brings you into the spiritual firing line more significantly in Bethnal Green than the fact of occupying an advantageous but stable social position.

Whereas *nozzor* causes wasting illnesses, failure to thrive, weakness and lassitude, *jinn*-possession illness is violent. Common manifestations of possession are headaches, fits and a feeling of one's head spinning (*matta gurray*). In more extreme cases people lose their minds (*mon nai*) and become psychotic (madness, *fagoll*). The hallucinations and delusions of acute schizophrenics of any background frequently feature indigenous religious discourses (Littlewood 1998: 197) and Bengali psychotics may be seen chanting religious texts, calling on Allah, dancing, praying with beads, their hair and clothes in shameful disarray. Their appearance and deportment is in sharp contrast with the habitual quiet piety of five times a day Islamic prayers (*namaz*). This contrast fuels the conviction among onlookers that a religious battle is being fought within the sufferer's body between forces of good and evil. *Jinn-bemar* may be quiescent (cf. Parry 1994: 235) or detectable in less flamboyant cases only by a change in character, subtle changes in habitual facial expression, and altered behaviour. Lastly *jinn* may be sent by others to cause illness without possession and these are catastrophic, life-threatening illnesses: unconsciousness, strokes, heart attacks and sudden death.

Possession for a *jinn's* capricious pleasure is well known and the subject of many typical stories. Music, dancing and loud noises attract the attention and interest of *jinn*, and once certain excitable individuals are in an emotional state, if not adequately protected, or despite efforts to shield them, *jinn* are very liable to take them (*jinn dowrse*; the passive construction, to be possessed, is expressed as *jinn lagse*). A *mullah* told me a story of events which took place in his village in Bangladesh:

> The youngest of six brothers, known to be volatile in personality, started behaving like a madman. A *mullah* was called and found that he was not mad but, as suspected, possessed by a female *jinn* who wanted to marry him. The use of *tabiz* did not rid the man of possession but attracted fourteen other *jinn*, each worse and more disfiguring than the last. These frightened the *mullah* who ran away. The fourteen *jinn* said they would not leave unless the female *jinn* came back and married the boy. Exorcism was finally achieved when another mullah advised ritual bathing in deep clean water. While the boy was in a possessed state, however, he provided an open conduit to the network of *jinn* knowledge and so the family was pestered by the needy who tried to get his *jinn* to answer questions about their own problems (cf. Parry 1994: 241).

Jinn are not wholly disliked: they can be devout and helpful as well as malicious but even irritating wilful *jinn*, if accessible through possession, can supply knowledge to those who lack the skills, resources and nerve to employ them on a regular basis. If someone is not possessed, those who want *jinn* assistance have to go to the trouble and expense of finding someone who can summon *jinn* through a medium or converse with them without being possessed.

The worst effects of *jinn* follow the malicious acts of a *jadhu-kor*, someone who practices black magic. Those who deliberately manipulate *jinn* to do others harm combine the worst effects of gossip and *jinn*. The *jinn*-communication system is much more effective than gossip and the harm they can do is more direct and dramatic than the chronic malaise engendered by *nozzor*. Those who suffer *jinn* effects are also likely to attract gossip.

> A woman staying temporarily in a refuge, hiding from her violent husband, new to my list of patients, told me in broken English that she suffered from bodily aches and pains as well as heavy periods. She used the English word 'tension' to describe her feelings. I asked if she meant *sintha* (anxiety), and she was startled by the Sylheti word. She switched to Sylheti and her face became grave, her voice lowered while she told me that her sister-in-law (*nonhori*) had used a *jadhu* and this had changed her husband's face (*mouk boddlaise*) overnight. Before, he had been so kind (*ze*

maya), but now he was violent and cruel. She did not know why the sister-in-law had done this.

Her story echoed many others of women in similar circumstances. Another woman, be it the husband's lover or his older sister, is often blamed for the changing fortunes of a married couple or the break-up of a marriage. Many couples or siblings do not get on and quarrel from time to time; the hallmark of *jinn* at work is the sudden volte-face as a husband or brother who had hitherto been so kind and loving alters overnight and becomes a fiend. This sudden change of face is an important theme in stories of possession. Sufferers commonly speak with longing and nostalgia for the days when their loved one returned affection and wore a kind expression. All at once the change seems to occur without any reasonable explanation; the ill-feeling does not grow slowly or build in paranoid schismogenesis like gossip but strikes all of a sudden.

The aspect of a person's face is given particular metonymic value as a key to Bengali notions of character and personality. During a séance I attended, the possessed medium (*tullarashi*) altered his physiognomy in a remarkable way, more like the skilled mimic's alteration of face than simply grimacing. In daily life, those who express one thing by facial expression but whose speech conveys another meaning are noticed and distrusted. Changeability of visage causes anxiety whereas the dead-pan dignified face of an elder is the hallmark of probity and reliability. In domestic settings I have observed Bengali people use abrupt change in face and vocal style in a teasing or admonishing way to cause consternation in others. The change does not denote an enduring change in mood: they slip back into casual conversational mode just as suddenly. Change of face thus takes on particular significance in stories of possession where it is a record of the effect of the *jinn* who cunningly displaces the real person. Aggrieved wives do not say of their possessed husbands that the spirit *made him* stop loving her but that possession has displaced their husband's personality within his body. A possessed person, the husband in the above case, may have no insight into the matter but the wronged wife knows exactly what has been at work to destroy their harmonious family life. In this way the loved husband or brother is not lost from view for there is hope that he will be restored if a remedy can be found and the *jinn* ejected. Successful exorcism allows the person to be restored to their normal state of individuality and relation to others without lengthy readjustment (cf. the arduous time-scale of psychotherapy).

In many cases where a woman has been abandoned or abused, however, the charms, spells and prayers do not work and such cases become chronic. The *mullah* may protest that the *jinn* in such cases are too powerful for their skills. A state of paralysis ensues whereby the woman has no-one else to turn to for redress. Living alone with her children she is considered with suspicion by neighbours whose friendliness is superficial. The gossips get to work and feed her paranoia. Her chronic 'neurotic' attitude only confirms their view that she is unstable. For many, the situation of poverty and marginalisation continues for years and the children are caught up in cycles of deprivation and dysfunctional relationships. It is useless, as with gossip and *nozzor*, to expose the wrong-doer for this will not prevent them from using black magic over and over again. From time to time the wronged woman hears from third parties, who do not try to spare her feelings, that she is still being cursed.

This is, in many ways, as accurate a description, or 'reflection' in a spiritual modality, of the social situation of many single Bengali mothers in Bethnal Green. These women cannot make use of the general supportive counselling which is offered by social workers or doctors or mental health nurses since the work of these professionals is premised on adjustment of a patient's attitude, feelings and conduct in relationships rather than prosecuting the wrongdoer (unless the woman wishes to undertake legal proceedings). In the Bengali view, however, unless the other party is halted in their wrongdoing, supportive therapy alone is unlikely to work and the victim remains mired in misery. Meanwhile it is not difficult for unknowingly possessed husbands to maintain a respectable position in society so that even 'known' wife-batterers and child-abusers can continue a normal life since the *jinn* ensures that others are taken in by his 'face' of respectability.

> The youngest of eight brothers, a waiter, told me that the restaurant owner often bullied him. He came to me for a certificate so he could stay at home because he felt *durbol*, (weakness, enervated). My exploration of his quiet, polite and meek personality and his previous experiences in similar situations prompted him to talk about his family. Being the youngest, his brothers were normally supportive and loving but one day the face of the second eldest changed. This man called a meeting of all the brothers to dispute their rights over jointly held land in their village in Bangladesh. Dismayed by the overbearing attitude of his brothers, the youngest offered to hand over his portion hoping to mollify them. He felt that giving up land would be a small price to pay in order to enjoy once again their *addor* (benignity of seniors towards juniors). His hopes were not fulfilled and his altruism was heartlessly overlooked so he consulted a *mullah* who told him that jealous villagers had ensorcelled his brothers against him. An article, taken on his brother's last visit to the village, had been ritually buried in order to allow manipulation of events through *jinn*. The young man now feels despondent: the *mullah* told him that his brothers are obdurate because they pretend not to believe in *jinn*. This makes the perpetrators' control all the more deadly, for unless the possessed man agrees to wear a *tabiz*, nothing can be done. Interestingly this stubborn brother has reason to despise the *jinn* system although he may not actually be a sceptic: he recently took his daughter to be examined by a *mullah* so that he could

declare her possessed but she told me that the *mullah* declined to do as her father wished.

6.5.2 REDRESS

The manipulation of *jinn* through unorthodox practices is frowned upon by Islamic specialists from mosques since it encourages a superstitious form of heresy which distracts the congregation away from the five pillars of Islam which are the only route to salvation. Mosque *mullahs* do not deny the existence of *jinn*, far from it, but to believe that they account for every kind of misfortune and to engage in séances and related activities is superstitious and sinful (cf. Parry 1994: 246). Pious Muslims should not stoop to credulousness and risky dabbling in the spirit underworld. Seeking information about others through *jinn* is foolish but the employment of *jinn* to hurt enemies is not only risky it is also *goona* (sinful). Despite such reasoning, many seek immediate help for their difficulties through magic rather than waiting for the slower and less certain outcome of devout prayer (cf. Gardner 1993b). Just as doctors do not hand over pills without some minimal notion of a therapeutic relationship, so the skills of adepts in *jinn* business cannot be exploited without the supplicant participating in the *mullahs'* therapeutic nexus.

A young man knocked on the door of an unorthodox *mullah* at midnight asking for help as his wife had run away. Theirs was a love match without the approval of their parents but they had had a mosque blessing as well as a registry office wedding. His father had become ill in Bangladesh so he went urgently to visit him. On his return to Bethnal Green he discovered that his wife had been brought home to her parents' house on the initial pretext that her sister was ill and then she had stayed or been kept there for unspecified reasons. The *mullah* told the young man that it was late and he was tired for he had had troubles of his own that week and doubted that he had the strength to do anything that night. The young man begged for help so the *mullah* made a *tabiz*. He wrote a spell, meticulously copying the Assamese text and diagram from a book his *ustaad* (teacher) had sent to him from Bangladesh. He wrote it in coloured ink on birch bark, aggravating his chronic writer's cramp. The scroll was sealed into a metal container, given to the man and money was refused, "You can pay me when your wife returns to your house". With scant regard for the older man's tiredness and generosity, the young man made a further request, "Can you see if anything is wrong with me?" Again the *mullah* tried to refuse but the man was insistent so he fetched some uncooked rice and put it into the young man's hand to hold. When the man then opened his hand holding the rice he shook all over and nearly collapsed. The boy gasped and said that he never knew this sort of thing could happen; the *mullah* then flicked water over him and sent him home. The *mullah* told this last part of the story with pride in his powers even when he had been in an exhausted state. The next day the young man returned and said he had not slept all night and felt very strange but was hopeful that he would be reunited with his wife. As he finished telling me the story, the *mullah* told me that he had seen that the boy had a *jinn* living within him, but he had refrained from making the *jinn* speak out, and he thinks the prognosis is poor.

Why does this particular man have a *jinn* possession diagnosis when he only asked for a magical charm of some sort to force his in-laws to release his wife once they had proved obdurate to negotiation? Until he knocked on the door of the *mullah,* the matter was apparently entirely social. The young man raised the notion of psychological manipulation through false news of a sick relative rather than the idea that his in-laws had used supernatural means. Once the charm had been made, however, he felt inclined to submit himself to the *mullah's* diagnostic process for an unspecified reason. We do not know enough to say who had suggested to him that there was something wrong. He appears to be judged as a naive and likely *jinn*-victim by the *mullah*: for his taking such an instrumental view of the adept's practice, for overlooking the adept's needs (his tiredness) and for his rushing in thoughtlessly to his own diagnostic ritual. The young man may have thought he was getting a quick fix, but became enmeshed in a more complex set of relationships than he could have anticipated.

It is quite legitimate for good Muslims, when faced with a chronic medical problem such as headaches or asthma, *nozzor* or *jinn-bemar,* to go to the mosque and ask for advice about spiritual help for their illness. Sylheti people are nearly all Sunni Muslims and do not need priests to perform ritual effects or to intercede between themselves and Allah. The various religious experts who are associated with the mosques (*ilima, mullahs, imams, muftis,* and so on) are resources of knowledge and not instrumental practitioners. Their roles include giving religious advice, guidance, leading prayer sessions (*zoomma*) and performing recitations of the Koran. A *mullah* will discuss supplicants' problems in social and religious terms and usually enjoin close observance of Islamic practice and prayer. They may also give a passage of the Koran to be worn within a small metal case on a thread on the body. These *tabiz* may look just like unorthodox charms but they differ in meaning: whereas unorthodox charms are thought to work in a magical sense, the orthodox *tabiz* are purely symbols of religious faith. They display in material form the protection afforded by Allah who recognises piety through such practices but they do not have intrinsic magical power. The wearers of orthodox *tabiz* should not expect immediate results as do those who wear the magical variety nor should they attend séances or other illicit rituals. Many do not have the patience to wait until ordinary piety bears fruit so there are plenty of customers for instrumental spirit practitioners.

The history of syncretism between Hinduism and Islam in Bengal, and notions of 'Great' and 'Little' traditions of Islamic orthopraxy and local customs has been debated extensively (see R. Ahmed 1988, Barton 1986, Eade 1994, Murshid 1995, Rozario 1992). Ahmad (1984) emphasises the importance of purely local analysis whereas Robinson (1983) and Ellickson (1972) stress the continuous tensions between orthopraxy and local traditions against Das (1984) and Minault's (1984) views (see also Barton 1986: 34). Eickelman (1982: 12) underlines the importance in ethnographic research of discovering why one interpretation of Islam is considered more normative than others at particular times and places, rather than looking for a comparative typology of 'islams' (see also Bowen 1993: 7, el-Zein 1977). The continued tension between two Islamic traditions, both in Bangladesh and London, is expressed in the contrast between the two largest mosques in Tower Hamlets. The East London mosque is multi-ethnic, representing 'World Islam' and looks to Saudi Arabia for support whereas the Brick Lane mosque has a Bengali congregation and is oriented to the state of Bangladesh (Eade 1994, Gardner 1995). In Bethnal Green, as in the United Kingdom as a whole, there is evidence of increasing interest and adherence to non-Bangladeshi World Islam, particularly among the younger generation (Eade 1998). Young Muslims educated in Britain who attend the East London mosque say that they have more confidence in a religious institution that does not have nationalist (Bangladeshi) connections. They also experience, positively, the *umma*, or world-community of Islam in multi-ethnic prayer sessions.

Gardner draws a parallel between the transformations that may be effected by religious intermediaries (*pirs*) in Bangladesh and those brought about by migration through economic intermediaries in the world. Successful emigrants returning to Bangladesh reinterpret the role of the *pirs* along orthodox lines, enhancing their own status as 'purist' Muslims, and giving further emphasis to the distinction between two forms of Islamic practice in Bangladesh (Gardner 1993b). Nonetheless there has not been a decline in demand for those who can offer help through unorthodox spiritual practices outside Bangladesh and so the same binary religious formation of Islam obtains in Bethnal Green as well as in Bangladesh.

Unofficial spirit manipulators are numerous in the East End and other cities with significant Bengali populations. Patients think nothing of travelling to Birmingham or Bradford to see a specialist with a particular reputation. These are experts in the use of *tabiz* and exorcism as well as having skill in commanding *jinn* to assist the afflicted. They may also be herbal and naturopathic practitioners (*khobiraj*). Their tasks are, broadly speaking, four-fold. Firstly they are diagnosticians of all kinds of illness. Secondly they use spells, charms and other techniques to treat illnesses whether they are wholly *uffri-bemar*, or partly physical. In the main these are chronic illnesses such as asthma, high blood pressure, stroke or skin complaints where ordinary medicines cannot effect a cure. Thirdly, informal *mullahs* use *jinn* to gather social information. They may do this through séances using a medium to divine a particular case, or they may communicate directly with *jinn* on an occasional or regular basis for specific enquiries or routine reports. Fourthly, the *mullah* can use *jinn* who are willing to be in their service to control the behaviour of other people. It is a serious sin to use *jinn* to harm others out of spite, but retrieving an errant wife or daughter, or striking down a delinquent son by *jinn*-control can be justified (not by the most orthodox). Likewise engaging a *jinn* to do battle with *jadhu-kor* who are sinfully attacking clients is also legitimate where a *tabiz* alone is insufficient.

The *mullah* may have an *ustaad* or mentor who updates and supervises their practice. There is no fixed canon of spells and magical practices. Many use similar techniques such as blowing on water, giving the patient a handful of rice to hold, writing out *tabiz* texts and so on, but there is a demand for newly imported, more powerful charms which are thought to outwit experienced *jinn*. These enable the practitioner to keep ahead of the competition for there are many *mullahs* in the business throughout the UK. Bengali newspapers carry advertisements posted by these practitioners. The imported spells are often Hindu, originating in Assam (a place particularly associated with magical lore) or other parts of India via *ustaads* in Bangladesh who send texts in foreign or ancient scripts accompanied by arcana, mantra or diagrams and drawings of powerful *jinn*. Whether these are true antiquities or invented 'traditional' mantra, they are more powerful than those currently in circulation. Reasonable *mullahs* with a social conscience or astute business sense accept payments on a no-win no-fee basis. Others ask for payments varying from £25 to £200 or more depending on the scale of the problem and the dangers involved for the practitioner.

Khobiraj and spiritual adepts are mostly, but not exclusively, male. It can be a vocation of the afflicted as already described. The families of those called to this sort of work are not usually happy about their career because it is not only arduous but also dangerous. There are many in *jinn* society who are not pleased to have their pitches queered: they watch the *mullah* and his family for any chinks in their armour of spells and *tabiz* and strike a blow whenever possible. During the management of one very difficult case the entire family of a *mullah* had to stay indoors without washing or cooking for a week. Doors are bolted and barred against lesser *jinn* and their spies but this is nothing for the more powerful spirits which appear at will in the guise of a human despite such precautions. The following notes give some idea of the variety of tasks that make up the casework of this type of *mullah*:

> A *mullah* and his wife felt generally poorly and out of sorts. They summoned a *jinn* and sent him to Bangladesh. In the family's village they found that jealous fellow villagers had buried an article as part of a spell to

cause them harm. The *jinn* took about an hour to go to Bangladesh and back retrieving the harmful object which was then destroyed.

A patient with chronic chest disease showed me an object that a *mullah* had obtained from her throat. It looked like a piece of bone which could not have lodged there for long without causing serious illness. The laboratory report said that it was non-specific organic material.

A client asked the *mullah* to help find the gangster who had mugged his son. *Jinn* assisted the *mullah* who was able to chase the gangster at speed in his car by making the police blind to his speeding.

A father knew that his daughter was possessed from her altered and excitable mood. The *mullah* eliminated two out of the three *jinn* but the last remained lurking in his own house and he had difficulty finding it.

A relative of the *mullah* felt hot all over and his head started to spin. He immediately called in the healer and during a short visit the blowing of water over his body eliminated the problem.

A lengthy séance using a *tullarashi* summoned a *jinn* to help diagnose a marriage problem. The conduct of the séance went awry because of the *jinn* teasing and messing about, impersonating other *jinn* and calling in his friends to take joint possession of the medium. The séance was abandoned.

On a daily basis, several of a *mullah's* clients can be dealt with on the phone by advising them to rotate the wearing of the several *tabiz* that have been already given, or promising to leave another *tabiz* for them. Others ring to report good results.

As with *nozzor*, it is not necessary to know exactly who is sending harmful *jinn* in order to effect a remedy. It is easier if you do know for certain but counter-magic operates by deflecting harm directly back on itself and will therefore hit the target with automatic precision. This is what makes dealings with *jinn* dangerous, for sudden death may strike the perpetrator if the spiritual weapon is deflected by a powerful *tabiz* or if a spiteful *jinn* is foiled by a protective spell and returns to kill the sender in anger. All who deal with *jinn* take care to perform their tasks in private, often at night, behind closed or locked doors. Here, as with primary preventative measures, the material and spiritual worlds merge from a technological perspective. Physical concealment is not an effective barrier to *jinn* who can irrupt into a house despite locked and bolted solid doors. The point is that the *attention* of *jinn*, and those who might conjure them can be evaded if your behaviour is unnoticeable. *Jinn* are powerful but they are not all-wise, all-seeing entities and can be manipulated by psychological means, coaxing, teasing, subterfuge and threats of violence as much as human beings. Careful attention to boundaries and coverings, if skilfully deployed, may conceal inner disturbances and perturbations which in their dramatic potential excite the careless gaze of others who just might be nearby.

Access to social information is key to the successful *mullah's* work and depends on the extent of the relationships they can sustain with unpredictable and risky *jinn*. Astute social judgement based on copious information garnered from a busy communication network ensures correct selection of the most amenable cases and good results. By report it is not uncommon for an adept to make a diagnosis but to decline to take on the case. The intractability of the problem (when they have learned of all the circumstances) is rationalised as denoting the power of the malignant *jinn*-in-service. Competition for business means that they cannot afford to have too many failures in their case-books and it is better to retire with dignity than to be defeated in public.

A *mullah's* reputation as spiritual healer is expressed in a deportment which impresses upon others a strong commanding personality, discriminating judgement and courage. Spirit practitioners act as if they were beacons of strength in a world of prevalent disease and misfortune and thus exaggerate the contrast between the strong and the weak. They strive to gain mastery over the most powerful rituals which cause people suddenly to collapse unconscious, or to follow their wishes immediately like automata. Their comportment differs subtly from other senior men in that the dead-pan facial expression of probity is altered by a powerful, almost threatening, gaze (cf. Pocock 1973: 30). The authoritative command of the *mullah* who takes risks in a drama of heroes and villains contrasts with the weak, surrendering, shaking victims. This is a strong version of the hierarchical *addor/shomman* axis of kinship relationships where benign compassionate love (*addor*) is bestowed on juniors who ideally offer unreserved respect (*shomman)* to senior kinspeople.

This integrated set of skills and practices faces new obstacles in Bethnal Green compared to Bangladesh. Although *jinn* are disembodied when not in possession of a person, they do live, partly at least, in the material world. Immigration officers do not hinder the movements of spirits, nor the pangs of jealousy, so misfortune is transposed from Bangladesh to Bethnal Green without the same degree of attenuation and distortion that affects kinship but it is altered nonetheless. Migration to cities affects *jinn* capabilities because of the geographical distances that they have to cover, the built-up city and confusing street lights. The trip to Bangladesh and back for a *jinn* is swift (about an hour) but not instantaneous. Within London, the task of tracing people to obtain information for a human master is not always easy for *jinn*. The cold hard pavements of the city lack the receptive impressionability and warmth of the mud paths in Bangladeshi villages so the trail may run dry, *jinn* lose the scent and fail to track down their quarry. Apart from these minor drawbacks, there is little diminution of the scope and power of *jinn* in London as compared to Bangladesh. If any aspect is thought to be lessened, it is the ability of *jinn* to assist would-be healers rather than their ability to harm.

These explanations of the added difficulties of manipulating *jinn* in Bethnal Green can be interpreted metaphorically to underscore the physical experiences of Bengali people who describe the cold and unsociable nature of the streets of London. The parallels between *jinn* and human sociability are analogous and illustrative but little more can be drawn from such parallels. Rather than making too much of these analogies, the contrasting moralities of human and *jinn* societies are of greater significance for Bengali people in Bethnal Green and should be emphasised.

6.6 Discussion

The commonplace finding that witchcraft and gossip thrive in 'small town' societies, where neighbourly relationships are easily soured, is modulated in this account by the attention paid to the dialectical (almost complicit) relationships between those people who are anxious and those who are willing to foment scandal and prosecute harm. Vulnerability to misfortune has been given as much prominence as the propensity and motivation to perpetrate harm. These kinds of negative relationships stand in contrast to others within the local and transnational Bengali population which do not have recourse to certain spiritual beliefs or the discourse of gossip. This piece of ethnography is not, however, primarily a contribution to the already ample anthropological literature about the nature of reason and belief through the ethnography of gossip, evil-eye, spirit possession, and witchcraft (Boddy 1989, Gluckman 1963, Kapferer 1991, Lambek 1989 and 1993, Lewis 1971, Middleton & Winter 1963, Pocock 1973). Rather, the material presented here serves to elucidate one of the ways in which the predicaments of Bengali people in Bethnal Green are differentially distributed among that population.

Among Bengali people in Bethnal Green a social slight may lead the victim to anticipate gossip or spiritual harm but often it is not until the victim falls ill that they realise such harm is afoot. Bengali people do not constantly dwell on who may be 'out for them' in paranoid fashion and then 'invent' symptoms. Once evil is uncovered it is only possible to send punishment back along the same channels rather than finding a mutually agreeable resolution. There are no witch-hunts although privately everyone knows that *jadhu-kor* will go to hell. This free-floating wickedness and the fact that gossips and the like are not commonly unmasked means that the scope of evil is theoretically unlimited.

The best protection is afforded by a robust personality. The simple act of wearing a *tabiz* already indicates a self-awareness of susceptibility to the harm of others and increases the likelihood of being a target. Even the most confident personalities cannot be entirely proof for a strong character may be attacked by affliction being visited upon close relatives who have more vulnerable personalities. I have referred to Giddens' (1991: 35ff.) notion of ontological security as a theoretical model for this effect. Indigenous understandings of anxiety (*sintha*) corroborate his theory.

If someone gives in to profound worry and despair (*sintha*), Bengali people perceive a risk of fatal sequelae in the form of heart attacks or madness. This is again clearly distinguishable by Bengali people from all other types of illness through reading the patient's facial expression. The altered physiognomy of the *sintha* sufferer betrays an internally generated illness, easily distinguishable from stress-related problems (*zamilla*, *zontoronna*) which are external in aetiology. *Sintha* represents the foundering of an individual's primary relationship in the world: their own self-regard and practical consciousness. This failure of one's primary relationship with self is the model from which all the other harmful social relationships follow. Any breakdown in ideally harmonious and loving relationships opens the door to disease and destruction. The difficulty lies in maintaining self-confidence in difficult circumstances while keeping a discreet weather-eye open for harm from others.

It can be seen that the role of *jinn* in cases of possession is analogous to those of *bhut*, *pey* or *preta* in India. There are, however, important differences most particularly in that pious Muslims do not believe that the ghosts of the dead can possess the living (excepting the ghosts of concealed infanticide victims). Some violent possession episodes in Bethnal Green and Bangladesh could be described as imaginative public demonstrations of social tensions, resistance, or the need for strong social control (Gardner 1995: 254) which lend themselves to dramaturgical re-ordering of local social relations (Kapferer 1991). There are, however, no voluntary possessions which bear comparison to Lambek's account of possession in Mayotte (1989 & 1993) or Boddy's account (1989) of *zar* cult practices (see also Nourse 1996 and Placido 2001). The Bengali mediums who submit to adepts' manipulations are not in the same accommodative relationship with the spirits which inhabit them as Mayotte mediums. The lack of emphasis on possession as a source of alternative social discourse does not mean that Bengali spirit affliction is entirely an anthropology of evil (Parkin 1985). *Jinn* may assist the pious Bengali person without possession and some involuntary possessions may assist those who can thereby gain access to the spirit world for entirely moral purposes. The fact remains, however, that the disruptive effect of possession on what are considered to be normative social relationships is far more prominent in my ethnography than anything which could be described as a socially useful communicative discourse.

Possession, in the Bengali spirit sense, takes people (*dowrrse*) and reconfigures networks of people and spirits (cf. Strathern 1996). Capricious *jinn* possession dissociates the victim from normal society: the flow of quotidian social connections is halted but, if the attack is not fatal, or if it is controlled, may open up useful spirit networks. Even more scandalous, then, is the deliberate action of an enemy who employs black magic directly or through an adept in order to interfere with the 'natural' course of relations.

The *jinn*-human creature, deliberately fashioned, does not merely *reflect* bad feeling in the family as is the case with *nozzor*, nor is it only a generic strain-gauge of social upset but represents a problem for which the exact causes can be divined by adepts (cf. Parry 1994: 233ff.). This does not, however, tell us why possession took place rather than an ordinary dispute, apart from the possibility of circumlocution and the drama of the exorcism (should it take place). In the change-of-face mode of possession, the victim is not crudely chopped off and completely dissociated from the whole human world. Rather, they are carefully excised by the *jadhu-kor-jinn* partnership from some branches of their social network and left connected to others, those favourable to the *jinn*-sender. Control of *jinn* is thus a powerfully precise remote (third-party) instrument of social technology (cf. Gell 1988 and 1998). The ruthless intention of the person using *jinn* through an intermediary contrasts with the near complicity of *nozzor* and gossip relationships.

An alternative to discourse theory in the analysis of gossip and spiritual harm is the decoding of the sociology of the multifarious and not always easily discernible patterns of human social relations through the more condensed and pungent spiritual events revealed through ethnographic research. The explanatory model is one where informants provide the anthropologist with an idiomatic rendition of social relationships which are troublesome or in crisis and are therefore awkward or difficult to express in blunt propositional speech. Circumlocution or displacement into a dissociated spiritual modality is read as an alternative, often preferred, strategy. This model has the merit of allowing the researcher to strengthen ethnographic insights by recursively cross-checking data from one modality (the quotidian patterns of social relationships) with those discovered in another (spiritual) setting (Gomm 1975, Nabokov 1997, Parry 1994: 191ff, Pocock 1973, Stirrat 1977). Placido points out that this type of analysis risks reflecting current anthropological concerns rather than the events taking place in the field (Placido 2001: 208).

I have not been specific in sociological terms beyond the notion that it is usually persons known to the victim who are suspected of being involved in spiritual harm. My ethnographic data yields a recurrent difficulty between husband's elder sister and younger brother's wife and also elder brother and younger brother (actual siblings or cousins) but cannot be considered extensive enough to make any summary generalisations about the shape of Bengali social problems which are recurrently expressed in spiritual modalities. Rather than large-scale epidemiological categories of persons who might have enduring propensities to do harm, consciously or otherwise, I have stressed the more immediate, moment by moment necessity for people to guard propriety through proper comportment if they hope to ward off spiritual harm in Bethnal Green. The difficulty for transnational families is that the direction of harmful missiles cannot be so easily predicted in the thick and thin distorted social world of Bethnal Green as opposed to the more readable mesh of Bangladeshi village life. It is also difficult to keep track of the tenor of relationships with villagers when living in Bethnal Green; this is another recurrent if diffuse category of likely perpetrators of harm and sources of jealousy.

I have been careful to emphasise that Bengali society, whether in Bethnal Green or Bangladesh, cannot be described wholesale as gossip-ridden, superstitious or envious. The population is diverse in patterns of belief and practice. Bengali informants themselves may generalise and say that strong belief in *nozzor* or habits of gossip are the preserve of the less-educated or those hidebound by superstitious custom; others, conversely, say that those who do not believe are foolish or snobs. It is clear, however, that as the Bengali population has only recently become established in Bethnal Green, the alignment of gossip, *nozzor* and *jinn* effects with particular sociological categories are not easily discerned by anyone. Relations with non-Bengali residents, who themselves make diverse judgements and generalisations about Bengali neighbours and their observable customs, compound these difficulties.

CHAPTER 7: RELATIONS OF DIFFERENCE

7.1 Introduction

Simple inspection of statistical data suggests that racism is the most important constraining factor in determining the salient predicaments of Bengali people in Bethnal Green. While they share with other residents the difficulties of living in an area of highly polarised wealth (for the few) and poverty (for the majority), Bengali people are found disproportionately among the most deprived (Carey & Shukur 1985: 416, Wrench & Qureshi 1996: 63). Given this social fact, it might be thought that this chapter should have been placed earlier in the thesis. The format of an ethnography of people whose lives are pervasively affected by racism (whether aggressive, institutional or banal in its expression) needs careful consideration. In addition to remarks made in Chapter 1, and before embarking on ethnographic illustration, I will discuss the approach which I am adopting with reference to other social science literature about racism. Space precludes a thorough review of such literature, even if it is confined to minority ethnic groups in Britain. Instead, certain themes are emphasised in order to contextualise my particular approach: I make further reference to other aspects of the literature throughout the chapter.

Knauft argues that anthropology pursues two objectives: one is to 'document and valorise the richness and diversity of human ways of life' and the other is to 'expose, analyse, and critique human inequality and domination.' (Knauft 1996: 48-50). These twin objectives are in practice opposed to each other and have opposite excesses. If too much attention is paid to cultural diversity this leads to endless relativity whereas an emphasis on inequality privileges discourses of dis-empowerment and is likely to obscure other kinds of argument and important social facts (ibid.: 52). Knauft notes that Gramscian themes may be recruited by authors who favour the discourse of inequality and Bakhtinian references by those who pay attention to cultural diversity. The problems posed by the dual aims of social science can be traced throughout the history of the discipline. The difficulty is stated succinctly by Durkheim with reference to errors in studies of phenomena generally deemed to be pathological, 'The common flaw in these definitions is their premature attempt to grasp the essence of phenomena' (Durkheim 1966 [1938]: 54). Essence, here, can be seen to refer simultaneously to what are called 'essentialising discourses' and to the nature of relations of inequality, i.e. to both arms of Knauft's dualism.

From the early days of sociology in the USA, the question of race attracted the attention of researchers because of the pressing social problem of 'race relations', particularly in urban settings. The problem of the 'colour bar' similarly prompted early research in Britain (see Banks 1996 for an anthropologist's review of this literature). Support from institutions such as the Commission for Racial Equality fostered extensive sociological research into racism in Britain (Brah 1996: 26). Anthropologists in Britain have studied South Asian populations more often than Afro-Caribbean groups (with the notable exception of Benson 1981, Abner Cohen 1993, Little 1947, and, more recently, Alexander 1996). Studies of black British populations are more usually the preserve of sociologists. This historical division of labour might lead the casual reader to assume that in Britain 'Asians have culture, West Indians have problems' (Benson 1996) and again reflects the conflict between the two arms of Knauft's dualism.

The advent of the notion of multiculturalism, in this sense an idealistic model of nation states containing harmonious mosaics of discrete, bounded cultures, allowed a move away from the baldly stated problem of 'race relations' (see Hesse 2000 for an ample review of the history of multiculturalism in Britain and America). Anti-racism was formerly the opposing term to what was sometimes seen as bland and conservative multiculturalism (Hall 2000: 211). Since 'mosaic' multiculturalism was premised on what some would describe as an old model of cultures (bounded, discrete, internally homogeneous) the notion was partly undermined by 'newer', post-modern ideas of the permeable, mutable and internally heterogeneous nature of cultures (Knauft 1996: 250ff., Wright 1998). The difficulty occasioned by efforts to incorporate fluid and relativistic models of culture to arguments seeking to challenge racial discrimination has already been noted. Another difficulty arises when the ethnographer finds that informants not uncommonly espouse older, bounded and distinctly primordialist version of culture themselves (Banks 1996: 107). This is especially likely to be found in situations (often urban) where the visibility of clearly differentiated cultures affects the deployment of material or political resources (Baumann 1996, Cohen 1974: xi). In order to resolve the contradiction between emic and etic versions of the status quo, multiculturalism has been reformulated as 'strategic essentialising' or 'critical multiculturalism'. This is understood to be a political strategy which actively seeks to redress discrimination by affirmative or other actions, but retains the possibility of theorising cultures along anti-essentialist lines (Turner 1993).

The incompatibility of the dual strands in humanist writings, as distinct from the sphere of political action, is recognised by others, apart from Knauft, as a recurrent source of difficulty which has no universal solution (Alexander 2000, Banks 1996: 178, Baumann 1996 & 1999, Cohen 1974: xvi, Geertz 1973: 30, Gilroy 2000: 241ff., Hall 2000, Hesse 2000, Kuper 1994 & 1999: 232, see also Durkheim's response to the racism of the Dreyfus affair (Durkheim 1973). The tension can be discerned in criticism and counter-criticism throughout the vast literature on racism, ethnicity and multiculturalism. Some see the vogue for recruiting 'anti-essentialising' positions to their argument as no more than 'intellectual pork-barrelling' or politically correct posturing on the part of a cosmopolitan elite (Friedman 1997, see also Caglar 1997, Gilroy 2000: 276, Keith 1995: 562, Kuper

1994). Criticism from the opposite direction is typified by Ballard (1992) who castigates the 'race relations industry', with its focus on oppression and the oppressed, neglecting the 'rich resources of culture' (see also Ballard 1994b: ix). Banton stands out from others in consistently advocating a Durkheimian analysis throughout his career. Racism, in his view, is undeniably a social ill, but for the researcher it is a 'normal social fact' requiring analysis (Banton 1999: 1). Banks notes the merits of Banton's approach in separating social problematics from sociological problems (Banks 1996: 94). Even such purely academic treatment which avoids any direct policy prescription is, however, vulnerable to appropriation and mis-reading by journalists, politicians, community-leaders and policy-makers alike (Bloch 1983: 10, Keith 1995: 552, Wright 1998). The ease with which journalists make self-evident the relationship between ethnicity and gang violence is a case in point (Alexander 2000).

How both goals might be brought together in a form of counterpoint or productive tension without losing sight of either is, of course, particular to each ethnography. It is unlikely that simple juxtaposition of cultural description with a chapter on racism would be sufficient. For that reason, I placed a case-book of episodes, many of which illustrated the unanticipated ways in which the cross-cultural aspect of a doctor-patient relationship intruded inappropriately, whether from myself, the patient, or both in dialectical fashion, before any description of Bengali 'culture'. The three descriptive chapters that followed placed relationships between the Bengali population and others largely in the background so that features of Bengali social life could be presented in a readable manner. I emphasised differentiation within the Bengali population but left any description of relations with non-Bengali residents undeveloped. Those three chapters thus represent an excursion along the cultural diversity arm of Knauft's dualism, namely the goal of a modest ethnographic contribution to existing accounts of the cultural diversity of humankind. This chapter pays attention to the other arm of Knauft's twin goals of research: the alignment of inequality and injustice with apparently discrete social groups. The case histories given in Chapter 3 can be revisited to illustrate the arguments discussed here.

The question for this chapter can be stated simply as, 'In Bethnal Green what effects do the patterns of relations between Bengali and non-Bengali sections of the population have on the distribution of social predicaments that are particular and salient to Bengali residents?' Unsurprisingly the answer will show that negative outcomes of racialised relationships prevail in Bethnal Green and have most significance for those who also suffer socio-economic deprivation and are politically weak. More than this can be said to illuminate the variability and polarisation of outcomes for those from similar social circumstances.

The references to non-Bengali people in this chapter are generalisations for the specific purpose of the argument about relations of difference. Bengali people make a variety of inferences about people of other backgrounds in Bethnal Green, especially about Muslims from Kurdish, Turkish, Pakistani and Somali populations as well as white people. The sense used here for 'British' is that of informants' perceptions of mainstream consensus cultural values, whether the representatives of that consensus are white, black or other.

7.2 Multicultural Bethnal Green and Dual Discursive Competence

In Bethnal Green, multiculturalism is used in common speech only as a descriptive term, usually with the positive connotations of harmonious co-existence of culturally distinctive groups (cf. Anthias & Yuval-Davies quoted in Hesse 2000: 7). In practice, the notion of harmonious co-existence continues to rest on an implicit assumption on the part of older, settled, groups that populations derived from recent immigrants will adapt to, if not assimilate, mainstream notions of a 'reasonable' balance between public (civic) and private (cultural) behaviour (Castles 1993: 28). Whilst it is imagined that white people may do no more than pick and choose from among a variety of material cultures (so called 'boutique multiculturalism' (Fish quoted in Hall 2000: 211)), immigrant groups are presented with the possibility or even coercion to think about alternative ways of life to that of their homelands. With the exception of occasional religious conversions, non-Bengali people in Bethnal Green do not consider adopting Bengali or Asian values as a solution to their problems. When in difficulty, such people talk mostly of moving out of the area, or blame those whom they see as responsible for the degeneration of the area. In other words, they imagine and desire a more idealised version of their British traditions. The youth worker in Chapter 4 (p. 64) thought that life was improving because *they*, the younger Bengali generation, were changing *towards* a more 'liberal' outlook. The changes he referred to were not simply a matter of bilingualism and styles of dress, but changes in deeply held attitudes towards the relation between the individual and society and modes of family life. His version of ideal multiculturalism is thus tied to the idea of incoming populations altering towards a particular liberal model of the place of culture in civic and private lives.

Such one-way views of immigrant assimilative or adaptive trajectories are commonplace and subject to criticism (Brah1996: 25ff., Caglar 1997). Gilroy looks to diaspora for a ready alternative to immutable primordialism but notes that in this context, terms such as hybridity and creolisation are too suggestive of prior situations of ethnic or cultural purity (Gilroy 2000: 275). Hall regards this as semantic quibbling since no-one is suggesting that hybrid *individuals* exist (Hall 2000: 226). Nevertheless I argue that biological metaphors too readily suggest that hybrids and creoles have only two different parents, whereas in practice, cultural variation may occur under the influence of a multiplicity of genealogical sources. In Bethnal Green, Bengali 'culture', World Islam and

Westernising discourse make up an important triad of influence even before local politics, Bangladeshi politics, the media, popular culture and racism have been considered. Moreover, it cannot be assumed that hybrid innovation will be always creative in a positive sense, nor that breaking down boundaries will necessarily lead to transcendence of the problems of difference (Caglar 1997).

A conjoining conceptual device for (primordial or essential) whole cultures and (instrumental or relativised) cultural admixtures is found in Gerd Baumann's notion of dual discursivity. Baumann (1999) argues that in socially mixed areas, people who have any sort of ethnic awareness have a 'dual discursive competence'. They have the ability to perceive their position as relative to other ethnic or cultural groupings, contingent, emergent and hybrid perhaps, but they are also able to feel a primordial sense of belonging to an immutable age-old substantial group whether it is known to them as their culture, race, tribe or ethnic community (Baumann 1999: 93, see also Allahar 1996: 17, Rex 1994: 4,). The ability to think of one's position as being relative to others, but also linked to a stable or primordial tradition, is aligned with Knauft's duality of critical humanism: in circumstances conducive to a relativistic frame of mind, many people may be receptive to ideas of cultural diversity, relativism and change; alternatively, primordial self-consciousness comes to the fore when awareness of relations of inequality and discrimination suffered because of 'accidents' of birth are awakened. It can be anticipated that not only is this dual discursivity likely to be unevenly distributed within and between populations but the contours of that distribution, the constraints and pressures to be more or less (or non-) dual, are likely to be relevant to an account of differential social predicaments in a mixed society.

'[P]eople can be observed to command a double discursive competence when it comes to their theories about culture, and they develop this dual discursive competence more strongly the more they expose themselves to everyday multicultural practice.' (Baumann 1999: 92).

The notion of a dual competence, variously expressed, side-steps the troublesome issue as to whether persons in mixed societies become hybrid, more conservatively traditional or live in a liminal, in-between state. It is a more widely applicable model than the notions of cultural code-switchers (Ballard 1994a: 30), cultural styles (Ferguson 1999: 97) or creoles and hybrids. Baumann (1996) finds in Southall that the granting of state resources to community groups favours instrumental formations of 'official' communities, leaving what he calls the 'demotic' cultural discourse more or less to its own devices. My perspective differs from Baumann in that my focus is on families and households rather than community politics and I wish to include the primordial side of discursive competence, that is, the reproduction of tradition (summarised into the 'domains' of preceding chapters) as well as Barthian construction of boundaries (Barth 1969), social upheaval and change.

I have made a 'rough-cut' assessment of forms of dual discursive competence which delivers a typology of three kinds of behaviour at cultural interfaces. I have called the three categories of practice 'cultural agonism', 'common-sense multiculturalism' and 'unsettled strategising', applicable to all residents in Bethnal Green. Each will be illustrated, but in summary, cultural agonism describes those with a strongly primordial sense of their culture which is to be preserved and defended at all cost. This practice discursively tends towards racism. Common-sense multiculturalism also favours a primordial feel for culture but with a pragmatic, non-violent attitude towards compromise and instrumental manoeuvres necessitated by living in a mixed-ethnicity world. Discursively it is centred on ethnicity and the issues affecting minority ethnic groups and some authors see it as aligned with 'cultural racism' (Lawrence 1982: 97ff., Wright 1998: 10). Unsettled strategising describes those with maximal dual discursivity and an unsettled position in relation to cultural values. Questions of race and ethnicity do not come to the fore so much as the notion of culture and cultural relativity. Before drawing together ethnographic illustration and detail from my field notes, a brief examination of the list of the eighty or so Bengali households with whom I am most familiar can provide a starting point for orientation. At a household level, allocation to the three categories (with all the obvious provisos as to the internal heterogeneity and inconstancy of this kind of generalisation) I found that the agonistic mode is the minority practice (less than one in ten), common-sense multiculturalism the majority (just over half) and those who fall into the unsettled strategising group make a large minority. This allocation exercise acts as a corrective to the bias inherent in a purely descriptive presentation which would tend to give prominence to the more dramatic case histories and perhaps underplay the unremarkable. Ethnographic illustration of each will include discussion of the issues of race, ethnicity and culture which can be seen to be aligned severally to each type of practice: race with agonism, ethnicity with pragmatism and culture with strategising.

Hall makes a similar categorisation of practices in relation to cultural boundaries in diasporic populations (see also Hannerz 1980: 255). Hall describes firstly those who are deeply committed to tradition, usually with a diasporic inflection; secondly he describes those whose traditionalism has intensified through racism or changing world conditions such as the rising salience of Islam; thirdly, he discussed those who evince advanced 'hybridisation' of culture (Hall 2000: 227). Whilst aligning myself with his intention and the form of his tripartite typology but leaving aside the problem of hybridity, I retain two criticisms. Firstly, there is an implicit evolutionary flavour to Hall's presentation whereby tradition is a stable state prior to diaspora which may then either hybridise or intensify in receiving countries. Secondly, Hall's typology presents only the individual diasporic migrant's outlook which is thereby traditional, intensified traditional or changing. This might be seen as quibbling when his intentions, which I support, are clear from the rest of his article, but in the arena of relations of difference, such details can crucially determine overall directions and political understandings of the argument, and hence their rhetorical use (Bringa 1995).

I add the following comments before embarking on ethnographic illustration. The categories presented here make up a typology of kinds of *relations*, not kinds of *persons*. Any categorisation is an abstraction but some are more useful than others in the context of marked socio-economic inequality. Within each category there is, of course, diversity but inter-group distinction remains more important than intra-group variety. Such a typology does not consist of watertight compartments but they rather shade into each other. The actors allocated to the different types may be groups, families or individuals. These actors may show one or more types of behaviour at different stages in the life-cycle of individuals or domestic groups, and may thus episodically inhabit one and then another of these categories. Households may be a useful unit of analysis for one category but not for another where age and gender are more relevant. This typology allows insights to be gained from those who are reproducers of 'culture-as-tradition' as much as from those who creatively or (more usually in my experience) painfully undergo socio-cultural change. Finally, they are to be seen only as routes into the workings of cultural effects in Bethnal Green and the distribution of social predicaments of its Bengali population and not a programmatic statement of correctness.

Where non-Bengali views and behaviour are described, they are the collated observations, remarks and conversations that I have been attentive to during fieldwork in the presence of non-Bengali patients, colleagues, my own social network and the media. While not amounting to any sort of systematic fieldwork of non-Bengali populations of Bethnal Green, they are systematic in the sense of being a set of data collected in the context of the relationships I have with Bengali informants.

7.3 Three Practices of Relations of Difference

7.3.1 UNSETTLED STRATEGISING (AND THE DISCOURSE OF CULTURE)

This way of managing relations of difference includes individuals and families where social or personal difficulty can be represented too easily in terms of cultural conflict, whether by themselves, by those who offer social assistance or the researcher. There is no settled view as to which 'system' offers better choices and the way to resolve dilemmas and conflict is elusive. Both sides (or none) of the dualities appear and recede. The lack of room for manoeuvre may lead some to switch to strategies offered by another category. The complexity of issues demanding immediate attention leaves little leisure for picking and choosing identities or modes of public and private life in a thoughtful, reflective manner. Disrupted marriages and disputes within neighbourhoods or extended families may demand precipitate action rather than a slower careful selection of an innovative cultural schema. Some in this group become chronic heart-sink 'cases', irritatingly non-compliant with institutional frameworks for social assistance, rather than evolving into so-called post-modern creative loci of heteroglossial culture.

Those who illustrate the theme of unsettled strategising most obviously are also those who come to the attention of people who feel responsible or empowered to advise and influence the outcomes of trouble cases and are, in general sociological terms the most disadvantaged by any measure. I found that those who are the weaker party to Bengali cultural hierarchies, women and junior male kin, were most likely to find themselves in predicaments where cultural dilemmas emerged, either because they sought an alternative discourse or because non-Bengali people who were involved with their problems found that raising alternatives to what they saw as 'Bengali tradition' was not ruled out. Disadvantage alone does not necessarily prompt actors to consider non-traditional discourses. It is where socio-economic disadvantage *compounds* the ill-effects of being placed by tradition in a lowly status position that people may be pushed across customary boundaries. Status can otherwise be improved by converting economic capital into social capital and vice versa: there is plenty of evidence that this takes place with or without deliberate strategic intent. Without either economic or social status resources, however, recruiting the political power of alternative discursive forms offers the chance of a way out. Thus single mothers, divorced women, those in ethnically mixed marriages and those who have dramatic rifts with kin, especially younger brothers of families with joint land holdings in Bangladesh, are all over-represented here. A culturally relativist view can be expressed by anyone but it has more force in the context of those whose lives will be immediately and materially affected by the way that the universalism-relativism debate plays out.

I am not suggesting through this formulation that culture in its most fluid, contested and processual manifestation might be reduced to a grammar of complaint, a yardstick of social disaffection or a false-consciousness form of cover-up for personal problems. The extent to which individuals do or do not depict their predicaments in terms of cultural difficulty might be a measure of personal disaffection or contentment, or it could be a measure of their vulnerability to a relativistic version of cultural meanings in Bethnal Green through a combination of social position and personal biographic moment.

The people discussed here represent the meeting point of specific Bengali customs, ideologies and cultural effects together with the adverse effects of gender, class, racist and socio-economic relations in the area as a whole. British and Bengali are not the only sources of the rhetoric that might be deployed in situations of dispute. The East London mosque, for example, may also try to influence the outcome of trouble-cases with an approach that is distinct from what I have typified as British and Bengali. Media influence, the arts, popular culture and alternative life-styles can also play a part. The people in this group show a particular kind of engagement with the contradictions evident in a mixed society. When faced with difficulty, they tend to stay with the problem rather than retreating to common-sense multiculturalism or defensive cultural agonism. Cultural relativism is, in this manifestation, not a yardstick of complaint, but a measure of a certain kind of resilience.

7.3.1.1 Episodes

It may take only a single episode to throw up a relativist perspective. Visiting a friend, I happened upon the mother berating her children for doing little to help with preparation for a party. She did not cut short her lecture while I sat down to drink tea in the kitchen. When she had finished I made a timid attempt at expressing sympathy with a general platitude, commenting that women had a hard life (*"Betinne lagi zibon hoshto"*). This prompted a more specific, culturalised diatribe, *"Bengali betinne, zibon nai!"* (Bengali women have *no* life!). Whatever the commonalities of all women in relation to households, our situations are radically different; my comparative remark precipitated a switch from her framing the problem as being that of a mother whose children had failed in their filial duties to that of a woman who by virtue of her cultural position had no life of her own, *compared to* others.

Jahanara, a married woman with school-age children received news that her brother was seriously ill in Bangladesh. Her parents-in-law decided that it was not possible to allow her to travel at present for a variety of reasons including financial. She asked me in some distress for my medical view about her brother's prognosis and used the opportunity to speak vehemently in English, "Bengali women have too hard a life", she said, "My culture is so stupid; I am so afraid for my brother, we are very close". We both knew that other Bengali wives in similar circumstances but with a more understanding husband and in-laws, are allowed to visit sick relatives. The money can usually be found somehow but in Jahanara's case, for whatever immediate reasons, the situation was formulated as one of a conflict of duties within Bengali family life. Her emotional outburst shows that although culturalised views are likely to find sympathy with an English doctor, she did not calculate or rehearse this presentation but felt it as such, *given the context*.

These small episodes include my presence, not to illustrate my fieldwork orientation, nor because of any obligatory sense of self-reflexivity being always a virtue in an ethnography. I place myself in these illustrations, as I did in Chapter 3, because I cannot efface who I am in an 'undercover' form of participant-observation and become a fictive Bengali woman. The contrast that cannot be displaced therefore becomes a research device. I am read differently by differently placed informants and it is particularly with housewives that I am read as a representative of women's choice *in other cultures*. Similarly, as many Bengali people ask if I am divorced as ask if I am married: they assume that it is likely that my own traditional, customary social context is neutral with regard to marital status. When worn down by sleepless or naughty children Bengali women ask how I manage, some with more curiosity than others, "It must be nice to work *and* be married" they say. Although some married Bengali women do work (few as yet, but increasing in number among the younger generation), the culturally mixed setting prompts these woman to vocalise their reflective thoughts about such matters.

7.3.1.2 Young men

Faruk, the youngest son of a Bengali widow, is in trouble with drugs, spending up to £200 daily on crack and heroin, and this made him to ask for medical help, "How had he started?" I asked, "Through school friends, mates who smoked regularly, and one day I bought some myself and that was that" he replied. Is this predicament surprising given that his father was a harsh man, given to beatings, so that as a child, he and his mother and sisters spent time in a refuge for battered wives? The drug world in Bethnal Green is culturally very mixed, forming a social nexus where close relationships between young men and women of all backgrounds are less marked by ethnic segregation than other social spheres. He spoke to me warmly of the egalitarian nature of loyalties and friendships among his addict friends in contrast to his father's racist attitudes to non-Bengali people. Rather than going to local drug counsellors (some of whom offer an 'Asian' service) as some of his fellow addicts had done, Faruk sought help within the Bengali community. He went to his uncle in Norfolk to escape local drug contacts and found work in a restaurant. The return to the community is a familiar story with Bengali drug-users for it is practical, the restaurant-kin network allowing easy travel within Britain and beyond. Others find renewed religious fervour through support from the East London mosque or they may deliver themselves up to family control which might include being sent to a locked institution in Sylhet.

Faruk did not make a clean break from drugs in Norfolk and when found to be in possession of cannabis was not only thrown out by his uncle but given a relatively harsh community service order by the courts. He said the county justice service was "very racist - because there weren't many Asians there". The probation officer, he said resignedly and bitterly, had done nothing whatsoever to arrange any help for him. He stays at home now with his mother although there are a lot of arguments and he could qualify for his own bed-sit given his current 'mental illness' status. He prefers an English doctor because Bengali doctors "won't take on druggies." Bengali doctors do, in fact, take on the problems of addicts: those patients who reject Bengali doctors often have a more specific difficulty for they assume that the doctor is likely, for cultural reasons, to break confidentiality and inform their parents. Faruk cares enough about his status in Bengali terms to inhibit him from leaving the community entirely, which he could do since he has reasonable qualifications and skills. He also has enough experience and insight into the workings of non-Bengali British society to be disillusioned of any notion he or others in his position might have about 'freedom' in the non-Bengali world.

This rather obvious example of a young man considering more than one solution to a common problem in Bethnal Green is given to show that trying one thing and then another without dismissing any avenue entirely is the more usual scenario than that of hybridity, code-switching or hovering in-between two cultures. Faruk is insightful about the virtues and drawbacks of Bengali family values, the mosque's religiosity, British liberality and British racism. His sense of identity - of how he would describe and comport himself - is not out of focus, even if we might call it multi-faceted. He became an addict primarily because drugs are easily available in Bethnal Green; he was predisposed or had an elective affinity for narcosis because his family life was painful and his awareness of local attitudes and experience of racism made him uncomfortably aware of the limits to his ambitions because of his social position. He is now singularly aware that his future way of life must be forged from diverse sources, none of which are wholly adequate.

7.3.1.3 Young women

School students find it relatively easy to efface cultural barriers between Bengali Muslim womanhood and those teachers and peers who are eager to read them as independent, modern young women. Strictly traditional students are, of course, just as worthy of educational opportunity but those who express a relativistic discourse are particularly noticed and celebrated from my assessment of actual and reported remarks of school and college teachers. If a student wishes to recruit support, whether in the form of advice or practical action, they will be more noticeable if they deliver a culturalised description of their family's attitudes so as to make their own, oppositional views more compelling. The teachers and social workers will then listen, and the girl's parents can be told that they are not just overlooking their daughter's personal feelings but that their cultural attitudes are incompatible with any young girl's right to independent choice. This strategy risks being found to be manipulative on the one hand (if her family are found in fact to be reasonable) or risks a hardening of the conflict between the child and the family in excessively cultural terms. Just as Bengali parents may sequester their daughters in locked bedrooms to preserve their honour for a groom, social workers can and do remove them to a place of safety, even to their own homes, in an attempt to effect a 'rescue'. There is sometimes little social space for the thoughtful child who would like to balance the competing interests of several factions more closely.

For young Bengali women brought up in Bethnal Green, their mettle is tested as the prospect of marriage approaches. Living in a plural social world does not in itself make acquiescence with an arranged marriage difficult. The banal racism that they are likely to suffer as 'Asian women' will not be noticeably alleviated by making a love-match, nor worsened by the fact of their arranged marriage. Once married, they will gain enhanced status in Bengali eyes. Some girls, especially those already deemed possible trouble-makers, or where family status is felt to be resting precariously on her particular marriage, are sequestered at home as soon as they can leave school. While the scope for romantic attachments is restricted by this process, there is then a stark choice between flouting the family and creating a rupture or marrying and achieving some independence and status as a married woman. Before any actual engagement, they may be coolly discursive about their ability to be strategic in the face of impending family control (Gavron 1998: 99ff.). Some assert that they will have a say in their future, while others speak with warmth of the trust that they willingly give to their family but most comply

The burden of conceptual and strategic issues that must be cleverly managed by these young women is immense (Brah 1996: 76ff.). They are likely to be critically, even cynically aware through their peer group that the grass is not greener on the other side of the fence and that non-Bengali classmates make equally hard choices at this stage about personal and family relationships. It is not surprising, therefore, that there is by no means a mass exodus from Bengali arranged marriages even nowadays.

7.3.1.4 Young mothers

An analogous predicament is found among young mothers in traditional marriages. There are considerable obstacles to conjugal harmony in any such marriage. To recapitulate: London-based women are likely to find themselves living with a young man who has only recently arrived from Bangladesh, ill at ease, unable to speak English and dependent on Bengali connections to find work and become 'established'. His peers, brought up in Britain, will be further advanced at the same age. He will be pressed to contribute some of his income to the joint family account, and although this might be a good long-term investment, in the short term it causes added strain within his household.

If marriageable girls are closely scrutinised in their public behaviour, the expectations of propriety placed upon young married women are even greater. Chaperones are mandatory and a *sari* or *shalwar kameez* and *burqa* the proper style of dress. The scrutiny of in-laws, if local, can be claustrophobic. Despite difficulty, many such marriages develop their own strengths and become happy households. If, however, there is conflict within the marriage then the stakes are raised dramatically. Divorce, as discussed in Chapter 4, affects women's status profoundly, but men, however they might suffer emotionally, are unlikely to lose personal status. In spite of a good connection spoiled, they can marry again relatively easily if resident in Britain as compared to a divorced Bengali woman. The balance of power is therefore weighted against women who mostly strive hard to rectify a bad situation. They can try to work alone, using force of argument to influence husbands to change their behaviour. If this is unsuccessful they may involve their own brothers and other male relatives to dispute with her husband and affines. If this does not work they can turn to British institutionalised support systems. If the situation is violent and small children are involved, such agencies are likely to move in of their own accord, as are the senior members of the two sets of in-laws or their representatives. Whatever the perceptions of the participants, at some point the problem is likely to be described in cultural terms, usually (in the non-Bengali view) as a stand-off between intransigent traditionalists and reasonable liberals. In effect, the women may be told, or feel that they are being told, by statutory agencies that their own and their children's welfare are not only more important than the views of their husband and his family, but that help can be given only if they agree to follow a strategy which contradicts customary Bengali family values.

Battered wives are exhorted to leave their husbands with the implied or explicit threat of their children being put into care on grounds of emotional abuse should they do not co-operate with statutory agencies (this was Rukshana's predicament, p. 51). Those Bengali women who reject separation in the face of violence are often regarded as 'culture-bound'. In such confrontations and negotiations, culture is given 'immodest causality', obscuring alternative approaches to resolution of a problem (Farmer 1999). It can be in the interest of the 'victim-client' to continue negotiations within this cultural paradigm for she can use the rhetoric of both sides strategically to manage a delicate situation. These young mothers are aware that they are a salient locus of negotiation between the competing socio-cultural zones of British social services and Bengali kinship. The more they dramatise the oppressive intransigence of the 'elders' of their 'community', the more they will deflect (often unconsciously) attention to problems at a personal level in relationships. This was how Rahela (p. 161) managed her problems at one stage for she allowed both family hierarchy and statutory services to pass judgement on her behaviour but avoided following the prescriptions of either group.

It is true that cultural values and customs may constrain personal relationships but it is possible to choose which aspect to discuss with whom and in what terms. Given the scarcity of support services for marital disharmony, it may be more strategic for a wife to engage practical help, child-care, enhanced benefits and better housing by concurring with her depiction as a cultural victim than to be on a long waiting list for relationship counselling with which her husband is unlikely to co-operate. While British institutions use the rhetoric of universal rights and duties, individual responsibility and support based on rational co-operation, other rhetorics are available. I have been told that the East London mosque, for example, offers to take on the role of arranging second marriages for divorced Bengali women who are 'abandoned' by their community should they take up the *hijab*.

As a group these young Bengali wives are not just dual or triple sufferers because of race, religion and gender, their cultural life is also held hostage to social support by those who uphold the civic-private divide in multiculturalist or religious modes. In large measure understanding and insightful as to the causes of their injustices, their powers of endurance and fortitude are to be admired. These examples demonstrate the effect of multiple influences on individuals or families who are able to think about, or cannot avoid dwelling on, the possibilities of more than one way of life rather than going to one or other 'camps'. They demonstrate dual discursivity coming under heavy fire from all sides: the pressure to conform to traditional Bengali values or Islamic orthodoxy or to prosecute a rational individualistic strategy in a multiculturalist paradigm. The constraint occasioned by such oppositional paradigms can be seen in less dramatic case histories on a daily basis.

Culture is immediate and personal not because individual wills are blocked by apparently arbitrary cultural rules. Cultural consciousness blazes forth when an attempt to negotiate change in certain circumstances precipitates a rapid divergence along cultural or culturalised lines between the protagonists. This divergence is often felt to be disproportionate to the scale of the matter in a personal sense. It is not that one side is right and the other wrong that is being examined here, but rather the way that a more complex and nuanced analysis of any problem is likely to be obstructed through nobody's particular fault. A more accurate and critical analysis of the matter is blocked by the ways that limited repertoires of available paradigms turns into a shadow-play of cultural stereotypes. The distress of the disadvantaged woman is increased by the poverty of such paradigms. Health Visitors, doctors and social workers are, for the most part, reasonably pragmatic and not overly ambitious about what can be achieved by their influence alone. Any outcome that is at least, 'good enough', if not optimal, will be considered but the *terms of the discussion* and its dialectical progression are likely to be constrained in ways that are not always anticipated nor desirable.

7.3.1.5 Culture

Diasporic populations underscore the importance of conceptualising culture in a relational way rather than as an autonomous explanatory domain (Kuper 1999: 246, see also Farmer 1999 passim, Knauft 1995 passim, Strathern 1995: 157). In such a changeable place as Bethnal Green, there is nothing obvious that we can mark off as a cultural sphere, no readable Geertzian' faded text nor any webs of meaning which can be used analogously as a generalised, separate backdrop for social action (Geertz 1973: 30 & 452). Life is not, however, blurred and unreadable in Bethnal Green: enduring customs and traditions are evidently a very solid part of the picture, particularly when examining relations of difference. Wright similarly finds that despite changing academic perspectives, older understandings of culture (bounded groups with shared meanings and values) persist in public parlance and are appropriated by New Right politicians in Britain (Wright 1998). Both old and new models of culture are appropriated by business and development workers (ibid. 1998: 7). Change and flux may complicate the conceptual work of researchers but they are not necessarily confusing to the people who live in such places, nor do they preclude the formation of solid social groups.

As an example of simultaneous endurance and change, Gavron has shown that marriage choices have changed for young Bengali women in Bethnal Green. She does not, therefore, generalise about arranged marriage but uses notions such as trends and directions which are, from her viewpoint, more useful analytical terms for discussing this issue (Gavron 1998). The enduring practice of arranged marriage is, however, a persistent diacritical feature of relations of cultural difference between sections of the population in Bethnal Green, no matter in what direction the cultural form of that practice is going (see also Bhopal 1999: 126). Likewise, the notion of Asian family values, variously interpreted and misunderstood, are a persistent and, relatively speaking, an unchanging feature of relations of difference (Sen 1997). Asian family values are an important component of the interfaces between different sections of the population in Bethnal Green and as such are distinguishable from, if intertwined with, other components of those interfaces such as racism, gender relations and economic issues. The observation of persistent features such as the practice of arranged marriage or the notion of Asian family values in the contours of cultural boundaries does not, however, permit the term culture to be detached from relationships and used as an independent explanation for the existence of the boundaries.

Anyone may reflect on what it is that constitutes difference living in such a varied place as Bethnal Green. I do not illustrate 'views': rather than using structured interviews which usefully record the scope of attitudes (for example towards identity, Islam, work or racism) I have tried to deploy consistent and structured attention to certain themes as well as a self-imposed discipline of checking field notes for silences and absences. In this way I have sought out evidence that people are, perhaps only for a moment or more enduringly, aware that their current predicament may be cast in more than one paradigm, and that it is hard to decide which is most likely to offer the best solution to the problems of their predicament. Those who are caught up in awkward predicaments may be very aware that some people see their problem as being mostly about backward-looking tradition which hinders progress and resolution, while others see the difficulties as being caused by British institutional attitudes undermining Bengali family values or Islamic orthodoxy.

This category of boundary behaviour can hardly be called an approach, although the actors may be strategic at times. The examples given in the casebook of Chapter 3 were mostly predicaments where the interface of cultural difference developed with events rather than being given by predisposition, habits or a settled view of things. There is no lack of trouble-cases among people whose habitual way of managing relations of difference are described as agonistic or common-sense multiculturalist but the lines of cleavage in those two categories are at least clear, not necessarily unchanging over time but nevertheless at any one moment, easily discernible. Even with clear-cut boundaries, however, these strategies may not be robust in all circumstances: bilateral multiculturalism sometimes contains thinly disguised cultural racism.

7.3.2 COMMON-SENSE MULTICULTURALISM (AND THE DISCOURSE OF ETHNICITY)

7.3.2.1 Ethnicity

When euphemisms were needed for the discredited notion of race (and in an analogous case, for caste (Beteille 1996: 171, Fuller 1996: 22,) ethnicity emerged as a usefully ambiguous term (Miles 1993, Ratcliffe 1996: 3, Strathern 1995 fn8). The emergence of 'ethnic cleansing' as a sinister technological descriptor for recent crimes against humanity in Europe and Africa has taken some of the warmth that was formerly associated with primordial understandings of ethnicity. It remains, however, as the institutional term of reference for relations of certain kinds of difference, at least in Britain. The possibility that ethnicity may slide backwards too easily into racial discourse is observable in Ratcliffe's careful reordering of the phrase 'ethnic minority group' to 'minority ethnic group' so as to ensure that ethnicity is thought of as a characteristic of all and not only of non-white populations (Ratcliffe 1996: 4, see also Bonnett 1996).

The term ethnicity, with a strongly bounded meaning encompassing that of more or less naturalised ethnic communities, persists in Bethnal Green particularly in institutional settings. Departments of housing, education, the police and medical services disavow racism but have not yet fully adopted the notion of culture and multiculturalism as an official labelling system for the minority communities whom they serve. Multiculturalist social policies have, as already discussed, been severely criticised, but many citizens of all backgrounds who are concerned about 'ethnic minorities' and racism find some form of multiculturalism a comfortable *modus vivendi*.

The standard multiculturalist model promotes a comfortable, if conservative or even static, view of cultural or ethnic origins. Customs and traditions are felt to be in a stable, 'natural' relation with the material, economic, educational and political possibilities of social life. This can be represented as a pragmatic relationship between cultural and civic life: culture becomes aligned with private life and civic conduct with public life. Spontaneous expression of the relativistic side of dual discursive competence is least apparent among followers of this model, Bengali or non-Bengali, middle-class or working-class, although many will be able to discuss its possibilities if questioned. None would consider participation in ethnic violence nor overt antagonism. This model is most valued among those who have the resources to maintain a rational strategic project for their family even in difficult circumstances. Notions of change, creolisation and hybridity, if apprehended at all, are given guarded or non-committal approval and there is evidence of anxiety about the relationship between ethnicity and violence. This results in strengthened adherence to the notion of civic virtue but potentially weakens culture as a creative resource. Instead we find unquestioned, if sequestered, tradition, heritage or a watered down, culture-as-arts, formulation. There is thus a secession of culture from a way of life, actively embraced, towards its manifestation as a set of residual cultural traits and artefacts. The idea that civic security might be bought at the expense of the potential for cultural innovation and creativity is not often explicitly recognised although a non-specific regret at the loss of cultural heritage may be expressed. The relativistic side of Baumann's duality is suppressed and efforts to resolve the effects of discrimination pragmatically is privileged over the celebration of cultural diversity. In so far as such attitudes facilitate relations with non-Bengali neighbours and colleagues it is an outlook that brings certain advantages.

7.3.2.2 Class effects

Reflecting on those Bengali families which I have identified as common-sense multiculturalist, there is roughly a half and half mix of the middle- and working-class families as judged by the occupation of the father. Since middle-class Bengali families are relatively few in Bethnal Green, they are not just over-represented in this category, it is almost a truism that being middle-class delivers you into a common-sense multiculturalist paradigm. I have already discussed intra-family diversity of emergent socio-economic and class position in Chapter 4. Here I will take a generalised household view in the first instance but this variability should be borne in mind.

Bengali families who had already achieved middle-class status prior to migration are unlikely to demonstrate boundary difficulties, at least not at household level. Education allows them to be discursive about multi-ethnic society in a way that promotes common-sense multiculturalism. This discourse need not disturb their own culturally specific world view. Cultural space safely allows them to compartmentalise their private cultural home life where a *lungi* can be worn and food eaten traditionally with fingers (but prepared with modern kitchen appliances rather than the utensils found in poorer households).

In their roles as community leaders they promote Bengali arts, literature and music within the bounds of Islamic propriety. They may feel sorry for those who deny themselves the riches of Bengali arts-culture because of unreflective Islamic orthodoxy.

Their religious practice is rarely fundamentalist (Alam 1988: 11, 45-52) and they are irritated by sections of the British media that often links Islam with fundamentalism. Education and career aspirations are valued on a par with non-Bengali families of similar socio-economic status. They are likely to thrive and usually outperform English working-class children in educational achievement. Within the family they sensibly allow for individualism and choice: some prefer to encourage European foreign language study to Bengali at GCSE level. However they recognise this as a potential point of momentum for the beginnings of apparently irreversible Westernisation. Special educational efforts in language and the cultural heritage of Bengal via community classes mitigate against cultural loss (Gregory & Williams 2000: 137).

These are the well-liked colleagues at university, work, in education, the health service, social and civil services. They retain enough cultural distinctiveness so as not to be regarded as completely assimilated but men in white-collar occupations are more likely to wear Western styles rather than Islamic clothes (this practice is changing and masculine Islamic styles are increasingly seen in mixed work-places). Working women wear *shalwar kameez* or Western dress, long or short hair but Islamic details such as scarves and veils are not taken to such a point that it would occasion difficulty in their work . They remark easily enough about their position relative to other sorts of Bengali people locally and may be pitying or disparaging about those that are unable to be flexible because they are 'stuck' in tradition. Racism affects everyone, but the views of such as these are likely to be shared with non-Bengali middle-class families. They are likely to feel that the unacceptable face of British society must be fought with a united front rather than partisan, ethnic action groups.

Among the working-class families in this set (for example that of Abdul Choudhury and Monowara Nessa Chapter 4, p. 68) the home language is Sylheti, spoken with familiarity and pleasure, but they strive to master enough English to be independent of state-provided interpreters. Home cooking is traditional *bhatt* (boiled rice and curry) but the children's school-acquired tastes for pizza, beans and chips are partially accommodated. Their style of dress is neither aspirational in Islamic, Bengali or Western styles but safe, conservative, pretty or smart but not with a view to impress others. They are not likely to be seen at large-scale staged cultural events such as the *mela*. They are not pushy about moving to a better standard of housing, nor do they make strenuous efforts to alter the education department's allocation of school places. Family strife is not made public. Culture and tradition are apparently thought of as having a greater effect on life choices than gender, class or even racism, and are not seen as obstacles to advancement. A rational upward trajectory whether cautiously step-wise or at a more aspirational velocity overwhelms other considerations.

Rabia Nessa, the eldest child of a widowed father who worked as a factory tailor, has married a mosque worker and although she did reasonably well at secondary school, did not go on to higher education but has settled to her housewifely status and the care of her children. Fluent in English and interested in current affairs, she is able to discuss points of cultural interest such how to take medicines during Ramadan without being sinful, or whether alcohol could ever be allowed for Muslims. These are not for her disturbing ideas - or, rather, they mark the limits of her relativism. When the occasion demands, such as her husband's lack of English, she can discuss cheerfully his poor progress and set it rationally against the background of their current minority-immigrant-status. Her expectations for her children are high and she is nervous of the more colourful sections of Bengali society locally. She is quietly outraged about racist behaviour but offers no radical solutions, "What can you do?" Easily reassured by myself in an adult compassionate professional role, she is the ideal young adult for a smooth relationship with a professional who has socially granted pastoral responsibilities and notionally higher social status than herself.

From the point of view of 'mosaic' multiculturalism, those working-class families who appear to have humble aspirations in the public sphere and who live their private lives in a way that is congruent with the homeland are ideal co-citizens. Undemanding beyond their rights to equal opportunity in health, employment and education, they do not disturb existing boundaries and are resignedly accepting of the vicissitudes of inner-city life and even racist violence as a necessary price to pay for the future opportunities of their children. Whether they could be classified as economic migrants or otherwise, they certainly cannot be construed as exploitative of the British benefit system and often sacrifice much for the sake of a better future for their descendants. Where physical health allows they are industrious, their substandard houses acceptable, neat and decorated within their means. The children are managed sensibly and professionals treated with respect. Doctor-patient relationships are conducted with decorum and beliefs about spiritual-illness, if they are even thought of, are kept in the background. Their misfortunes invite sympathy from other surgery staff because they are always polite and personable.

In kinship terms, marriages are stable and safe and their children conform to parent's arrangements. There is a disproportionately large number of families in this group with few local kin connections and this 'floating island' status must account for their relative freedom from immediate personal strife (cf. Bott 1971). This apparent rational ease does not just happen to some but is achieved despite difficulty. The event of marriage and the arrival of children concentrates the minds of those who at one time thought of breaking away because their older siblings or they themselves followed non-traditional paths outside the community. Different life stages present alternative strategies in a different light (fairly predictably). Setting course for common-sense multiculturalism promises well and the current climate of attention to racist harassment means that the police can now be relied upon, at least to a greater extent than in the recent past, to protect persons and property of all citizens. This strategy can be the refuge of those who have had difficulties within the extended family so some 'floating islands' are those who have cut themselves off from the patrilineage. The past rupture may then be revealed in a hypersensitivity to references to their 'Bengali culture'.

These are the ideal neighbours allowing English people to say that they are not racists, "They're just different". These white neighbours may not be particularly intimate but they do not show hostile behaviour. They tolerate pungent cooking smells in densely populated housing blocks for the sake of racial harmony. These neighbours are as upset as anyone about racist attacks but discriminate carefully between honest citizens and those they suspect of unfair encroachment of 'normal' civic values, "Why should they just come over here and demand a house right away, sickness benefit and all that?"

At the hands of the service sector, attention to the ethnicity of Bengali clients occludes a more holistic appraisal of their needs (Smaje 1995: 121). The patronising nature of 'special needs' treatment can be quietly side-stepped by clients in this group rather than challenged impolitely. Other obstacles are not so easily negotiated: even a family which has achieved naturalisation status remains affected by immigration restrictions when it comes to the marriage of their children. Their benefits are curtailed when they save up for prolonged visits to Bangladesh. Their housing needs are limited as the local stock does not provide for large households, and these needs are seen by some housing officers in racist terms (see Chapter 4, p. 88).

7.3.2.3 Different Languages

Although non-Bengali and Bengali people follow this common-sense model and share outlooks, this does not prevent a clash of views when boundaries are threatened. The limits of common-sense multiculturalism are demonstrated amply by the issue of teaching mother-tongue languages in the borough. The preservation and celebration of diverse but separate cultural customs, languages, crafts and arts (together with anti-racist laws and the politics of tolerance) is thought of as being the most practical way of demonstrating comfortable multicultural relationships. The street festivals in Banglatown (the area surrounding Brick Lane in Spitalfields) are relaxed and enjoyable and give the lie, superficially, to the idea that there is a fundamental unease in the relationship between Bengali and British cultures. Older Bengali people, however, see the *Mela* festival (Bengali New Year) as an invented tradition arising from the influence of Hindu India after Bangladeshi independence.

Teaching Bengali to Tower Hamlets' children of Bangladeshi origin is accepted as a good thing by parents, politicians and educators. Many Tower Hamlets' secondary schools teach Bengali to GCSE level. Until 1999, foreign languages were rarely taught in British primary schools. Since then, an early language learning initiative has been launched in some areas to extend this to all schools. East London primary schools which enrol multi-ethnic student populations, including recent refugees from Kurdistan, Somalia, the former Yugoslavia as well as immigrants from Commonwealth countries, provide extra support geared towards achieving bilingualism and fluency in English but no formal foreign language classes. Because of this unmet need, volunteers have set up after-school community classes providing Bengali and other mother-tongue language tuition as well as support for mainstream curriculum subjects to children from families where English is not the first language. This voluntary sector is now supported with grants to some, but not all such projects from the Local Education Authority towards the hiring of venues, teachers' wages and the purchase of teaching materials. Full-time administrators run the Mother Tongue department of the LEA and provide monitoring, support and supervision for the classes. In addition, they have drawn up a Bengali curriculum framework for 5-11 year olds following national curriculum standards for other subjects. Currently about 5000 Bengali children attended such classes in Tower Hamlets (grant-aided or otherwise) out of a total Tower Hamlets Bengali children's population of about 20,000 (LBTH 2001).

One difficulty is that the classes teach Standard Bengali but the children come from homes where the Sylheti dialect is spoken. Sylheti has no current written form, the old Sylheti Nagari script having fallen into disuse, so all texts are published in Standard Bengali. The modern Bengali alphabet does not fully allow a written form of Sylheti and English-script phonetic transliteration may be just as appropriate (or inappropriate, depending on your view). Many parents may understand Standard Bengali but are neither fluent nor literate in that language. Chalmers (1996: 5) has argued that Standard Bengali and Sylheti are separate languages but while I have not found any Sylheti speaker who would agree with this, his idea carries some force with English educationalists. As young children find Standard Bengali quite difficult to learn, the suggestion was made that Standard Bengali texts should have parallel English-script Sylheti as well as English translations. This is accepted as qualified necessity, and such a trilingual picture vocabulary book has been produced, but in linguistic terms this is seen as an insensitive blunder. The analogy would be to produce a vocabulary for Scottish children using the transliterative spellings of heavily accented and dialect words for the sake of promoting fluency in Received

English among Scottish children, and perhaps even a Scottish language distinctive both from Gaelic and English.

The second difficulty touches on moral issues in relation to language education. While the Syhleti dialect is sometimes, semi-jokingly, called a raw language *'khassa basha'* by its speakers, the parent language, Standard Bengali, is referred to not only as *shuddor* (proper) but often as *shundor*, (beautiful). Educated Bengali friends have elaborated on this, describing Bengali as a 'deep' language, suited to poetry, exceptionally expressive of emotions and profound ideas. Its usage is considered as being constitutive of a particular moral outlook, and a vehicle for correct social conduct. It was the cause of martyrdom and of a civil war when West Pakistan sought to impose Urdu as an Islamic national language on both provinces of post-partition Pakistan. Bilingual Bengali Mother Tongue educators, in light of such issues, would like to include a two-way dialogue with mainstream education so as to influence foreign language teaching in state schools. They give two reasons in favour of this arrangement: firstly, overall educational achievement is improved by placing Mother-Tongue tuition within mainstream schools. Where such tuition is relegated to low-status community venues, the potential benefits are reduced through the devalued position of the classes (Frost 2000). Secondly, it is felt that the methods of Mother Tongue tuition in Bengali was likely to inculcate desirable moral values because of the particular qualities of Bengali as already discussed. This, however, has proved to be a sticking point for the Local Educational Authority, at least in terms of their immediate reaction, which gave the impression that they saw no association between modern foreign language learning and moral education.

The idea that language contains in a microcosm the morality of Bengali life (distinct from the tenets of Islam) is at the very least misunderstood, and for some I suspect it is repugnant. Linguistics scholars may explore such relationships but on a day to day level, in the sphere of children's education the two are separated; good citizenship, it is suggested, should be taught as a separate, soon to be compulsory, curriculum subject. School assemblies have multicultural formats, but the idea of embedding moral education in language lessons sounds unacceptable to most educationalists. The idea of depth in a language, of a moral as well as an aesthetic beauty which illustrates a partnership between the expressive capabilities of a language and moral aspects of the relationships of its speakers raises suspicions of indoctrination. I do not think that the (imperial) tradition of Classics education in British public schools, which deliberately fostered inculcation of 'high culture' (Kuper 1994: 539) contributes to contemporary educators' distaste, but rather that this principle of one tradition of English education has been forgotten.

Education is an institution where racism is most carefully avoided and liberal practices of tolerance and understanding are valued and promulgated. A firmly exclusive tone, however, is suggested by the resistance to incorporating an understanding of the comparative moral values of different cultures unless clearly labelled as World Religions. Alternative values are more easily accommodated by multi-ethnic institutions the nearer they are to being objects, or if they are cultural practices that can be objectified such as dress, dance, poetry, crafts and music. Given the straitened finances of state-sector education in Tower Hamlets, however, it is difficult to know how far the coat is being cut to suit the cloth and how much the constraint on language tuition within schools is determined by economic stringency. Many other subjects that are not strictly part of the National Curriculum are similarly constrained.

Both within and outside education in Britain, different moralities can be accommodated if retained within some kind of ethnic enclave. Religious differences are likewise accommodated because they can be contained on the whole within institutional boundaries. Arranged marriages and the customs and values of 'Asian families' are also acceptable as long as excessive proselytising behaviour is curtailed and the rights of the individual are respected. More than that, British workers with social responsibilities such as teachers, social and health workers feel able to make incursions into areas such as family values, not only when it is suspected that the law is being broken (the issue of child abuse) but when a particular view of the moral value of individualism is threatened.

What I am describing here is the way that the experience of racism is not only the bomb in Brick Lane, the breaking of windows, the mugging or cursing in the street and the 'institutionally racist' attitudes of officials behind desks, but it is also the polite but firm rejection of those values which most closely affect social relationships by persons who might be expected to be sympathetic towards minority ethnic groups. This rejection may not be conscious, but the inability or unwillingness to entertain the Bengali point of view can be felt as a slight or as cultural racism: the example of language education given above is a case in point. In my own experience of health care it is not uncommon to find that clinicians of all backgrounds confess to a persistent sense of difficulty in doctor-patient relationships with Bengali patients to a greater extent and degree than that with patients from other minority ethnic groups. This difficulty is not simply related to linguistic problems, nor to differences in the expected social etiquette of doctors and patients behaviour, since many of these 'difficult' patients have grown up in Britain. Commonly these clinicians feel guilty, inadequate or exasperated in the face of their inability to overcome this problem rather than expressing any generalised negative opinions about Bengali people, society or culture, however they formulate such matters. It is possible that the relative size of the Bengali population compared to other ethnic groups contributes to this effect rather than any unique characteristic of relationships between doctors and Bengali patients. Were the Somali or Vietnamese population to expand, the same phenomenon might occur, but the fact that the phenomenon is observable because of the prevalence of such encounters does not detract from the worth of scrutinising the dynamics of relationships deemed to suffer from such difficulty.

Flattery, extravagant or overly elaborate politeness are mannerisms which are shown by patients of all sorts of backgrounds in the face of what is often seen to be an authoritarian or at least hierarchically-ordered medical establishment and is relatively easily set aside or put into perspective by well-disposed clinicians. Rather than the problem being to do with a disquieting but essentially superficial mismatch of etiquette or expected role-behaviour, the discomfort, as I have experienced it, arises because mutual expectations as to the usual parameters for such encounters are not always congruent and the differences cannot be analysed with any precision. When there is an *awareness* that this is so, discomfort arises and becomes a difficulty which affects the consultation.

Rina Bibi is a cheerful, energetic middle-aged woman who speaks English with relative ease although she came here as an adult. She is usually accompanied by her husband and they are comfortable in each other's company, sitting close together, talking back and forth, filling in for each other when any details are forgotten. Her persistent problems with sinusitis and nasal allergy prove difficult to control with conventional medicines; there is no hint of any psychological element in her illness nor any expressed anxiety about spiritual causes: the problem is simply how to improve a chronic condition. I feel that I have expressed sufficient sympathy and outlined the limits of conventional medicine for this annoying, chronic but not serious disease; they will have the benefit of a specialist opinion in due course. I also prescribe willingly. After all this has been discussed Rina pleads with me, "Doctor, this problem is really upsetting, you know, my head feels heavy and spins; when I walk I feel dizzy, I cannot manage at all (*soltam fari na*)" The full range of symptoms is rehearsed once more.

Many patients with troublesome symptoms cannot reach a mutual understanding with their doctor about treatment and prognosis. With a bit of thought, the doctor can usually say why this is so, for example because they are afraid of cancer despite reassurance, or because they are depressed, or their family life is difficult and their illness-behaviour is altered in a negative way because of this. With Rina Bibi, none of the usual factors seems to apply when thinking about the reason for her extending an already lengthy consultation. She does not apparently have irrational fears, psychological disturbance or a dysfunctional family life; she is, in fact, a rather jolly personality and I feel, with an uncomfortable mixture of self-doubt and self-pity, that she has rather overlooked my needs (my time-schedule) and not appreciated my efforts to help; on the other hand, perhaps I had overlooked something and failed to answer her needs in some important respect. In Rina's case, and other similar encounters with Bengali patients I feel that she is unable to fully trust my judgement because she is cannot be sure that I have fully appreciated her predicament. It is not that she is habituated to repeating herself and that I have set an irritating limit to her customary mode of presentation; her facial expression is one of doubt and slight disappointment that *there is not something more* in my response to her. For my part I feel that I would be showing favouritism and a patronising attitude if I were to go further in demonstrating my sympathy and willingness to help. There is an uneasy lack of resolution.

The separability of British and Bengali cultures is therefore expressed in this mode through different perceptions of the *possibilities* of social relationships. The scope of these possibilities may be enlarged in a meaningful way if there are grounds for a shared moral outlook, that is, a reasonable degree of congruence in expectations about the parameters of the relationship, and not just a mutual tolerance and understanding of different 'customs'. On the other hand, respect and tolerance of what are seen to be very different sets of customs may work reasonably well in a limited way because the boundaries are clearly drawn. Bengali-speaking English professionals are popular, I suspect, not just because of their linguistic skill, but also because it is assumed that in speaking the same language they are cognisant of, and susceptible to Bengali moral relationships. The British-Bengali interface turns on the contrast between the idea that moral principles can exist as abstractions, separate from actual social relationships, and the alternative idea that morality is instantiated within the prosecution of social relationships and cannot be abstracted from them, even though the guiding principles may be found in a code or constitution. In philosophical terms this is perhaps a narrow distinction but in terms of the possibilities for relationships between persons of different backgrounds it is an important difference. Taken further, tolerance of moral, ethnic and cultural differences that relies heavily on restraining civic boundaries may harden into defensive or antagonistic postures. The suddenness of ethnic conflict among people who had lived peacefully together is a case in point (Bringa 1995).

7.3.3 CULTURAL AGONISM (AND THE DISCOURSE OF RACE)

7.3.3.1 Racist violence

While there is a clear distinction between racist violence and racist attitudes that fall short of violence, both share an agonistic outlook in the maintenance of sharp boundaries between different groups of people. Such attitudes connect individuals such as David Copeland, who set off a nail bomb in Brick Lane in April 1999 but did not at the time belong to any political group, to the large-scale ideologies of overtly racist organisations. This connection allows the discussion to consider both violent and non-violent behaviour within one framework.

The history of racism in the East End of London begins centuries before the

Bengali population settled there and was particularly significant in the time when the Jewish refugee population expanded rapidly at the end of the 19th century. The history and contemporary problem of East End racism has been described in outline in Chapter 2 and is well described by other authors (BG & STC 1978, Cohen 1996, CRE 1979, Husbands, 1982, Gavron 1998, Runnymede Trust 1993)

Although most informants could talk about personal experience of racism, there have been no more than three or four episodes of racial violence against Bengali patients that I witnessed as their doctor during the last five years. Although few, the incidents have important repercussions. The awareness of the threat of violence and the way that this impinges on daily life is palpable if difficult to quantify. All inner-city residents are habituated to restrictions on their mobility and the need for a burdensome amount of security technology for their homes, cars, places of work and person, such that it becomes unremarkable, everyday and normal - a social fact. The awareness of susceptibility to racial attack, however, is of a different order to this general fact of city life. In a community survey (LBTH 1999: 9) the majority of people of any background said that they would avoid going out alone at night but Asian respondents were significantly more likely to restrict their mobility in the evenings and would avoid public transport and particular areas even in company. The same report finds a steady decrease in (criminal) racial incidents since 1994, the figures for 'Asian' victims falling from over 400 per year to less than 200 (the category 'Asian' is not sub-divided). In 1997 in Bethnal Green (the second most populous neighbourhood in the borough) there were approximately 50 episodes of racial incidents against all ethnic categories, compared to 150 in the less populated and less mixed nearby area of the Isle of Dogs. Crimes of violence against the person have risen steadily from 1995 onwards to a level of over two hundred serious assaults each year in the borough (LBTH 1999: 13). The reporting and collection of the most appropriate data for the levels and trends of racist attacks are difficult since only racial crimes (not all racist events) are counted, victims who suffer recurrent incidents are not recorded and it is likely that some people are less likely to make a report to the police. If the prevalence of violence against the person has increased, as reported by the police, it is hard to imagine that racist behaviour has declined.

National figures obtained from the British Crime Survey (BCS) and police reports form a larger set of data but, in fact, are more difficult to interpret than local figures. The BCS interviews representative samples of the national population in order to uncover the prevalence of crime that may not have been recorded by the police. The BCS consistently reports higher figures for racial crimes than the police but also show less variation over time. Between 1988 and 1993, Home Office statistics (2001) showed an 80% rise in racial incidents, while the BCS reported no increase between 1987 and 1991 (Virdee 1995: 17ff.). The most recent BCS reports a marked fall of the order of 30% in all racially motivated incidents and a similar fall for those crimes specified as being against minority ethnic victims from 1995 to 1999 (Home Office 2001: 49). The number of all racially motivated incidents *reported* to the police rose four-fold in the same period (without breakdown according to ethnicity of perpetrator or victim). In many areas the numbers doubled between 1998 and 2000 (Home Office 2001: 49).

The parameters used to produce these figures alter frequently, making comparisons from region to region or from one year to another inaccurate. Figures are affected by alterations in policy for classifying and recording incidents. This changed significantly in light of the 1999 Macpherson report of the inquiry into the murder of the black teenager Stephen Lawrence in 1993. The report drew attention to institutionalised racism in the British police. The terms 'racial' and 'racially-motivated' were found to be ill-understood by police officers (Macpherson report quoted in Banton 1999: 2). Crime statistics are now collected on the basis of Macpherson's suggestion that 'A racist incident is any incident which is perceived to be racist by the victim or any other person' (Macpherson, quoted in Banton 1999). Racist crime figures are also affected by altered behaviour of citizens with regard to reporting incidents, whether to the police (which is obviously affected by the anticipated response to such reports) or to BCS interviewers. All that can be seen from the accumulated police data is that just as London contains 40% of the national non-white population (Rees & Phillips 1996: 48), so reported racially motivated incidents in London consistently represent between 40% and 50% of all reported racially motivated incidents in Britain in all years from 1994 to 2000.

Against this general and imprecise data my experience from the 1990s of specific episodes of racial attacks on individual Bengali people as already stated is few. In my presence, Bengali people are unlikely to bring up the subject of White racism except with regard to institutional attitudes, for example those of the police and housing departments. The incident described in Chapter 3 (p. 44), where a waiter was the victim of a near fatal racist attack, showed that the victim chose to adduce the area rather than anti-Bengali racialised discourse as the most proximate reason for the event. While it is unwise to generalise from one incident, his reasoning points to the important issue of it being easier to talk about the area as actor or agent rather than pointing to particular groups of people within the area as being responsible for such attacks.

An anthropological readership does not need to be told that the human race has no sub-sets of different biological races. Whilst the biological idea of race has become redundant, the descriptive words, 'racial', 'racist' and 'racialised' continue to be important terms in any study of relations of difference. It is generally understood that unequal relations of power are facilitated and embedded through naturalising discourses such as those of race and gender (Hertz 1960 [1909], Knauft 1996: 256ff., Moore 1994). Gilroy writes forcefully of the need to transcend 'raciology' (his neologism for the entire discourse of race, overt and covert) in all its manifestations. He argues that attention to 'raciology' makes visible the unlikely political alliances between black nationalists and white supremacists in their shared habits of mind (Gilroy 2000: 221). 'Raciological' thinking, he argues, allows an undesirable, strong version of ethnicity to emerge together with proto-fascist potentials 'secreted inside familiar everyday patterns of government, justice, thought and action' (ibid.: 229). His argument, which is attentive on the whole to black rather than Asian groups in Britain, can be seen as privileging one side of the duality that Knauft describes, that of relations of inequality, and so the issue of cultural diversity remains for him problematic. His views remain relevant here, however, where it is not difficult to see how the common experience of overt as well as banal and institutionalised racism fosters agonistic reactions within the Bengali population.

7.3.3.2 Banal Racism

Banal racism in the form of comments, gestures and other aggressive behaviour that stops short of actual violence is common and easily overheard and observed in Bethnal Green particularly in relation to women wearing formal Islamic covering. References to 'Pakis' (or 'Pakis or whatever'), which too easily recalls the phrase 'Paki-bashing', demonstrates a continuing affiliation with a racialised commentary on local life (Cohen 1996). Racist views of black and Jewish people are not uncommonly expressed by Bengali people, especially by older men. Even if this is mildly challenged, there is little consideration of the way in which their views contribute to the racist discourse that oppresses them locally.

Casual snubs to Bengali fellow students or workers, derogatory comments to passers-by, parents who do not stop their children dropping litter (including glass) into the gardens of Bengali neighbours are typical, almost unremarkable components of chronic stressful and damaging racist behaviour. If young men are arrested for racial violence the rest of their family are unlikely to be entirely condemnatory if they showed equivocal or even antagonistic behaviour towards other ethnic groups beforehand. In these ways a non-violent but hostile discourse ensures that racial violence remains a permissible form of behaviour and a part of the local repertoire of social facts rather than the pathological acts of certain individuals. This basic Durkheimian observation (Durkheim 1966 [1938]) warrants emphasis since it has not, in my opinion, displaced the preference, outside the academic establishment, for labelling certain kinds of behaviour as pathological *tout court*. In fact, Banton (1999) has recently found the need to rehearse the Durkheimian argument (see also Keith 1995: 552). The actions of the nail-bomber, David Copeland, were described by journalists as those of a pathological individual who acted independently of any social formation, thus underplaying the contribution of individual behaviour in the production of systematic social discursive practices. It should be stated that most residents of Bethnal Green do not behave in a racist manner, but those who do, however infrequently, are not sporadic aberrations, but intimately connected to local discourses that support their behaviour as well as the nation-wide discourses that persistently shape the East End through the lurid chiaroscuro of sentimentality and violence. Media accounts of the enormities of racism in the East End not only overplay their use of the area as a metonym for all British racism but also tend to depict the white working-class population as entirely reprehensible, their faults only visible to the better educated middle classes. Those white working-class families who get on perfectly well with their neighbours are overlooked. Where ethnic conflict in the inner-cities is manifest as violence on both sides, the notion of deprivation as some form of economic determinism serves as a catch-all explanation, rather than being only one of several contributing elements in violent relationships.

7.3.3.3 Traditionalism

Non-violent agonistic boundary behaviour is found in those families and households who see themselves as strongly traditional in outlook, whether British, Bengali or other. Defensive boundary expression is often seen in conjunction with the possibility of increased cultural status within the self-determined enclave. Here, then, we find 'Asian values', 'British' or 'English' traditions, Islam and Christianity adduced to naturalise boundary problems (Keith 1995: 557). Any ideas of closer co-operation let alone assimilation are seen as risking contamination of cultural values. Some Bengali families speak directly of the harmful effects of the juxtaposition with local non-Bengali, non-Muslim society, and this is a prominent theme informing family strategies. Class and gender issues are accorded less importance than race, ethnicity, tradition and culture. This sort of agonistic boundary practice favours conservative orthodox masculine traditions which may nevertheless be strongly supported by women. Pursuing family interests is paramount and attention to status markers in dress marriage and public comportment is obvious.

Here are found the stiff *murubbis* (senior Bengali men) and strict rules for womenfolk and family roles in general. Male employment is more inclined to business, mosque or community work than to middle-class professional careers that are prosecuted in mixed-ethnicity workplaces. Father is also less likely to be concerned with non-Bengali society other than a utilitarian view of local rights and resources. Uncompromising attitudes prevail even though these risk gaps in pastoral care for teenagers and young adults who must find social advisors among their friends or non-Bengali people. This group forms a significant part of the resource by which certain Bengali traditions are reproduced or strengthened. Money is spent on expensive imported Bengali food, Koranic instruction and (for a few) fee-paying Islamic secondary schools. Parents encourage their daughters to continue with Islamic dress, even if they are taunted in the street, as a show of pride. Although their children are by no means unquestioning conformists, they generally know where they stand with such single-minded parents.

When comparative attitudes are elicited, for example in general conversation or, more tellingly, in the context of conflict between Bengali parents and non-Bengali institutions, the contours of incompatible cultural difference come to light. In Bangladesh, I am told, wrong-doers are dealt with through informal but powerful kin and village groupings of wise and knowledgeable elders. British laws, they feel, are applied rigidly, regardless of social context. Family law particularly arouses comment since they can be invoked by children or wives if they report domestic violence to social workers or the police. I am not suggesting that this is ever done capriciously but those who expect a continuation of what they see as their natural authority as fathers and *sassas* (father's brothers) are dismayed when those who should be subject to their rule are able to mobilise others with the power to challenge their authority by what appear to them to be mere catchwords. In Islam, a *mullah* or family *murubbi*, may listen to moral arguments from both sides and give a wise judgement. Under British law, trip-wires seem to trigger standard responses regardless of the persons involved: victims of domestic violence are removed to a place of safety leaving arguments and discussion until later. Rules and abstract codes appear to be salient parameters governing British family life when compared to Bengali family norms. The rule of law limits the scope of strategies for parental control of children and the moral basis of family life is rendered inflexible, straitened by a body of abstract law codes. Parental advice and influence are felt to be impotent when thus separated from the practical steps needed to guarantee compliance. Those with least resources are most likely to become more firmly entrenched against non-Bengali mores if they cannot exercise customary control in the discipline of their children. The better off can afford to be more liberal but not necessarily Westernised in this matter for they may also express regret and criticism for the way British society has apparently made Bengali family relationships impersonal.

It is not true, of course, that British family life is determined and shaped only by the legal parameters of the law. The relationship between Bengali and British parents' perspectives on the family can be seen as a differential willingness or resistance to submit to the external agency and abstract principles of the law. British parents do not necessarily feel this a constraint. The Bengali parents' consensus view within this agonistic group is that these laws are not simply a practical solution for some, unsuited to others, but by their very existence undermine the 'natural' moral authority of parenthood and kinship.

There is often a feeling of a lack of fit between what are seen as British family values and British family law, neither of which support ideal Bengali family norms (cf. Jeffery 1976: 95ff.).

A father is frustrated because the police told him that his runaway son could not be brought home forcefully because he is almost sixteen yet the school threatened to prosecute him for his son's truancy. Another father is exasperated when repeatedly called to the police station to be told that his son is in need of discipline for minor incidents, "If he is a criminal then why don't you lock him up, if he is not then why don't you leave him alone and allow me to beat him?"

Those who are proof to British norms are Bengali families where father and his male kin are confidently authoritative; together they form an effective cordon against the state. This is not a guaranteed strategy to ensure family discipline: they are likely to estrange those daughters who feel the contrast with other local family models just as acutely but make a different inference from that of their male kin and their stance may provoke rebellion.

In summary, an agonistic mode of behaviour at the interfaces of different groupings in a mixed society is a strategy that carries risk. In its mildest form there is a risk of family break-up as different members perceive the alternative strategies for managing race relations differently. In violent expression, the risk of damaging confrontations and large-scale conflagration as seen in the English towns of Oldham, Bradford and Burnley in 2001, is easily related to this kind of boundary behaviour. For those who recoil from agonistic confrontation, a common-sense multiculturalist stance appears to offer more fruitful consequences.

7.3.3.4 'Asian gangs'

The 'Asian gang' has not yet been placed within my typology of modes of managing racialised, ethnic or cultural boundaries. Young British-Asian men do not consistently evince a distinctive approach to boundary behaviour. They are themselves often a rhetorical resource for discussions about the problems of multicultural Britain. Alexander, in her study of young Bengali men in London, argues that their representation as 'Asian gang' members conflates the discourses of 'assumed raced, gendered and generational deficiencies which constitute a 'triple pathology' of young black and Asian men' (Alexander 2000: 125). The complexities of the lives of these young men, she argues, is falsely simplified and naturalised in the media into the sound-bite of 'masculinity-in-crisis'. Media emphasis on the issues of inner-city streets and Muslim fundamentalism can be added to Alexander's list rendering such young men beyond the pale as 'folk devils' (Keith 1995: 558ff.).

To deny the reality of gangs, white or Bengali is naive, but juvenile delinquency does not exhaust the analysis of contemporary Bengali youth (Keith

1995: 560ff). Alexander (2000) likewise critiques essentialising discourses that have brought the Asian gang into the public imagination as a fully fledged moral panic about ghetto subcultures. This moral panic distorts and obscures the complex subjectivities of gang members. These subjectivities or identities are, she argues, constructed differently to those of their white counterparts primarily because they are formed in the context of relations of inequality and racism. Like Keith, she argues that this constraint has not, however, effaced ties formed through Bengali kinship customs, community welfare groups and shared territory. Such ties and connections offer alternatives to strategies of violence and reprisals for violent attacks. The examples given of Jahangir (p. 52) and Faruk (p. 196) illustrate this complex mesh of connections and resources. Alexander (2000) demonstrates that mediators can and do work effectively between different masculine groups. The fact that problems remain does not gainsay the usefulness of such interventions, nor undermine the way in which street violence has been focussed through the lens of racist political and media discourse (Keith 1995).

In Bethnal Green, large-scale violent episodes between white and Bengali groups of young men have receded. In the 1980s and early 1990s, any attack on a young man recurrently occasioned reprisal attacks by the opposite group (Keith 1995). My observation of a decline in inter-ethnic *group* violence has been corroborated by discussions with young men who describe a territorial truce in inner-London. Young men may walk in any area on their own but a group that looks purposeful and steps over territorial boundaries implicitly declares that they are open to violent engagement. Swaggering machismo and stand-offs between different sub-groups of Bengali young men for a variety of proximate reasons (offences against their own or their sister's reputation, threats to their friends, episodes of disloyalty) continue in various inner-London areas that are considered territorially as a middle-ground for young men of all backgrounds.

Alexander (2000) notes the difficulties of writing meaningfully about masculinity in conjunction with ethnicity or racialised behaviour: all too often one theme erases the other. Attempts to articulate the two along the lines of 'intersection', 'layering', 'transruption', 'transversalism' or the dialectics of cultural hybridity struggle to present a clear explanation of what actually goes on in a sociological sense. Despite such difficulties, work such as Alexander's is important for keeping readers' minds open as to the particularities of any one social fact, whether it is one of a prevalent public image or the material facts of violent crime.

Discussion of subjects such as 'Asian gangs' often brings out what might be called the 'hard-core' of modern British sociological writing on race and culture, stretching the limits of language and expression. The difficulty echoes Knauft's recognition of the conflict between the dual goals of a critical humanist stance: the celebration of difference and the exposure of relations of inequality. The predicaments of a minority of young Bengali men are certainly aggravated by their being 'essentialised' as pathological alien gang-youths but they do represent a limit case for the skills of critical humanists whose positions remain largely within the territory of cosmopolitan academic institutions.

7.4 Summary

This chapter has demonstrated that of the several possible modes of managing relations of what might be called racial, ethnic or cultural difference discussed here, none is guaranteed to consistently deliver a happy outcome. Aggressive behaviour is always a social ill, but traditional, agonistic separatism and liberal multiculturalism may each cause as many problems as they solve. Those who fall into the unsettled category may do so by default rather than design but could be said to be the most open to creative solutions in the face of difficult predicaments.

Large-scale effects of class, gender and socio-economic resources shape the elective affinity that any individual or household may have for one or other strategy as well as the success of any one approach. Within any of the three modes of behaviour described, and particularly for the unsettled strategisers who remain open by choice or necessity to more than one set of influences, outcomes are configured not only by the social facts of Bethnal Green, but also by the pragmatic resources that lie to hand for the actors involved. In the long term, changes in social or juridical policy may have significant effect on relations of inequality. At a more personal level, the scope of available resources for any individual is enlarged or diminished, not simply by a lessening of racist attitudes by those with pastoral or statutory duties and responsibilities for social welfare, but by a greater range of paradigms that might be adduced to frame the predicaments they seek to address.

CHAPTER 8: CONCLUSIONS

8.1 Introduction

The kinds of data that have been presented in this thesis include those from the fields of history, geography, statistics, and sociology in conjunction with my own ethnographic data of Bengali household life, positive and negative sociability and relations of difference. Each source presents one aspect of the lives of those who identify themselves as belonging to the Bengali population in Bethnal Green and which can now be brought together. In this concluding chapter I present briefly a standard account of the position and likely future trajectories for different sections of the Bengali population in Bethnal Green. I then present a set of predicaments which are of particular relevance to a more complex understanding of the ways in which Bengali cultural issues interact with the effects of history, geography, socio-economic issues and relations of difference. There are many other 'facts of life' which are particular to Bengali residents in Bethnal Green but which are not described here. As I have already said, this is not intended to be a complete survey of contemporary Bengali 'socio-cultural life-styles', but an attempt to uncover salient and recurrent constellations of effects and events particular to Bengali people and are illustrative of the consequences of their living in Bethnal Green.

8.2 Static and dynamic I: position and trajectory

Starting with a consideration of statistical data alone, the position of Bengali populations in Britain is one of maximal disadvantage by any measure. Modood and Berthoud's close-grained examination of survey data for British minority ethnic populations, in accordance with data discussed in earlier chapters, finds that Bengali households are consistently worse off in socio-economic terms compared with other ethnic groups, only the Pakistani populations in Britain coming close to a similar level of disadvantage (Modood and Berthoud 1997: 343).

> 'The full scale of the economic plight of the Bangladeshis and Pakistanis becomes apparent when one analyses household incomes and standard of living. The new data reveal that there is severe and widespread poverty among these two groups. Thus more than four out of five Pakistani and Bangladeshi households have an equivalent income below half the national average - four times as many as white non-pensioners.'

The scale of disadvantage prompts the use of the word 'plight'. The intention is clearly to emphasise injustice, but as I noted earlier, plight is a word that has connotations of lack of power or resources to ameliorate the situation described. Statistical data are crucial for shaping policies aimed at eradicating inequalities and so the analysis demands strong language to emphasise the import of its findings. It would be wrong, however, to infer from such data (and this is not, of course, Modood and Berthoud's intention) that the majority of

Bengali households in Bethnal Green or Britain as a whole are places of unremitting misery. Complementary to this kind of data, then, are surveys which systematically collect the views of samples of the Bengali population. These show that it is possible to be successful or optimistic despite pervasive disadvantage. The interviewees in *'Routes and Beyond'* are a group of successful young Bengali adults who are shown to be able to use Bengali, British and Islamic resources combined to shape their future trajectories in a positive manner (Centre for Bangladeshi Studies 1994).

Bethnal Green has been described here as a place conducive to both upward and downward trajectories for all kinds of residents who may have a variety of starting positions at birth or on migration to the area. The position of the wealthy cosmopolitan couple who buy a gentrified loft apartment in Bethnal Green is clearly different from a middle-class professional Bengali couple who arrive from Sylhet via university degrees in Dhaka to take up teaching or research posts in London. Their position is again very different from any working-class family reliant on local authority housing and welfare benefits. It is not difficult, however, to find people who have moved from top to bottom, or bottom to top in a relatively short time-scale while living in Bethnal Green. Position only describes a synchronous conjunction of effects such as gender, class and other socio-economic parameters. My purpose is to go beyond statistics and social position so as to examine the ways in which broad social facts operate with cultural effects and relations of difference in producing successful or unsuccessful strategies and outcomes. The causal chain of events that takes people from similar positions to very different outcomes, or from different positions to similar outcomes can be elucidated by paying attention to trajectories and the strategies available to those who provide examples of recurrent social predicaments for one section of the local population.

To reiterate the findings given in Table 7 (p. 99), for a large minority of Bengali households their future in Bethnal Green looks favourable. The majority are likely to continue to be over-represented among the most disadvantaged in the area. Position plus trajectory form a simple two-dimensional progression away from the passive stasis of plight. Predicament and strategy form a model of greater complexity, but also of greater explanatory potential. It is complex to think about in its dimensions and format, but not difficult to describe.

8.3 Static and dynamic II: predicament and strategy

8.3.1 INTRODUCTION

The predicaments of the Bengali people in Bethnal Green which best illustrate the constellations or interactions of multiple social facts fall into three broad categories: those related to violence, the problems of parents of older children and the difficulties of young married couples. Many particularities can be elaborated and will be discussed in more detail after a descriptive outline of each category.

8.3.2 VIOLENCE AND RACISM

The most widespread, almost universal, predicament that Bengali people face in Bethnal Green is vulnerability to racism. The chance of someone being violently attacked in any one year in Bethnal Green is lower than for other neighbourhoods in Tower Hamlets. Awareness of such vulnerability, however, and the more common experience of aggressive behaviour which stops short of violence is significant enough to curtail the lives of Bengali people to an uncomfortable extent. This shared vulnerability is one of the factors that makes a commonality of the Bengali experience in Bethnal Green, even in the absence of any other population-wide shared trait such as language, custom or kinship structure. Although there are other prevalent 'facts of life' for any Bengali person in Bethnal Green, such as the likelihood of a significant relationship to Islam, the Bengali language and the nation-state of Bangladesh, vulnerability to racism is more immediate, pervasive and significantly negative in its effects. As discussed in Chapter 7, even when an accommodative bilateral multiculturalist approach is espoused as an ideal, misunderstandings and omissions are commonplace in settings where Bengalis and non-Bengali people negotiate over a common problem. In this way opportunities are lost, or at least narrowed down to a few standardised scenarios.

The common experience of racism is an important factor which engenders the second predicament to be considered here, namely that of young single Bengali men who are too readily typified as 'Asian gang' types caught up in inner-city racial tension. The risk of severe physical violence outside the home is greatest for young men, whereas women and men of all ages are likely to suffer non-physical racial abuse in the street. Within the home, women are most vulnerable to violence at the hands of male relatives but this is a universal and not a specifically Bengali predicament. Agonistic response to racism and stereotyping in the context of limited socio-economic opportunity is the predicament of only a minority of young Bengali men but they in turn form part of the predicament faced by their families, as well as the residents of the area taken as a whole. Among the single Bengali men known to myself in this study about a fifth of those aged fifteen and over, and almost two fifths of those over eighteen are, or have been, involved with crime, violence or the law in a way that could be described as typical 'cases' of this predicament. Other young men might be thought of by their parents or friends as being difficult in some way but are not, or never have been involved in criminality or alleged criminal behaviour. Almost one in ten Bengali households are dealing with a young male relative who has attracted the attention of the police for one reason or another.

Some of these young men have died since this study began and their excess mortality rate leads to an under-estimation of the prevalence of the problem. Although difficult sons are found more commonly in broken homes, they are not exclusively from what are usually called 'dysfunctional' backgrounds, but may have grown up in large 'traditional' families with dense inter-household networks (albeit altered by transnational movement). Involvement with illegal drugs increases the danger of physical and psychological morbidity as well as exposing such young men to a risky, if exciting, alternative nexus of relationships which include other drug users, dealers and the police. This nexus is in sharp opposition not only to legal British citizenship, but also to the orthodoxies of the patrilineage and Islam. Unorthodox, criminalised young men may gain social capital in an alternative, more egalitarian social sphere, but at the risk of violence and self-harm.

8.3.3 FAMILIES WITH OLDER CHILDREN

Next is the perspective of older Bengali couples and their older children. In this predicament the particularities of the migration history of this population, and the way this affects kinship patterns and positive networks of social knowledge and support, are noticeable. These parents sustained their own marriages at a distance and brought up young children without the familiar (or at least expected) support of their paternal grandparents, or others in the extended family. They now face the difficulties of managing children of marriageable age or who are already married in the context of an overall social atmosphere that feels thin, distorted and inimical to the ideals of patrilineal joint households and the norms of extended families. The empty space in the kinship sphere, which should be filled by someone like a *bhabi* to act as intermediary between parents and their children, is sometimes usurped by outsiders. These cannot always be trusted with the interests of the patrilineage and do not seem to offer an acceptable alternative moral framework. Although migration away from village life can bring opportunity and a greater degree of freedom than for non-migrants, the possibility of losing status and a good reputation through the effects of gossip and negative spiritual harm is not always lessened for transnational families.

The changes wrought by migration and the juxtaposition with non-Bengali society, particularly in its institutionalised formations, make family life additionally difficult in circumstances where material resources are scarce and unequally distributed. The children of these couples, as they enter adulthood, contend with several competing discourses. Several versions of ideal Bengali family life, British citizenship, local popular culture, the imagined or real community of Bangladesh and more than one pattern of Islamic practice offer possible alternative ways of life. Within any household these discourses may be fruitfully aligned each with the other so that there is, essentially, no particular difficulty or predicament. Where this is not the case, then negotiations between child and parent, each of whom may recruit the rhetoric and people whom they identify as belonging to these discursive formations, becomes more than a standard account of generational tension and is instead, in the eyes of all concerned, a particularly Bengali predicament. Again, reviewing the lists of households and of the young adults in this study, about a quarter face explicit difficulties of this kind, sufficient to come to the attention of statutory authorities. This number includes the sons already discussed and those daughters whose conflicts are concerned with marriage arrangements and peer relationships. Young women who have observed the predicament of a divorced or abused mother are likely to be challenging in their behaviour, as are the outspoken and assertive children of upwardly mobile families where the older generation is particularly anxious about family status.

8.3.4 YOUNG MARRIED COUPLES

Lastly, the young married couples which include a wife born or educated in Britain are the locus where the interplay of wider social effects and Bengali cultural matters are shown with greatest force. They contend with the same factors that affect unmarried young adults, but given the fact of established marriage (and thus potential divorce) and parenthood, the outcome of the interaction of these factors carries greater weight for all concerned. Of the young couples which comprise a wife born or educated in Britain and a Bangladeshi-born husband, about half present difficulties with marriage as an explicit part of their predicaments, with the corollary that half are not in a degree of difficulty that would amount to a predicament, let alone a plight. In the main these wives shoulder the greater part of the burden of managing household problems: their Bangladeshi-born husbands may have very limited employment opportunities, at least initially. They are often sheltered from family difficulties, and dealings with outsiders by their wives and by the general support of Bengali masculine networks.

Divorce and marital difficulty causes particular disadvantage to Bengali wives. Although abandoned Bangladeshi-born wives are the most disadvantaged of all, divorced British-born wives do not find it easy to manage as single parents and remarriage remains difficult. The local kin of the husband are likely to exacerbate marital difficulties; the kin of a young wife may concur with their son-in-law's family for the sake of propriety or they may be ineffectual in their protests. Occasionally a wife's family are able to exert influence that actively assists their daughter. Couples without local kin but with reasonable finances and a good conjugal relationship can be generally free of concern caused by conflict between the differing goals of patrilineal and conjugal relationships (cf. Bott 1971).

8.4 Discussion

This is not a list of all the particularly Bengali predicaments that could be described, but in broad outline they are those which are found recurrently and are important considerations in relation to life in Bethnal Green. The predicament of small children entering school for the first time, for example, is noticeable, but given that the educational achievements of older Bengali children now exceed those of all other ethnic groups in the borough, I have subsumed the difficulties of young children into the predicaments of the household and also in the discussion of education from a general point of view.

The routes out of an unsettled phase where the state of predicament is more or less consciously felt may be one that leads to betterment or to a worsening of problems. None of the categories of predicament described is consistently aligned with an upward or downward trajectory although the threat of violence is a constant background constraint. Even recidivist young men who are demonised as 'Asian gang' youths demonstrate the ability to use multiple resources to move away from street violence to further education, or a successful career. The risk of suffering through violence and drugs-related crime and illness remains high, however, while they are involved with aggressive street-life. Older couples, whose family strategies are aligned productively with garnering support and material resources from local institutions and the local economy, can achieve all-round stability. However, the gradient of effort is likely to remain steeper for Bengali families in comparison with others, despite local popular opinion that government services now unfairly discriminate in favour of minority groups. Likewise, younger Bengali couples who contend successfully with multiple pressures can be upwardly mobile, but again despite a steep gradient of difficulty. This gradient may not be easy to discern with well-to-do households but it is measurable by consideration of those who slide downwards. Nothing is regularly predictable from a static view of current predicament alone, but an overview of the polarisation of household fortunes allows some educated guesses to be made as to the likelihood of certain outcomes.

The availability of different routes or strategies out of predicament towards a more favourable way of life depends, firstly, on social position given by class, gender and socio-economic resources. Secondly, the regard of others, and the ways in which a predicament may be mis-read as a plight with its causes in 'culture-bound' attitudes, opens or closes potential routes to change. Thirdly, the mode of managing relations of ethnic and cultural difference strategically sets the limits of any individual's or household's strategic intent.

Social position has already been described and its differential effects are relatively easy to imagine and categorise. The second set of considerations, the regard of others, is demonstrated not only by racist behaviour but also by the behaviour of sympathetic outsiders. Several examples of this were given in the case-book histories in Chapter 3 and can be reviewed here. The hospital consultant who diagnosed psychosomatic stomach pains, for example, favoured the notion of plight rather than noticing the habitual (in Aliya and Mohammed's case p. 38) and unhelpful way of negotiating social connections. This regard led to a systematic over-attribution of Bengali culture and migrant status as causes of their apparently irremediable plight. Mohammed's behaviour with myself, which at times felt like manipulative flattery, can be seen as a misjudgement on his part of the expectations that British professionals have of appropriate patient conduct. His enthusiasm for making adventurous connections with Bengali neighbours as well as professionals also misfired, so that they were read, socially, as troublesome loose cannons. What is significant here is that while they were relatively free of immediate pressure from local kin, this rendered them vulnerable to stereotyping by their Bengali neighbours (who were unable to assess their social position without kin knowledge) as much as by British doctors. Muffasir and his wife (p 43) were less ambitious than Mohammed and Aliya about recruiting social support through personalising relationships. This left them in the lurch when one of them was absent but by the same token they avoided the harmful effects of over-attribution of culture in professional relationships. Muffasir's limited employment opportunities, however, made him more vulnerable to racial violence through working late at night.

From a therapeutic point of view, containment and reassurance were thought to be more appropriate for Aliya than any kind of psycho-dynamic or behaviour modification approach even though the diagnosis was of a psychosomatic illness. This might be thought to be an esoteric analysis of the management of a patient with stomach-ache but it is an example of widespread similar mis-reading, especially by institutional staff concerned with education, employment, justice and housing. These apparently slight mis-readings obstruct access to practical assistance. As another small example, Bengali mothers whose children are at school and who receive sickness benefit are unlikely to be told that they could work for what are termed 'therapeutic hours' without compromising their benefits, because of mistaken assumptions about Muslim women and attitudes to paid work. She might find socially acceptable employment in a Bengali shop relatively easily for a few hours a week during school-time. It is very unlikely, however, that she will hear about such a programme from the social security office, because of this cultural mis-reading and so she will be denied potential psychological and financial gains.

The regard of others is not, of course, a one-way affair, and the bilateral mode of managing relations of difference is finally the most interesting dimension of the model of predicament and strategy. It should be remembered that with regard to the modes of managing boundaries of cultural difference an agonistic mode was the minority practice, common-sense multiculturalism the majority, and unsettled strategising, the mode for a large minority. Domestic violence, drugs problems and mental ill health predominate among the unsettled strategisers who are in families with a younger head of household, whereas the older common-sense multiculturalist households have fewer of these problems overall. All types show similar levels of health and unemployment problems. With regard to kin support, again the unsettled strategisers show fewer supportive kin relations and more mixed or difficult ones, whereas the common-sense multiculturalists are likely to be characterised by supportive kin relations or a lack of any local kin. Not all British-educated housewives married to Bangladeshi husbands are unsettled strategists - about half are currently managing without excessive difficulty. The husbands and wives who arrive from Bangladesh are particularly difficult to define in this typology given their dependency on their spouses and affines.

The limitations set by an agonistic mode of boundary management are reasonably obvious. Clearly defined principles, strictly upheld, determine which available resources can be used to manage a problem. Their success or failure depends on economics, density of supportive kin and ensuring a balance between strictness about family behaviour and the risk of alienating junior relatives. The unsettled strategisers on the other hand are open to the widest range of resources and possible outcomes so that although their predicaments often appear to be the most complex, they do, in fact retain the greatest number of choices of all categories. For those who adopt a form of pragmatic common-sense multiculturalism, life appears to run smoothly. This is only so by chance rather than design. A lack of access to important practical information has been described, a lack that is compounded by the Bengali experience of a mixed society blocking ordinary, informal information channels. This experience is felt most acutely in the contrasts that are shown up between British family law and institutional attitudes to family life and Bengali family norms. It is also thrown into sharp relief by the differing attitudes towards the place of moral education in schools. A similar effect is perceptible, if difficult to describe accurately, in the conduct of daily social relationships across cultural boundaries: those informants who reflect discursively on the contrast say that Bengali social networks feel intense and thickly meshed (which can bring its own problems) whereas British social networks are less involving, but may thereby allow greater room for manoeuvre. In this way, cultural differentials in the parameters of social encounters limit the free flow, not only of knowledge of other persons, but also of ordinary but very necessary practical information. This is likely to be the final operator (once economics and racism have been factored out of the equation) that accounts for residential segregation of the Bengali population. The everyday pathology of bilateral multiculturalism can be seen to be the most stifling of combinations except where good fortune favours both parties.

A return to the case-book again illustrates the contrast between common-sense multicultural encounters and those with unsettled strategisers. With

Fatima (p. 45), a comfortable British-educated young housewife, I noted that I tend to reinforce what might be characterised as a common-sense multiculturalist attitude to our relation of difference such that I often concurred with her mode of managing relations of difference. I never questioned the basis of her attitudes for I found that in general she appeared to be managing well, given the circumstances. My 'tender regard' for her could be a hindrance if her circumstances alter and she needs more than simple reassurance. This wariness of giving offence leads to neglect of equal access to services and the most subtle form of cultural racism, with plentiful examples throughout the health service (Smaje 1995: 80ff., 109ff. and passim) and probably in other public service institutions as well. With Rahela, the *bodnami* (p. 161), on the other hand, as with Salema who suffered domestic violence (p. 115), I found myself easily drawn into a discussion of cultural relativity and of the arbitrary and harmful nature of their cultural status in a mixed society. Reading their predicaments as one of struggle within the parameters of several discourses (Bengali gossip, British statutory agencies, Islamic orthodoxy) I paid attention to, and explored preferentially, the basis for their adherence to or subversive rejection of the doxa of each discursive formation. In this I was displaying a willingness, once they had opened up the discursive space, to entertain their notion of creative cultural innovation.

Rahela's persistent juxtaposition of one discourse with another, her unwillingness to rescind one in favour of the other, speaks of a remarkable ability to juggle dual discursivity in the course of the daily life of a housewife. What might be caricatured as manipulative or even hysterical behaviour can more usefully be interpreted as selective testing out of combinations and sequences that might produce a resolution to her problems in a form that would be both acceptable to her and in the best interests of her children. She could, alternatively, have resigned herself to patrilineal or statutory agency control or (this did not feature in her story but is not uncommon) Islamic orthodoxy supported by the East London mosque's services for women.

With Fazlul Ahmed, the father who although normally conservative in his customary practice, crossed the boundary to ask me directly for help with his daughter (p 54), I was taken aback, being used to a comfortable, if limited mutual relationship. He demonstrates that it is not only those who are exposed to the rhetoric and ideology of 'the free world' through a liberal education who can entertain a comparative and relativistic view of cultures and traditions. At other times he marks the conversation with comments such as, "In your culture" or "In my culture such and such is or is not permitted". In that mode he displays a conservative multicultural view of separate bounded constellations of practices and beliefs, but in practice he is willing to pragmatically engage my help because he trusts me not to upset the whole apple-cart. Given that masculine control of junior women is evidently a central concern of traditional Bengali families, this apparently unremarkable request for help 'from the other side' assumes greater significance than might otherwise be thought. There is an added poignancy to Fazlul Ahmed's gesture of trust when it is considered that men like himself represent to local British institutions the quintessence of intractable Bengali Muslim masculine dogmatism and antagonism towards notions of individual (and especially female) freedom of choice. Despite his conservatism he does not stereotype all British professionals as being purveyors of a loose form of morality which runs counter to Bengali norms. Others in his position, habitually traditional in outlook, would not and do not risk crossing such boundaries.

In an account of street-corner life of Italian immigrants in an American city in the 1930s, Doc and his gang turn out to have limited opportunity for self-advancement compared to Chick and his companions, because 'they don't mesh' with wider society (Whyte 1943: 273). The explanation appears to be that in the absence of economic capital, people like Doc devote their energies to social capital, thereby losing opportunities for economic advancement; similar predicaments for young Bengali men have been described here. I have observed that although large Bengali joint households can provide an economy of scale which favours material as well as social advancement, isolated Bengali couples can concentrate on their own resources productively precisely because they lack the distraction of a local extended family. The crucial contextual factor in these three ethnographies is the wider society, the beyond-neighbourhood world which, in an ecological metaphor, favours certain kinds of households and neighbourly networks rather than others (cf. Bott 1971 [1957]).

Diasporic populations manage well if they can take into account necessary changes to familiar social customs as a result of migration. They measure the gap between the possibilities and practicalities of reproducing such customs and act accordingly with greater or lesser success. Werbner (2001) notes the reduction in tolerance for irony, humour and dissent within minority ethnic groups (particularly Muslims in Britain) who suffer discrimination and oppression. She calls this the limits of cultural hybridity. Rather than paying attention to the limitations of minority populations in their tolerance of a majority discourse, the mirror can be reversed to show the limitations in tolerance of the majority population. 'Boutique multiculturalism', 'cultural tourism' and a liberal rhetoric of tolerance thrive in 'metropolarities' like Bethnal Green and adjacent Spitalfields. This celebration of distinct 'cultures' and 'heritage' limits the potential for the majority population to engage in open discourse with the cultural values revealed by the lives and experiences of ordinary people from minority ethnic populations. A tendency to maintain a 'healthy' distance between culture and citizenship prevails, spatial metaphors are prominent in such impoverishing discourse and common ground forsworn.

BIBLIOGRAPHY

Abrahams, R.D. 1970. A performance-centred approach to gossip. *Man* (N.S.) **5**, 290-301.

Abu-Lughod, L. 1986. *Veiled Sentiments: honor and poetry in a Bedouin society*. Berkeley: University of California Press.

Acharya, S. 1996. Women in the Indian Labour Force. In *Women and industrialisation in Asia* (ed) S. Horton. London: Routledge.

Adams, A. 1987. *Across seven seas and thirteen rivers*. London: Tower Hamlets Arts Project.

Addams, J. 1917. *The long road of woman's memory*. New York: Macmillan.

Ahmad, I. 1984. Introduction. In *Ritual and religion among Muslims in India* (ed) I. Ahmad. Delhi: Manohar.

Ahmed, R. 1988. Conflict and contradictions in Bengali Islam. In *Shari'at and ambiguity in South Asian Islam* (ed) K.P. Ewing. Berkeley: University of California.

Alam, F. 1988. *Salience of homeland: societal polarisation within the Bangladeshi population in Britain*. Coventry: Centre for research in ethnic relations. University of Warwick.

Albury, D. & C. Snee. 1996. Higher education and East London: a case for social renewal. In *Rising in the East* (eds) T. Butler & M. Rustin. London: Lawrence & Wishart.

Alexander, C.E. 1996. *The art of being black*. Oxford: Oxford University Press.

Alexander, C. E. 2000. (Dis) entangling the 'Asian Gang': ethnicity, identity, masculinity. In U*n/settled multiculturalisms* (ed) B. Hesse. London: Zed Books Ltd.

Allahar, A. 1996. Primordialism and ethnic political mobilisation in modern society. *New Community* **22**, 5-21.

Anwar, M. 1979. *The myth of return*. London: Heinemann.

Asghar, M.A. 1996. *Bangladeshi community organisations in East London*. London: Bangla Heritage Limited.

Augustins, G. 2000. A quoi servent les terminologies de parente? *L'Homme* **154-155**, 573-598.

Aziz, K.M.A. 1979. *Kinship in Bangladesh*. Dhaka: ICDDR.

Back, L. 1996. *New ethnicities and urban culture: racisms and multiculture in young lives*. London: UCL Press.

Baker, T.F.T. 1995. *A history of the county of Middlesex. Vol. 11, Early   Stepney with Bethnal Green*. Oxford: Published for the Institute of   Historical Research by Oxford University Press.

Ballard, R. 1992. New clothes for the emperor? the conceptual nakedness of the race relations industry in Britain. *New Community* **18**, 481-492.

Ballard, R. 1994a. Introduction: the emergence of Desh Pardesh. In *Desh Pardesh. The South Asian Presence in Britain* (ed) R. Ballard. London: Hurst & Company.

Ballard, R. 1994b. Preface. In *Desh Pardesh. The South Asian Presence in Britain* (ed) R. Ballard. London: Hurst & Company.

Bandolier: evidence-based health care. Oxford: Anglia & Oxford RHA. 1996. (published monthly).

Banks, M. 1996. *Ethnicity: anthropological constructions*. London & New York: Routledge.

Banton, M. 1999. Reporting on race. *Anthropology Today* **15**, 1-3.

Barth, F. 1969. *Ethnic groups and boundaries: the social organisation of culture difference*. London: George Allen & Unwin.

Barton, S.W. 1986. *The Bengali Muslims of Bradford*. Leeds: Department of Theology and Religious Studies, University of Leeds.

Baumann, G. 1996. *Contesting culture: discourses of identity in multi-ethnic London*. Cambridge: CUP.

Baumann, G. 1999. *The multicultural riddle: rethinking national, ethnic, and religious identities*. New York: Routledge.

Benson, S. 1981. *Ambiguous ethnicity: interracial families in London*. Cambridge: CUP.

Benson, S. 1996. Asians have culture, West Indians have problems: discourses of race and ethnicity in and out of anthropology. In *Culture, identity and politics: ethnic minorities in Britain* (eds) T. Ranger, Y. Samad & O. Stuart. Aldershot: Avebury.

Berrington, A. 1996. Marriage Patterns and inter-ethnic unions. In *Ethnicity in the 1991 census. Vol. 1, Demographic characteristics of the ethnic minority populations* (eds) D. Coleman & J. Salt. London: H.M.S.O.

Beteille, A. 1996. Caste in contemporary India. In *Caste Today* (ed) C.J. Fuller. Delhi: OUP.

Bethnal Green & Stepney Trades Council (BG & STC). 1978. *Blood on the Streets*. London: Tower Hamlets Council (updated 1994 Tower Hamlets Trades Council).

Bhopal, K. 1999. South Asian women and arranged marriages in East London. In *Ethnicity, gender, and social change* (eds) R. Barot, R, H. Bradley & S. Fenton. Houndmills: Macmillan.

Bleek, W. 1976. Witchcraft, Gossip and Death: a Social Drama. *Man* (N.S.) **11**, 526-541.

Bloch, M. 1983. *Marxism and anthropology*. Oxford: OUP.

Boddy, J. 1989. *Wombs and alien spirits: women, men and the Zar cult in northern Sudan*. Wisconsin: University of Wisconsin Press.

Bonnett, A. 1996. Anti-racism and the critique of 'white' identities. *New Community* **22**, 97-110.

Booth, C. 1891-7. *Life and labour of the people in London*. London: Macmillan.

Bott, E. 1971[1957]. *Family and social network*. London: Tavistock Publications.

Bowen, J.R. 1993. *Muslims Through Discourse*. Princeton: Princeton University Press.

Bowes, A., N. Dar and D. Sim. 2000. Citizenship, housing and minortiy ethnic groups: an approach to multiculturalism. *Housing, Theory and Society* **17**, 83-95.

Brah, A. 1996. *Cartographies of diaspora: contesting identities*. London: Routledge.

Brimicombe, A.J., M.P. Ralphs, A. Sampson, H.Y. Tsui. 2001. An analysis of the role of neighbourhood ethnic composition in the geographical distribution of racially motivated incidents. *British Journal of Criminology* **41**, 293- 308.

Bringa, T. R. 1995. *Being Muslim the Bosnian way: identity and community in a central Bosnian village*. Princeton, N.J: Princeton University Press.

Brison, K. 1992. *Just talk: gossip, meetings, and power in a Papua New Guinea village*. Berkeley: University of California Press.

Burgess, E.W. 1968 [1925]. Can neighbourhood work have a scientific basis? In *The City* (eds) R.Park, E.W. Burgess & R.D.McKenzie. Chicago: University of Chicago Press.

Caglar, A.S. 1997. Hyphenated Identities and the Limits of 'Culture'. In *The politics of multiculturalism in the new Europe: racism, identity, and community* (eds) T. Modood, & P. Werbner. London & New York: Zed Books.

Cameron, S & A. Field. 2000. Community, ethnicity and neighbourhood. *Housing Studies* **15**, 827-843.

Carey, S. & A. Shukur. 1985. A profile of the Bangladeshi community in East London. *New Community* **12**, 405-417.

Carsten, J & S. Hugh-Jones. 1995. *About the house*. Cambridge: Cambridge University Press.

Castles, S. 1993. Migrations and Minorities in Europe. Perspectives for the 1990s: Eleven Hypotheses. In *Racism and Migration in Western Europe* (eds) J. Solomos & J. Wrench. Oxford: Berg.

Centre for Bangladeshi Studies (CBS). 1994. *Routes and Beyond: voices from educationally successful Bangladeshis*. London: Roehampton Institute & Queen Mary and Westfield College.

Chadwick, E. 1965 [1842]. *Report to Her Majesty's Principal Secretary of State for the Home Department, from the Poor Law Commissioners, on an inquiry into the sanitary condition of the labouring population of Great Britain*. Edinburgh: Edinburgh University Press.

Chalmers, R. 1998. Paths and pitfalls in the exploration of British Bangladeshi identity. In *A question of identity* (ed) A.J. Kershen Aldershot: Ashgate.

Chandavarkar, R. 1994. *The origins of industrial capitalism in India: business strategies and the working classes in Bombay, 1900-40*. Cambridge: Cambridge University Press.

Cohen, A. 1974. Introduction. In *Urban ethnicity* (ed) A. Cohen. London: Tavistock.

Cohen, A. 1993. *Masquerade politics: explorations in the structure of urban cultural movements*. Berkeley: University of California Press.

Cohen, A.P. 1993. Introduction. In *Humanising the city* (eds) A.P. Cohen & K. Fukui. Edinburgh: University of Edinburgh Press.

Cohen, P. 1996. All White on the night? Narratives of nativism on the Isle of Dogs. In *Rising in the East* (eds) T. Butler & M. Rustin. London: Lawrence & Wishart.

Cohen, P. 1997. Out of the melting pot into the fire next time: imagining the East End as city, body, text. In *Imagining cities: scripts, signs, memories*. (eds) S. Westwood & J. Williams. London: Routledge.

Collard, C. 2000. "Kinship Studies" au tournant du siecle. *L'Homme* **154-155**, 635-658.

Collier, J.F. & S.J. Yanagisako. 1987. *Gender and kinship: essays toward a unified analysis*. Stanford, CA: Stanford University Press.

Commission for Racial Equality (CRE). 1979. *Brick Lane and beyond: an inquiry into racial strife and violence in Tower Hamlets*. London: C.R.E.

Cooper, J &. T. Qureshi. 1993. *Through patterns not our own: a study of the regulation of violence on the council estates of East London*. London: University of East London.

Crapanzano, V. 1992. Some thoughts on hermeneutics and psychoanalytic anthropology. In *New directions in psychological anthropology* (eds) T. Schwartz, G.M. White & C.A. Lutz. Cambridge: CUP.

Creed, G.W. 2000. Family values and domestic economies. *Annual Review of Anthropology* **29**, 329-355.

Csordas, T.J. 1994. Introduction: the body as representation and being-in-the world. In *Embodiment and experience* (ed) T.J.Csordas. Cambridge: CUP.

Das, V. 1984. For a Folk-Theology and a Theological Anthropology of Islam. *Contributions to Indian Sociology* (n.s.) **18**, 293-300.

Dube, L. 1997. *Women and kinship: comparative perspectives on gender in South and South-East Asia*. New York: United Nations University Press.

Dundes, A. 1981. *The evil eye. A folklore casebook*. New York: Garland Publishing.

Durkheim, E. 1966 [1938]. *The rules of the sociological method*. Glencoe: Free Press.

Durkheim, E. 1973. Individualism and the intellectuals. In *Emile Durkheim on morality and society: selected writings*. Edited with an introduction by Robert N. Bellah. Chicago: University of Chicago Press.

Eade, J. 1990a. *The politics of community: the Bangladeshi Community in East London*. Aldershot: Avebury.

Eade, J. 1990b. Nationalism and the quest for authenticity: the Bangladeshis   in Tower Hamlets. *New Community* **16**, 493-503.

Eade, J. 1994. Identity, nation and religion: educated young Bangladeshi Muslims in London's "East End". *International Sociology* **9**, 377-394.

Eade, J. 1996. Nationalism, community and the Islamization of space in London. In *Making Muslim space in North America and Europe* (ed) B.D. Metcalf. Berkeley: University of California Press.

Eade, J. 1998. The search for wholeness: the construction of national and Islamic identities among British Bangladeshis. In *A question of identity* (ed) A.J. Kershen. Aldershot: Ashgate.

Eade, J & R. Momen 1995. *Bangladeshis in Britain: a national database*. London: CBS.

Eade, J., T. Vamplew & C. Peach. 1996. The Bangladeshis: the encapsulated community. In *Ethnicity in the 1991 census Vol 2 The ethnic populations of Great Britain* (ed) C. Peach. London: HMSO.

Eickelman, D. 1982. The study of Islam in local contexts. *Contributions to Asian Studies* **17**, 1-16.

el-Zein, A.H. 1977. Beyond ideology and theology: the search for the Anthropology of Islam. *Annual Review of Anthropology* **6**, 227-254.

Ellikson, J. 1972. Islamic institutions: perception and practice in a village in Bangladesh. *Contributions to Indian Sociology* **6**, 53-65.

Fabian, J. 1983. *Time and the other: how anthropology makes its object*. New York: Columbia University Press.

Farmer, P. 1999. *Infections and Inequalities: the Modern Plagues*. Berkeley: University of California Press.

Ferguson, J. 1999. *Expectations of modernity: myths and meanings of urban life on the Zambian Copperbelt*. Berkeley: University of California Press.

Finnegan, R. 1998. *Tales of the city: a study of narrative and urban life*. New York: Cambridge University Press.

Foucault, M. 1979 [1975] *Discipline and punish*. London: Penguin Books.

Foucault, M. 1982. Afterword. In *Michel Foucault: beyond structuralism and hermeneutics* (eds) H.L. Dreyfus and P. Rabinow. Hemel Hempstead: Harvester Wheatsheaf.

Friedman, J. 1997. Global crises, the struggle for cultural identity and intellectual porkbarrelling: cosmopolitans versus locals, ethnics and nationals in an era of de-hegemonisation. In *Debating cultural hybridity* (eds) P. Werbner & T. Modood. London & New Jersey: Zed Books.

Frost, E.D. 2000. Bilingualism or dyslexia - language difference or language disorder. In *Multilingualism, literacy and dyslexia: a challenge for   educators* (eds) L. Peer & G. Reid. London: David Fulton Publishers.

Fuller, C.J. 1992. *The Camphor Flame*. Princeton:Princeton University Press.

Fuller, C.J. 1996. Introduction In *Caste Today* (ed) C.J. Fuller. Delhi: OUP.

Gardner, K. 1992a. Londoni-gram. *New Community* **18**, 481-2.

Gardner, K. 1992b. International migration and the rural context in Sylhet. *New Community* **18**, 579-590.

Gardner, K. 1993a. Desh-bidesh: Sylheti images of home and away. *Man* (N.S.) **28**, 1-15.

Gardner, K. 1993b. Mullahs, Migrants, Miracles: Travel and Transformation in Sylhet. *Contributions to Indian Sociology* (n.s.) **27**, 213-235.

Gardner, K. 1995. *Global Migrants, Local Lives. Travel and Transformation in Rural Bangladesh*. Oxford: Clarendon Press.

Gardner, K. 1998. Identity, age and masculinity amongst Bengali elders in East London. In A *question of identity* (ed) A.J. Kershen. Aldershot: Ashgate.

Gardner, K & A. Shukur. 1994. "I'm Bengali, I'm Asian, and I'm living here. In *Desh Pardesh: the South Asian presence in Britain* (ed) R. Ballard.   London: Hurst & Company.

Gavron, K.S. 1998. *Migrants to Citizens: Changing Orientations among Bangladeshis of Tower Hamlets, London*. Thesis (PhD) University of London.

Geertz, C. 1973. Thick description: towards an interpretive theory of culture. In *The interpretation of cultures*, C. Geertz. New York: Basic Books Inc.

Gell, A. 1988. Technology and Magic. *Anthropology Today* **4**, 6-9.

Gell, A. 1998. *Art and agency: an anthropological theory*. Oxford: Clarendon Press.

Giddens, A. 1991. *Modernity and Self-identity*. Cambridge: Polity Press.

Gilroy, P. 2000. *Between Camps: Race, Identity and Nationalism and the End   of the Colour Line*. London: Allen Lane, Penguin Press.

Gilsenan, M. 1989. *Lords of the Lebanese Marches: violence and narrative in an Arab society*. London: Tauris.

Gluckman, M. 1958 [1940]. Analysis of a social situation in modern Zululand. *Rhodes-Livingstone Papers* **28**. Manchester: University Press for the Rhodes-Livingstone Institute.

Gluckman, M. 1963. Gossip and Scandal. *Current Anthropology* **4**, 307-316.

Godelier, M. Trautmann, T.R. & F.E. Tjon Sie Fat. 1998. *Transformations of kinship*. Washington: Smithsonian Institution Press.

Gomm, R. 1975. Bargaining from weakness: spirit possession on the South Kenya coast. *Man* (N.S.) **10**, 530-543.

Goodman, R.F. 1994. Introduction. In *Good Gossip* (eds) R. Goodman & A. Ben-Ze'ev. Lawrence, Kansas: University of Kansas Press.

Gould, H. 1968. Time-Dimension and Structural Change in an Indian Kinship System: a problem of conceptual refinement. In *Structure and Change in Indian Society* (eds) M. Singer & B. Cohn. Chicago: Aldine Publishing Company (Wenner-Gren Foundation for Anthropological Research, Inc.).

Greenhalgh, T., C. Helman & A. Mu'min Chowdhury. 1998. Health Beliefs and folk models of diabetes in British Bangladeshis: a qualitative study. *British Medical Journal* **316**, 978-983.

Gregory, E. & A. Williams. 2000. *City Literacies: learning to read across generations and cultures*. London: Routledge.

Gupta, A. & J. Ferguson. 1997a. Beyond "culture": space, identity and the politics of difference. In *Culture, power, place* (eds) A. Gupta & J. Ferguson. Durham and London: Duke University Press.

Gupta, A. & J. Ferguson. 1997b. Discipline and practice: "The Field" as site, method and location in anthropology. In *Anthropological Locations* (eds) A. Gupta & J. Ferguson. Berkeley: University of California Press.

Hall, S. 2000. Conclusion: the multi-cultural question. In *Un/settled multiculturalisms* (ed) B. Hesse. London: Zed Books Ltd.

Hamnett, C. 2001. London's housing. *Area, Institue of British Geographers*. **33**, 80-83.

Hannerz, U. 1980. *Exploring the city: inquiries toward an urban anthropology*. New York: Columbia University Press.

Hannerz, U. 1992. *Cultural complexity: studies in the social organization of meaning*. New York: Columbia University Press.

Harris, O. 1984. Households as natural units. In *Of marriage and the market: women's subordination internationally and its lessons* (eds) K. Young, C. Wolkowitz & R. McCullagh. London: Routledge & Kegan Paul.

Hertz, R. 1960 [1909]. *Death and The right hand*. Aberdeen: The University Press.

Hesse, B. 2000. Introduction In *Un/settled multiculturalisms* (ed) B. Hesse. London: Zed Books Ltd.

Holland, M.G. 1996. What's wrong with telling the truth? An analysis of gossip. *American Philosophical Quarterly* **33**, 197-209.

Holmstrom, M. 1984. *Industry and inequality: the social anthropology of Indian labour*. Cambridge: Cambridge University Press.

Home Office. 2001. *Statistics on race and the criminal justice system*. London: The Home Office.

Husbands, C. 1982. 'East end Racism' 1900-1980. *London Journal* **8**, 3-26.

Jackson, M. 1983. Knowledge of the body. *Man* (N.S.) **18**, 327-345.

Jeffers, S., P. Hoggett & L. Harrison. 1996. Race, ethnicity and community in three localities. *New Community* **22**, 111-126.

Jeffery, P. 1976. *Migrants and refugees*. Cambridge: Cambridge University Press.

Jeffery, P. 1979. *Frogs in a well : Indian women in Purdah*. London: Zed Press.

Kabeer Naila, 1994. Women's Labour in the Bangladeshi Garment Industry: choices and constraints. In *Muslim women's choices: religious belief and social reality* (eds) C.F. El-Solh & J. Mabro. Oxford: Berg.

Kanaaneh, M. 1997. The anthropologicality of indigenous anthropology. *Dialectical Anthropology* **22** 1-21.

Kapferer, B. 1991. *A celebration of demons*. Oxford: Berg.

Keith, M. 1995. Making the street visible: placing racial violence in context. *New Community* **21**, 551-565.

King, J. 1994. *Three Asian Associations in Britain*. Coventry: University of Warwick Centre for Research in Ethnic Relations.

Knauft, B. 1985. *Good company and violence*. Berkeley: University of   California Press.

Knauft, B.M. 1996. *Genealogies for the Present in Cultural Anthropology*. New York: Routledge.

Kolenda. P. 1968. Region, caste and family structure. In *Structure and change in Indian society* (eds) M. Singer & and B.S. Cohn. Chicago: Aldine Publishing Company (Wenner-Gren Foundation for Anthropological Research, Inc.).

Kuper, A. 1994. Culture, identity and the project of a cosmopolitan anthropology. *Man* (N.S.) **29**, 537-554.

Kuper, A. 1999. *Culture: the Anthropologists' Account*. Cambridge: Harvard University Press.

Lambek, M. 1989. From disease to discourse; remarks on the conceptualisation of trance and spirit possession. In *Altered states of consciousnes and mental health* (ed) C.A. Ward. Newbury Park, Calif.: Sage.

Lambek, M. 1993. *Knowledge and practice in Mayotte: local discourse of Islam, sorcery and spirit possession*. Cambridge: Cambridge University Press.

Lawrence, E. 1982. In the abundance of water the fool is thirsty: sociology and black 'pathology'. In *The Empire Strikes Back: Race and Racism in 70s Britain*. Centre for Contemporary Cultural Studies. London: Hutchinson.

Levy, R. 1994. Person-centered anthropology. In *Assessing cultural anthropology* (ed) R. Borofsky. New York: McGraw-Hill Inc.

Lewis, I. 1971 *Ecstatic religion: an anthropological study of spirit possession and shamanism*. Harmondsworth: Penguin.

Little, K. 1947. *Negroes in Britain: a study of racial relations in English   society*. London: Routledge & Kegan Paul.

Littlewood, R. 1998. *The butterfly and the serpent: essays in psychiatry, race and religion*. New York: Free Association Books.

London Borough of Tower Hamlets (LBTH). 1999. *Tower Hamlets crime and disorder audit 1998/9*. London: Tower Hamlets & Metropolitan Police.

London Borough of Tower Hamlets (LBTH). 2001. *People & Profile*. LBTH: The Housing Diretorate.

London, J. 1903. The people of the abyss. London: Isbister &Co Ltd.

Maloney, C. 1979. Foreword In K. Aziz *Kinship in Bangladesh*. Dhaka: ICDDR.

Mascarenhas-Keyes, S. 1987. The native anthropologist. In *Anthropology at Home* (ed) A. Jackson. London: Tavistock Publications.

Massey, D. S. & M.J. Fischer, 2000. How segregation concentrates poverty. *Ethnic and Racial Studies* **23**, 670-691.

Mauss, M. 1973. Techniques of the body. Translated by Ben Brewster. *Econ. Soc.* **2**, 70-88.

Mayhew, H. 1968 (1861-2). *London labour and the London poor*. New York: Dover.

Mearns, A. 1970 (1883). *The bitter cry of outcast London*. Leicester: Leicester University Press

Menski, W. 1999. South Asian women in Britain, family integrity and the primary purpose rule. In *Ethnicity, gender, and social change* (eds) R. Barot, R, H. Bradley & S. Fenton. Houndmills: Macmillan.

Middleton, J. & E.H. Winter. 1963. *Witchcraft and sorcery in East Africa*. London: Routledge and Kegan Paul.

Miles, R. 1993. The Articulation of Racism and Nationalism. In *Racism and Migration in Western Europe* (eds) J. Solomos and J. Wrench. Oxford: Berg.

Minault, G. 1984. Some Reflections on Islamic Revivalism vs. Assimilation among Muslims in India. *Contributions to Indian Sociology* **18**, 301-305.

Modood, T. & R. Berthoud 1997. *Ethnic minorities in Britain*. London: Policy Studies Institute.

Moore, H. 1988. *Feminism and anthropology*. Cambridge: Polity Press.

Moore, H. 1994. *A passion for difference*. Cambridge: Polity Press.

Morreall, J. Gossip and Humor. In *Good Gossip* (eds) R. Goodman & A. Ben-Ze'ev Lawrence, Kansas: University of Kansas Press.

Morrison, A. 1982 [1896]. *A child of the Jago*. Woodbridge: Boydell.

Murphy, M. 1996. Household and family structure among ethnic minority groups. In *Ethnicity in the 1991 census. Vol. 1, Demographic characteristics of the ethnic minority populations* (eds) D. Coleman & J. Salt. London: H.M.S.O.

Murphy, M.D. 1985. Rumors of identity: gossip and rapport in ethnographic research. *Human Organization* **44**, 132-137.

Murshid, T. 1995. *The Sacred and the Secular, Bengal Muslim Discourses 1871-1977*. Calcutta: Oxford University Press.

Nabokov, I. 1997. Expel the lover, recover the wife: symbolic analysis of a South Indian exorcism. *J. Roy. anthrop. Inst.* (N.S.) **3**, 297-316.

Nourse, J.W. 1996. The voice of the winds versus the masters of cure: contested notions of spirit possession aamong the Lauje of Sulawesi. *J. Roy. anthrop. Inst.* (N.S.) **2**, 425-442.

Okely, J. 1996. Own or other culture. London: Routledge.

Ong, A. 1987. *Spirits of resistance and capitalist discipline: factory women in Malaysia*. Durham, NC: Duke University Press.

Park, R., Burgess, E.W. & McKenzie, R.D. 1968 (1925). *The City*. Chicago: University of Chicago Press.

Parkin, D. 1985. *The anthropology of evil*. New York: Basil Blackwell.

Parkin, D. 1995. Latticed knowldege: eradication and dispersal of the unpalatable in Islam, medicine and anthropological theory. In *Counterworks* (ed) R. Fardon. London: Routledge.

Parry, J. 1979. *Caste and Kinship in Kangra*. London: Routledge.

Parry, J. 1994. *Death in Banaras*. Cambridge: CUP.

Parry, J. 1999. Lords of labour: working and shirking in Bhilai. *Contributions to Indian Sociology* **33**, 111-140.

Passaro, J. 1997. "You can't take the subway to the field!": "village" epistemologies in the global village. In *Anthropological Locations* (eds) A. Gupta & J. Ferguson. Berkeley: University of California Press.

Peach, C. 1998. South Asian and Caribbean ethnic minority housing choice in Britain. *Urban studies* **35**, 1657-1680.

Peach, C. & D. Rossiter, 1996. Level and nature of spatial concentration and segregation of minority ethnic populations in Great Britain, 1991. In *Ethnicity in the 1991 Census. Vol 3. social geography and ethnicity in Britain* (ed) P. Ratcliffe. London: HMSO.

Phillips, D. 1986. *What price equality?: a report on the allocation of GLC   housing in Tower Hamlets*. London: Greater London Council.

Phillips, D. 1988. Race and housing in London's East End: continuity and change. *New Community* **14**, 356-369.

Phillips, D. 1998. Black Minority Ethnic Concentration, Segregation and Dispersal in Britain. *Urban Studies* **35**, 1681-1702.

Placido, B. 2001. "It's all to do with words": an analysis of spirit possession in the Venezuelan cult of Maria Lionza. *J. Roy. anthrop. Inst.* (N.S.) **7**, 207-224.

Pocock, D.F. 1973. *Mind, body and wealth : a study of belief and practice in an Indian village*. Oxford: Blackwell.

Pollen, R. 2001. Cultural aspects of sexual difficulties. *Institute of Psychosexual Medicine Journal* **26**, 4-11.

Porter, R. 1994. *London, A Social History*. London: Penguin Books.

Raheja, G.G. & Gold, A.G. 1994. *Listen to the heron's word*. Berkeley: University of California Press.

Ratcliffe, P. 1996. Social geography and ethnicity: a theoretical, conceptual and substantive overview. In *Ethnicity in the 1991 Census Vol 3. Social geography and ethnicity in Britain* (ed) P. Ratcliffe. London: HMSO.

Rees, P & D. Phillips, 1996. Geographical spread: the national picture. In *Ethnicity in the 1991 Census. Vol 3. Social geography and ethnicity in Britain* (ed) P. Ratcliffe. London: HMSO.

Rex, J. 1994. Ethnic Mobilisation in Multicultural Societies. In *Ethnic Mobilisation in a Multi-Cultural Europe* (eds) J. Rex & B. Drury.   Alderhot: Avebury.

Reyna, S.P. 1994. Literary anthropology and the case against science. *Man* (N.S.) **29**, 555-581.

Risebero, B. 1996. Architecture in East London. In *Rising in the East* (eds) T. Butler & M. Rustin. London: Lawrence & Wishart.

Rix, V. 1996. Social and demographic change in East London. In *Rising in the East* (eds) T. Butler & M. Rustin. London: Lawrence & Wishart.

Robertson, R. 1995. Glocalization: time-space and homogeneity-heterogeneity. In *Global Modernities* (eds) M. Featherstone & S. Lash. Thousand Oaks, California: Sage Publications.

Robinson, F. 1983. Islam and Muslim Society in South Asia. *Contributions to Indian Sociology* **17**, 185-203.

Rogers, A. & S. Vertovec. 1995. *The urban context: ethnicity, social networks, and situational analysis*. Oxford: Berg.

Rosaldo, R. 1989. *Culture and truth: the remaking of social analysis*. Boston: Beacon Press.

Rozario, S. 1992. *Purity and communal boundaries: women and social change in   a Bangladeshi village*. Sydney: Allen & Unwin.

Runnymede Trust. 1993. *Neither unique nor typical: the context of race relations   in the London borough of Tower Hamlets*. London: Runnymede Trust.

Russell Bernard, H. 1994. Methods belong to all of us. In *Assessing cultural anthropology* (ed) R. Borofsky. New York: McGraw-Hill, Inc.

Rustin, M. 1996. Introduction. In *Rising in the East* (eds) T. Butler & M. Rustin. London: Lawrence & Wishart.

Ryang, S. 1997. Native anthropology and other problems. *Dialectical Anthropology* **22**, 23-49.

Sahlins, M. 1999. Two or three things that I know about culture. *J. Roy. anthrop. Inst.* (N.S.) **5**, 399-421.

Sangren, P.S. 1988. Rhetoric and the Authority of Ethnography. *Current Anthropology* **29**, 405-424.

Schneider, D. 1984. *A critique of the study of kinship*. Ann Arbor: University of Michigan Press.

Sen, A. 1997. Human rights and Asian values. *New Republic*, July 14 &21, 33-41.

Sheikh, A. & A.R. Gatrad. 2000. *Caring for Muslim Patients* Abingdon: Radcliffe Medical Press.

Sibley, D. 1995. *Geographies of exclusion*. London: Routledge.

Singer, M. 1968 The Indian Joint Family in Modern Industry. In *Structure and Change in Indian Society* (eds) M. Singer & B. Cohn. Chicago: Aldine

Publishing Company (Wenner-Gren Foundation for Anthropological Research, Inc.).

Smaje, C. 1995. *Health, 'Race' and Ethnicity: Making Sense of the Evidence.* London: King's Fund Institute.

Soja, E.W. 1997. Six discourses on the postmetropolis. In *Imagining cities: scripts, signs, memories.* (eds) S. Westwood & J. Williams. London: Routledge.

Sperber, D. 1985. *On anthropological knowledge.* Cambridge: CUP.

Sperber, D. 1996. *Explaining Culture, a Naturalistic Approach.* Oxford: Blackwell.

Stedman-Jones, G. 1989. The 'cockney' and the nation 1780-1988. In *Metropolis London; histories and representations since 1800* (eds) D. Feldman & G. Stedman-Jones. London: Routledge.

Stirrat, R.L. 1977. Demonic possession in Roman Catholic Sri Lanka. *Journal of anthropological research* **33**, 133-157.

Stocking, G. 1983. *Observers Observed: essays on ethnographic fieldwork.*   Madison: University of Wisconsin Press.

Strathern, M. 1987. The limits of auto-anthropology. In *Anthropology at Home* (ed) A. Jackson. London: Tavistock Publications.

Strathern, M. 1995. The nice thing about culture is that everyone has it. In *Shifting contexts* (ed) M. Strathern. London: Routledge.

Strathern, M. 1996. Cutting the network. *J.Roy. anthrop. Inst.* (N.S.) **2**, 517-535.

Summerfield, H. 1993. Patterns of adaptation: Somali and Bangladeshi women in Britain. In *Migrant women: crossing boundaries and changing identities* (ed) G. Buijs. Oxford: Berg.

Trautmann, T. 2000. India and the study of kinship terminologies. *L'Homme* **154-155**, 559-572.

Turner T. 1993. Anthropology and multiculturalism - what is anthropology that multiculturalists should be mindful of it? *Cultural anthropology* **8**, 411-429.

van Kempen, R & A.S. Ozuekren, 1998. Ethnic segregation in cities: new forms and explanations in a dynamic world. *Urban Studies* **35**, 1631-1656.

Vatuk, S. 1972. *Kinship and urbanization: white collar migrants in North   India.* Berkeley: University of California Press.

Virdee, S. 1995. *Racial violence and harrassment.* London: Policy Studies Institute.

Visram, R. 1986. *Ayahs, lascars and princes: Indians in Britain 1700-1947.* London: Pluto.

Werbner, P. 2001. The limits of cultural hybridity: on ritual monsters, poetic licence and contested postcolonial purifications. *J. Roy, anthrop. Inst.* (N.S.) **7**, 133-52.

Weston, K. 1997. The virtual anthropologist. In *Anthropological Locations* (eds) A. Gupta & J. Ferguson. Berkeley: University of California Press.

Whyte, W.F. 1943. *Street corner society; the social structure of an Italian slum*. Chicago: Chicago University Press.

Wilce, J. M. 1998. *Eloquence in trouble: the poetics and politics of complaint in rural Bangladesh*. New York : Oxford University Press.

Wirth, L. 1938. Urbanism as a way of life. *American journal of Sociology* **44**, 1-24.

Wirth, L. 1998 [1928]. *The Ghetto*. New Brunswick & London: Transaction Publishers.

Wolf, D. 1992. *Factory daughters: gender, household dynamics, and rural industrialization in Java*. Berkeley: University of California Press.

Wrench, J. & T. Qureshi. 1996. *Higher horizons: a qualitative study of young men of Bangladeshi origin*. London: The Stationery Office.

Wright, S. 1998. The policization of 'culture'. *Anthopology Today* **14**, 7-15.

Wright, T. 1875. *The great army of the London poor*. London: T. Woolmer.

Yan, H. 1997. On three major dichotomies. *Dialectical Anthropology* **22**, 51-78.

Yanagisako, S.J. 1977. Women-centered kin networks in urban bilateral kinship. *American Ethnologist* **4**, 207-226.

Yanagisako, S. J. 1979. Family and household: the analysis of domestic groups. *Ann. Rev. Anthropol.* **8**, 161-205.

Young, M. & P. Wilmott. 1957. *Family and kinship in East London*. London: Penguin Books.

Yuval-Davis, N. 1997. Ethnicity, gender relations and multiculturalism. In *Debating cultural hybridity* (eds) P. Werbner & T. Modood. London & New Jersey: Zed Books.